Caribbean Without Borders

Caribbean Without Borders:
Literature, Language and Culture

Edited by

Dorsia Smith, Raquel Puig,
and Ileana Cortés Santiago

Cambridge Scholars Publishing

Caribbean Without Borders: Literature, Language and Culture,
Edited by Dorsia Smith, Raquel Puig, and Ileana Cortés Santiago

This book first published 2008

Cambridge Scholars Publishing

12 Back Chapman Street, Newcastle upon Tyne, NE6 2XX, UK

British Library Cataloguing in Publication Data
A catalogue record for this book is available from the British Library

Copyright © 2008 by Dorsia Smith, Raquel Puig, and Ileana Cortés Santiago and contributors

All rights for this book reserved. No part of this book may be reproduced, stored in a retrieval system, or transmitted, in any form or by any means, electronic, mechanical, photocopying, recording or otherwise, without the prior permission of the copyright owner.

ISBN (10): 1-4438-0039-2, ISBN (13): 978-1-4438-0039-6

TABLE OF CONTENTS

List of Images vii
List of Tables viii

Introduction ix

Chapter One: Unveiling Constructs: Caribbean Literature, Language, and Culture... 1

The Caribbean Without Frames: Narrative Structure in Samuel Selvon's London Novels
Karen Mah Chamberlain 3

Ghost Know No Borders: A Look at the Functions of Ghosts in Wilson Harris' Fiction in General and the Ghost of Memory in Particular
Suzanna Engman 17

Drenched: Wet Poetries of Lorna Goodison and Olive Senior
Yasmine Shamma 30

The Use of English Lexified Creole in Anglophone Caribbean Literature
Marta Viada Bellido de Luna 42

Si-Dieu-Veut: Vodou as Catalytic and Fatalistic Religion in *Masters of the Dew*
Dara Green 58

Chapter Two: Drumming Up the Nation: Representations in Caribbean Music, Drama, and Dance Performance 77

Going Bananas on the New York Stage: Representations of the Caribbean as Seen in J. Robinson's *The Yorker's Stratagem; or, Banana's Wedding*
Juan R. Recondo 79

Bomba Trigueña: Diluted Culture and (loss of) Female Agency in AfroPuerto Rican Music and Dance Performance
Melanie A. Maldonado 95

Bob Marley: Postcolonial Activist and (R)evolutionary Intellectual
Adam M. Loyd 118

Chapter Three: Mapping the Caribbean: Migration, Landscape, and Identity 137

Disjunctions and Deformations: Memory and Landscape in the West Indies
Lavina Liburd 139

Staging Transculturation: Border Crossings in Josefina Baez's Performance Texts
Liamar Durán Almarza 161

Deconstructing Cuban Identity: Senel Paz's *The Wolf, the Woods and the New Man*: and its Film Adaptation *Strawberry and Chocolate* by Tomás Gutiérrez Alea
Tania Cepero López 175

Caribbean Women Writers and the Strategy of Memory
Aida Luz Rodríguez 194

Feodor Dostoyevsky and Claude McKay: Cross-Cultural Dialogue with the Dominant Western Ethnocentrism
Tatiana Tagirova 219

The Imagined Nation in Cristina García's *Monkey Hunting*
Raquel Puig 236

LIST OF IMAGES

ILLUSTRATION 3.1 AERIAL VIEW OF BASSETERRE 141
ILLUSTRATION 3.2 BASSETERRE, INDEPENDENCE SQUARE 142
ILLUSTRATION 3.3 TOWNHOMES IN BASSETERRE 143
ILLUSTRATION 3.4 THE 1792 COURTHOUSE 144
ILLUSTRATION 3.5 THE 1893 TREASURY BUILDING 144
ILLUSTRATION 3.6 NATIONAL HOUSING CORPORATION 145
ILLUSTRATION 3.7 1965 GOVERNMENT HEADQUARTERS AT LEITH 146
ILLUSTRATION 3.8 WEST SQUARE STREET, CIRCA 1990 147
ILLUSTRATION 3.9 CENTRAL STREET, 2004 147
ILLUSTRATION 3.10 PHOTOGRAPH BY ACWORTH CIRCA 1951 152
ILLUSTRATION 3.11 KASSAB AND RAM'S BEFORE RECOVERY 153
ILLUSTRATION 3.12 KASSAB AND RAM'S AFTER RECOVERY 153
ILLUSTRATION 3.13 GOVERNMENT HEADQUARTERS: BEFORE RECOVERY. 154
ILLUSTRATION 3.14 GOVERNMENT HEADQUARTERS: AFTER RECOVERY ... 155
ILLUSTRATION 3.15 FOUNTAIN AT INDEPENDENCE SQUARE 157
ILLUSTRATION 3.16 FOUNTAIN AFTER BEING VANDALIZED 157

LIST OF TABLES

Table 1: Gravlee, Clarence C. "Ethnic Classification in Southeastern
 Puerto Rico,'" 956.. 96-7

INTRODUCTION

The Caribbean region can be defined as "all the islands between North America and Mexico, plus Belize and the northern South American territories of Guyana, Suriname, and French Guiana."[1] Yet, the influence of the Caribbean can be felt as far away as places like Europe, Asia, Africa, and the United States. By having this evolution of an intercultural process, it is difficult to restrict the Caribbean to a simple conceptual area. Instead, the Caribbean is a complex region, "a meta-archipelago, . . . and as a meta-archipelago it has the virtue of having neither a boundary nor a center."[2] This view with regard to the diversity of the Caribbean geographical boundaries also parallels the field of Caribbean Studies. According to Kevin Meehan and Paul B. Miller, "literature, functions in the Caribbean, as elsewhere, as a documentary source that reveals the cultural patterns and social history that make up a civilization."[3] As such, the areas of Caribbean literature, language, and culture overlap and construct multiple representations of Caribbean societies.

It is with this wide-encompassing range of the Caribbean as well as the emerging fields in Caribbean Studies that the "Caribbean without Borders Conference: Literature, Language, and Culture" was developed in 2007. Noted Jamaican linguist, poet, writer, and academic, Velma Pollard gave the keynote presentation and addressed the mélange of cultures, history, and languages in the texts of Caribbean writers. In her address, Pollard refers to the Caribbean ethos as a trans-continental journey where the traveler recollects instances and experiences, thus, describing the essence of the Caribbean as a conglomerate of geographical locations, literatures, languages, and cultures. Like Pollard's address, the papers presented in this collection reflect the Caribbean's various regions, social issues, migratory experiences, cultural identities, creolized linguistics, and literary landscapes. They add also dimension to the myriad of Caribbean experiences and provide a novel examination of the Caribbean in its complexity. This pioneering collection is the result of selected papers presented at the "Caribbean without Borders Conference," which was hosted by the University of Puerto Rico, Río Piedras, on March 19-21, 2007.

In addition to discussing some prominent issues of the Caribbean, the papers in this collection examine the extensive field of Caribbean Studies and Caribbean scholars from the Anglophone, Hispanophone, and Francophone Caribbean. This text also demonstrates the breadth of Caribbean culture by including its diverse manifestations of poetry, fiction, film, architecture, theater, music, and linguistics. In many instances, these manifestations are a testament to a transnational consciousness that permeates Caribbean borders. Essays featured in this collection like Claude McKay and Dostoyevsky and Afro-Puerto Rican music and dance performances in the United States show the fluidity and transgressive quality of the Caribbean. As such, these essays connect the worlds of Europe, the United States, Africa, and Asia with the Caribbean.

The Caribbean in its complexity is represented in this collection through an exploration of topics that are divided into three major sections. The first section, "Unveiling Constructs: Caribbean Literature, Language, and Culture," examines various themes within the emerging disciplines of Caribbean Literature, Language, and Culture. The collection of essays in this section represents an intersection of the Caribbean experience and addresses the numerous frameworks in diaspora texts by Caribbean writers. For example, the exploration of the multiple representations of ghosts in the novels of Wilson Harris exemplifies the erasure of boundaries that runs as a leitmotif in this collection. According to Suzanna Engman, Harris' ghosts "embody cross-cultural beliefs that span four continents and meet in Guyana." In addition, Harris' ghosts "disregard borders of time, space, and logic" by being permeable, fluid, and impermanent. Yasmine Shama also addresses the theme of fluidity in "Drenched: Wet Poetries of Lorna Goodison and Olive Senior." Shama explores "uprootedness and violation" in relationship to the idea of wetness and focuses on "water in its quenching power."

Karen Mah-Chamberlain in "The Caribbean Without Frames: Narrative Structure in Samuel Selvon's London Novels" shows how Selvon creates "novels which break free from the frames of European perspectives by allowing speakers and listeners to discourse directly." Mah-Chamberlain demonstrates how Selvon's diasporic novels invert "the frame of European perspectives" with a narrational style that prioritizes West Indian discourse. From a linguistic perspective, Marta Viada Bellido de Luna analyses the use of Creole in Anglophone Caribbean literature. From the basilectal expressions of Anansi characters, to the pioneering efforts of Samuel Selvon to render dialect in narration, the inclusion of Creole, according to Viada, has been pivotal to the development of a Caribbean literary discourse. Finally, Dara Green examines the relationship of religious fatalism in vodou and revolutionary action in Jacques Roumain's "Masters of the Dew."

The second chapter of this collection, "Drumming up the Nation: Representations of Caribbean Music, Drama and Dance Performance," problematizes the evolution of these quintessential Caribbean forms. The development of the Puerto Rican *bomba* costume is analyzed as directly related to the commercialization of the form, Puerto Rico's relationship with the United States, and diasporic practice in Melanie A. Maldonado's essay "Bomba Trigueña: Diluted Culture and (loss of) Female Agency in AfroPuerto Rican Music and Dance Performers." Maldonado discusses how the trope of the mammy infiltrated the *bomba* costume, converting the use of the costume into "an act of colonial mimicry" that produced a "whitening" of the genre.

Moreover, in "Bob Marley: Postcolonial Activist and (R)evolutionary Intellectual," Marley's revolutionary ideals and their subsequent evolution from strict adherence to *negritude* to a transcendence of race and nationality through universal love are examined against the commercialization of his music. Lastly, representations of the Caribbean in J. A. Robinson's "The Yorker's Stratagem; or, Banana's Wedding," a play staged in New York during the second half of the eighteenth century, are explored as a "deformation of the North American system." In the tradition of the Caliban/Prospero trope, the play aims to present the image of the adventurous white Capitalist North American that arrives in "an unidentified Caribbean island" and experiences the depravation and corruption of West Indian society. Juan R. Recondo argues that "various carnivalesque elements, such as inversion, the grotesque, and hybridization, which are diversely present in "The Yorker's Stratagem; or, Banana's Wedding," become disruptions to various markers of North American identity such as republicanism, capitalism, and race." Further, the construction of the Caribbean as "other" in "The Yorker's Stratagem" enables a discourse between dominant (North American) and peripheral (black West Indian) that perpetuates "the unstableness of identity."

"Mapping the Caribbean: Migration, Landscape and Identity" introduces the theme of Caribbean identity formation and its struggle with unsettlement, mobility, border crossings, and change. As such, the text asks whether there is a Caribbean identity that can be used as a homogenizing factor for the region. By the mere diversity of its subject matter, the studies in this chapter seem to reject the homogenization of a Caribbean identity and veer towards the heterogeneous and fluid. Fragmented selves inhabit the studies of McKay and Dostoyevsky, and Josefina Báez's performance texts. Furthermore, the study on the works of Paule Marshall, Zee Edgell, Michelle Cliff, and Elizabeth Nuñez-Harrell prioritizes their use of memory to challenge fixed identities. Memory, as applied to the architectural environment of Basseterre, the capital of St. Kitts, further opens a discussion to conceptions of local identity. While, a close analysis of Crisina García's *Monkey Hunting* questions the homogenizing concept of nation. Finally, Tomás Gutierrez-Alea's film *Strawberry and Chocolate* initiates a discussion on the construction of identity based on binary oppositions and the necessity to deconstruct all binaries to attain a state that resembles Fernando Ortíz's notion of *Cubanía*.

Caribbean Without Borders: Literature, Language, and Culture is a pioneer compilation that highlights the perspectives and visions of emerging scholars in Caribbean studies, and paves the way for further studies that, instead of fragmenting the Caribbean archipelago in different linguistic regions, will provide a holistic view of an area that, albeit its differences, is inter-connected by a common sea and history. Benítez-Rojo expresses the region's interconnectedness thus: "within the sociocultural fluidity that the Caribbean archipelago presents, within its historiographic turbulence and its ethnological and linguistic clamor, within its generalized instability of vertigo and hurricane, one can sense the features of an island that "repeats" itself, unfolding and bifurcating until it reaches all the seas and lands of the earth, while at the same time it inspires multidisciplinary maps of unexpected designs."[4] The breath of this collection is, then, an attempt to provide a "multidisciplinary map" that bridges territories and shows the richness and variety of a region that has no boundaries.

Bibliography

Benítez-Rojo, Antonio. *The Repeating Island*. Durham: Duke University Press, 1996.

Boswell, Thomas D. "The Caribbean: A Geographic Preface." In *Understanding the Contemporary Caribbean*, edited by Richard Hillman and Thomas J. D'Agostino, 19-50. Boulder: Rienner, 2003.

Meehan, Kevin and Paul B. Miller. "Literature and Popular Culture." In *Understanding the Contemporary Caribbean*, edited by Richard Hillman and Thomas J. D'Agostino, 305-332. Boulder: Rienner, 2003.

Notes

[1] Thomas D. Boswell, "The Caribbean: A Geographic Preface" in *Understanding the Contemporary Caribbean*, 19.
[2] Antonio Benítez-Rojo, *The Repeating Island,* 4.
[3] Kevin Meehan and Paul B. Miller, "Literature and Popular Culture," 305.
[4] Benítez-Rojo, *The Repeating Island,* 3.

CHAPTER ONE

UNVEILING CONSTRUCTS: CARIBBEAN LITERATURE, LANGUAGE, AND CULTURE

"Unveiling Constructs: Caribbean Literature, Language, and Culture" examines various themes within the emerging disciplines of Caribbean Literature, Language, and Culture. The collection of essays in this section represents an intersection of the Caribbean experience and addresses the numerous frameworks in diaspora texts by Caribbean writers. Karen Mah-Chamberlain's essay engages the texts of the Caribbean writer Samuel Selvon in order to assess the lives of West Indian immigrants in London. By doing so, she explores the West Indian migratory experience and their narratives which move beyond traditional literary constructions. Similarly, Suzanna Engman focuses on transformative frameworks in her essay entitled "Ghosts Know No Boundaries." Engman notes that ghosts act as "as a metaphoric expression of presence in absence, repressed trauma, colonial guilt, and historical loss and recovery." Ghosts, when viewed from this perspective in *The Ghost of Memory* by Caribbean writer Wilson Harris, embody "linguistic, cultural, and literary theories," serve as the site of "collective unconscious memories," "forgotten cultures," and "alternate realities," and defy binaries. The discourse connecting literature, constructions, and boundaries is also addressed through an investigation of Caribbean poetry. Yasmine Shamma's paper analyzes the various representations of water in the poetry of James Berry, E.A. Markham, Lorna Goodison, and Olive Senior. Shamma contends that "employing water in contemporary Caribbean poetry" creates fluidity—"a banking against erosion through coating and recoating words and ideas, though actually, sometimes not moving at all, but staying still awhile." As such, water images in these texts range in form from "reflections of being wet, of feeling dry, warnings of thunder," to "the relief of bathing."Addressing the intersection of the use of Creole in Caribbean literature, Marta Viada Bellido de Luna draws attention to the sociolinguistic tendency to relegate Creole to the margins in "The Use of English Lexified Creole in

Anglophone Caribbean Literature." Her essay unites folk tales and fiction to explain the significant role of Creole in Caribbean texts and how the use of Creole "reflects the cultures and experiences of its speakers" and "asserts their Caribbean identity." Like the multiple perspectives presented in the employment of Creole, these approaches have promoted a plurality of insights into Caribbean culture. Proceeding to the aspect of the practice of the vodou religion in Haiti, Dara Green examines the use of vodou as an agent of social change in Jacques Roumain's *Masters of the Dew*. As Green's essay illustrates, "vodou plays the dual roles of being both fatalist and catalyst." Bound by the vodou beliefs, the characters in this text must weigh collective action with their consciousness of faith.

THE CARIBBEAN WITHOUT FRAMES: NARRATIVE STRUCTURE IN SAMUEL SELVON'S LONDON NOVELS

KAREN MAH CHAMBERLAIN

Few novels have attracted more linguistic and quasi-linguistic scrutiny than Samuel Selvon's *The Lonely Londoners*. The book about West Indian immigrants to post-World War II Britain has been widely praised for its innovative use of Creole language structures. Yet, the modification of Standard English morphology and syntax and the inclusion of idiomatic words and phrases is only one aspect of linguistic experimentation in the novel. The overall effect has been described by former University of the West Indies lecturer Roydon Salik in *The Novels of Samuel Selvon: A Critical Study* as "almost totally dialectical in style, episodic in structure, and minimal in plot."[1] In his introduction to *The Lonely Londoners*, Kenneth Ramchand, another Trinidadian and a pioneer in the study of West Indian literature as an academic field, takes issue with this characterization of the novel's form: "From looking at the narrator we are drawn to recognise in Selvon's literary artefact a tightness of structure (the way the parts are put inevitably together); subtlety of development and revelation of theme; linguistic cunning; and an appropriateness in the presentation and deployment of the characters.[2] Although it has received less critical comment, another of Selvon's novels, *The Housing Lark*, has a similar overall organization—a series of vignettes separated by rows of asterisks—a similar blend of Creole and Standard morpho-syntactical features and idiomatic phrases, and a similar cast of West Indian characters. The integrity of this narrative structure, which Ramchand asserts in the face of suggestions that it is loose, episodic, or generally exiled from European novelistic traditions, becomes clear when Selvon's London novels are contrasted with the overt and highly-structured organization of European frame narratives.

Form, whether in literature or conversation, is essentially a matter of whom is speaking and listening. Even the most basic communicative interaction, like that of two strangers exchanging comments about the weather, is determined by the relationship and identity of the participants.

In the Caribbean, the weather varies less than in England, and, as a result, this topic has less currency in small talk. Differences between West Indian and British meteorological discourse become apparent in a passage from *The Housing Lark*: "I mean, you think it have a lot of obeah and black magic in the West Indies, but if you listen to some of these Nordics. They say red sky is shepherd's delight, and if the dog fall asleep that mean rain coming, and if the cat start play frisk that mean sunshine."[3] Here the narrator defamiliarizes British proverbs and exposes them as superstitions, showing differences between the two forms of discourse.

In the face of this interaction between British and West Indian cultures and climates, it is interesting to pause and notice whom the narrator is addressing in this soliloquy on the weather. The implied interaction is clearly between one West Indian immigrant and another. The narrator is not speaking *to* "you Nordics," but speaking *about* "these Nordics." The addressor and the addressee share a set of experiences which separates them from the people back home: "you think it have a lot of obeah and black magic in the West Indies" and from the "Nordics" in London. The narrator of the novel and the narratee share a discursive space because they draw on a similar set of cultural knowledge and norms to communicate with one another.

This communication should not be confused with the communication between the author Selvon, who is a West Indian immigrant to London, and the reader, who may or may not be West Indian, an immigrant, or in London. The narrator is an implied, rather than an actual author, and the narratee is an implied, rather than an actual reader. The narrator and narratee communicate on a level in the text which lies between the level of author/reader and the level of most character interactions. In his framework for interpreting narrative fiction, *Narratology: The Form and Functioning of Narrative*, Gerald Prince explores how inferences can be made about narrators and narratees based on various linguistic signs including personal pronouns, spatio-temporal markers, and evaluative utterances.[4] The character of the narrator is especially accessible in instances of first person narration, but the character of the narratee and the purpose of the narration are often harder to determine.

It is possible to learn more about the participants and the purposes of narration by examining frame narratives, stories which have one or more other stories embedded in their structure. By describing the circumstances under which an embedded or interior narrative is told, frame narratives offer information about narrators, narratees, and the communicative interactions between them. For example, communicative purposes are illustrated well by Geoffrey Chaucer's 14th century work *Canterbury*

Tales in which the pilgrims tell stories to moralize and to entertain one another. The interactions between narrator and narratee illustrate why an interior narrative is worth telling and how an audience might respond to an interior narrative at the center of a literary work.

At the same time, frame narrators, whom Prince terms "main narrators,"[5] literally frame stories by selecting the boundaries of representation. For example, the frame narrator in Joseph Conrad's early 20th century novel about the disturbing effects of the ivory trade in colonial Congo *Heart of Darkness* could have constructed the story of Kurtz, the European ivory trader who "goes native", from Kurtz's own writings, could have chosen a different sailor's yarn, or could have listened for the voices of Congolese slaves in order to portray the *Heart of Darkness*. Instead the unnamed frame narrator relates the tale told by Marlow, a steamboat captain who brings Kurtz out of the Congolese interior, and interprets Marlow's story, perhaps in order to place the perspective from which the story is told closer to the sensibilities of an audience which Conrad assumed to be middle class and British. Kurtz's voice of warning and alteration becomes embedded beneath the voices of both Marlow and the frame narrator, reduced to a mere echo in layered quotation marks:" 'The horror! The horror!' "[6] The African characters in this text are even more silenced, than the European who sympathizes with them, because their voices are represented only as part of Kurtz's story not as active perspectives or participants in the Congolese drama. The power of the frame narrator to control the interior narrative is clear in the frame narrator's choice of which interior narrator to represent.

The main narrator not only frames the interior narrative through the selection of the narrator, but also exercises control over the interior narrator by representing the language of the interior narrative. In Emily Brontë's 19th century novel *Wuthering Heights* the frame narrator Lockwood says of his representation of the interior narrator Nelly Dean: "I'll continue in her own words, only a little condensed. She is, on the whole, a very fair narrator and I don't think I could improve her style."[7] The main narrator may claim to transcribe the interior narrative faithfully, but transcription itself involves numerous decisions about what to include and exclude. If an interior narrative is written, for example in a letter, then the main narrator need only make editorial decisions about whether to include the interior text in its entirety and perhaps correct a few misspellings. However, when interior narratives are spoken, it is up to the main narrator to convey the pronunciation, intonation, volume, gestures, and expressions of the interior narrator. In general, the accuracy of scribal representations of oral language relies on the language attitudes and experiences of the writer.[8] In frame narratives, part of this responsibility is passed on to the frame narrator.

In written representations of oral narrative, quotation marks often serve as the boundaries between voices, and Standard English frames literary dialect. For example, in Joel Chandler Harris' 19th century fictional portrait of an emancipated slave in the southern United States *Uncle Remus: His Songs and Sayings*, a standard English writing narrator records in literary dialect a series of stories told by a former plantation slave: "This is what 'Miss Sally' heard: " 'Bimeby, one day, atter Brer Fox bin doin' all dat he could fer ter ketch Brer Rabbit, en Brer Rabbit bein doin' all he could fer ter keep 'im fum it.' "[9] This contrast between the language of the frame narrative and the language of the interior narrative reinforces the sense that the frame narrator is needed as an interpreter between the dominant discourse and the subordinate discourse, between England and Africa in *Heart of Darkness*, between London and the moors in *Wuthering Heights*, and between the white metropolis and the black plantation in *Uncle Remus*. The use of eye-dialect, such as the apostrophes indicating the elision of "h" and "g" sounds which would be pronounced in Standard English, in addition to the frame created by the quotations marks, distances the narrator from speech which is not rendered according to middle class British and North American norms.

The technique of the frame narrative is related to other metanarrative devices such as the epistolary novel or pseudo-autobiography. Quoted speech, letters, and memoirs are forms of mimesis in that they imitate and illustrate the discourse of the characters rather than simply reporting or summarizing it (diegesis). Although he is primarily interested in the concepts as they relate to the work of Russian literary theorist Mikhail Bakhtin, David Lodge provides a good discussion of mimesis and diegesis. He points out how these techniques create layers of narration in a novel: "making the narrative discourse a mimesis of an act of diegesis, diegesis at a second remove."[10] The imitation of oral storytelling in frame narratives serves two almost contradictory functions. It estranges the reader of the novel from the world of the interior narrative by inserting an additional narrator and narratee into the process of interpretation, but it also makes the mechanisms of narration and the manipulations of subjective narrators more transparent.

Whereas traditional storytelling and oral communication more broadly occur in familiar social contexts with the possibility of interaction or at least non-verbal communication between the speaker and the listener, novels are almost by definition abstracted from the surrounding reality. In his discussion of the transition from orality to literacy, Walter Ong in

Orality and Literacy: The Technologizing of the Word describes the need for transition: "The nineteenth century novelist's recurrent 'dear reader' reveals the problem of adjustment: the author still tends to feel an audience, listeners, somewhere, and must frequently recall that the story is not for listeners but for readers, each one alone in his or her own world."[11] Frame narratives might play a particularly important role for readers who are still growing accustomed to more abstract forms of communication. Yet contrary to this possibility, most frame narratives work to orient a literary audience to an oral story world, rather than working to orient readers more familiar with oral traditions to the literary world. The subtle implication is that the interior narrator cannot communicate directly with the reader because of differences in culture or social status (as represented by literacy) which are mediated by the frame narrator.

Frame narration works as more than a technical device for introducing a story. The types of stories embedded in frame narratives in the nineteenth and early twentieth century are generally removed from a genial English middle class sensibility. To some extent, authors like Harris, Brontë, and Conrad should be commended for including the voices and stories of marginalized people in their novels, as Taylor Hagood commends Thomas Nelson Page for using a frame narrative structure similar to that found in *Uncle Remus* to create a dialogue between the white, metropolitan North and the black, plantation South in which the latter answers back to the former.[12] The inclusion of marginalized voices in cultural discourse is a corollary to representing their interests to people in power and seeking equity and justice in society. However, it is important to recognize that the decision to write about alternative perspectives is separate from the decision to delimit these perspectives in a frame narrative structure which empowers the frame narrator with the last word. In "Can the Subaltern Speak?", an article about the dangers of mainstream academics claiming to represent the position of marginalized subjects, Gayatri Spivak, points to the affinity between artistic representation and political representation and argues that in both cases the interests of the people being represented are subordinated to the perspectives of the more powerful members of the society who create the representations.[13] Spivak also explores the significance of interpolated narratives in the chapter on literature in *A Critique of Postcolonial Reason: Toward a History of the Vanishing Present*.[14] When the voices of marginalized people are represented by more politically powerful, socially prominent or culturally acceptable individuals, it is impossible to know whether the actual perspectives of the marginalized subjects are even being recorded at all.

The issues of representation and the mediation between oral and scribal literature described above are especially pertinent in the Caribbean context. The representations and restrictions of interior narrators by main narrators occur frequently in early Caribbean literature, despite the absence of formal frame narratives in early Caribbean fiction. Journals, histories, and ethnographies abstract and interpret Caribbean stories and discourse in the frame of European travel narratives, and C.L.R. James's *Minty Alley*, is an example of a novel in which a middle class narrator is called upon to frame the stories and language of lower class, Creole-speaking characters. The main narrator Haynes records the story of the residents of #2 Minty Alley based partially on his own observations and largely on the interior narratives brought to him in his role as confidant to the other residents. Haynes represents these interior narratives in quotation marks. The main structural difference between *Minty Alley* and a traditional frame narrative, like *Wuthering Heights*, is the sheer volume of informants whose stories Haynes frames and the subsequent brevity of each installment. The ability to view *Minty Alley* as a frame narrative also suggests that the analysis of the relationship between main narrators and interior narrators can be extended, even to instances in which narratives in direct speech constitute a relatively small percentage of a novel as a whole.

Selvon's *The Lonely Londoners* and *The Housing Lark* contain many vibrant short narratives or "ballads" in direct speech. A consideration of the way these ballads are framed in narration leads to a greater appreciation of Selvon's linguistic and structural achievement in these novels. The conversations in which these ballads are embedded reveal the communicative purpose of the narratives. The characters tell stories about people they know as a way of entertaining one another and more importantly as a way of creating a sense of solidarity among West Indians. In *The Lonely Londoners*, ballads are exchanged between Moses and Galahad which express this sense of solidarity. Moses has lived in London for several years and Galahad is a newcomer from Trinidad. At one point, Moses asks Galahad if he knows a man named Brackley. Galahad replies, " 'But how you mean?' " ("Of course") and proceeds to tell Moses a story about Brackley: " 'You ever hear bout the time when Brackley sleep with a whore?' "[15] Like many of the interior narratives in the traditional frame-story novels, Galahad's interior narrative embeds quotations into the direct speech narrative. In this case, this layered representation of speech occurs as the narrator represents the speech of Galahad who in turn mimics the voices of the other whores in the yard: " 'A-a! Brackley sleep with Tina, me child!' "[16] This compounding of voices, perspectives, and quotation marks reveals the structure of representation taking place in the novel. The

West Indians tell stories about mutual acquaintances and familiar character types rather than relating stories across boundaries of difference as is the case in many of the European works examined above.

The representation of direct speech in particular becomes even more interesting when Moses replies to Galahad's story with another ballad about Brackley: " 'You hear bout the time they nail Brackley to the cross?'"[17] Moses and Galahad use a similar variety of language in their narrations. For example, both use the base forms of verbs for the foregrounded action of the story with past tense inflections like "was" and "it had" for background information. Their speech is also marked by various Trinidadian usages, like the semantic shift in "Tina *carry* him home"[18] (meaning to escort rather than to lift and transport) and lexeme in "them boys start to make *rab*" (meaning trouble or fuss).[19] However, Brackley's quoted speech differs in the two narratives. In Galahad's narrative, Brackley also uses the base forms of verbs with a past or perfective meaning: " 'What the hell happen to you? I give you money and I sleep with you and everybody know.' "[20] Whereas in Moses' narrative Brackley uses the standard English past tense: " 'They didn't stone Christ on the cross!' "[21] In contrast to Galahad, Moses seems to mimic Brackley in a different code from the Creole, which predominates in his narrative as a whole.

Although it is possible that both Galahad's and Moses' quotations of Brackley are accurate transcriptions of Brackley's actual words, it seems more likely that each narrator has manipulated Brackley's speech to fit with the style of the retelling. The quotation of Brackley's speech in the narrative about his rendezvous with Tina re-encapsulates the narrative, allowing Brackley to narrate for himself. Brackley, Galahad, and the narrator of *The Lonely Londoners* share the joke and share the Creole language in which they tell it. Moses' narrative, on the other hand, pokes fun at Brackley rather than sympathizing with him. The code switching in direct speech signals the distinction between the voice of the character and the voice of the narrator (Moses). The use of Standard English also underscores the broader comic purpose of the tale. The humor in the story revolves around the ironic contrast between the solemnity of Christ and the crucifixion and the absurdity of Brackley's vulnerable position on the cross. The contrast between the Creole features of the ballad and the Standard English features of Brackley's protest extends this irony. The Trinidadian masquerades as Christ, but winds up playing the fool, despite his use of Standard English. However, neither Moses nor Galahad creates a contrast between the code of narration and his representation of the character's speech in order to exercise linguistic or moral authority over him. Similarly, no contrast exists between the code of narration in the novel and the code used in direct speech. This concordance between narrator and character is very different from the practice of using Standard English to frame representations of Creole language as in *Uncle Remus* or *Minty Alley*.

Not only does Creole language escape the boundaries of quotation marks in *The Lonely Londoners* and *Housing Lark,* but the narratives often break through the frame of direct speech. In some instances, the main narrator simply steps in to provide background information for the interior narrator's story, a classic movement from mimetic to diegetic discourse, which is seen in the following example from *The Lonely Londoners*:

> (Moses) "Eh-heh! You know Mahal?"
> (Narrator) Mahal was a mad Indian fellar who used to go around town playing as if he driving car, putting in gear and stepping on the x and making hand signals and blowing horn.
> (Galahad) "But how you mean? Everybody know Mahal!"
> "He must be catching arse with the new type of gear it have on them cars now!" Moses laugh.
> Galahad laugh. "He still driving old-model."[22]

As noted with the previous examples, Moses and Galahad share stories about characters they both knew in Trinidad to fulfill specific communicative purposes. One of these purposes is to entertain, but an even more important purpose is to identify with the same social network. It is not actually true that "Everybody know Mahal!" Therefore, the narrator must step in with a digest of the common knowledge shared by the two characters. This not only enables the narratee to understand the joke about Mahal pretending to drive a particular type of car, but also involves the narratee in the process of solidarity building among the West Indian immigrants.

A much more dramatic transgression of the quotation marks occurs in *The Housing Lark*. Harry Banjo, a Jamaican calypsonian who has just arrived in London, expresses surprise that Fitzwilliams, a member of the wily group of Trinidadians he has just met, is married. His roommate Battersby or Bat starts (in the quotation marks of direct speech) to tell Harry the ballad about how the tough-talking Fitz became the most henpecked husband of all: (Harry) "I didn't know he was married. Bat chuckle. 'Was a big thing. Let me give you the ballad . . . ' "[23] At the end of the ellipses in quotation marks, a line of asterisks signals the end of the chapter or episode in which Harry and the Trinidadians become acquainted. The next chapter or episode is the ballad Bat tells Harry. The narrative includes Bat's asides to Harry, "Boy," and Bat's first person pronouns "we" and "my". The main narrator is absent, except for the parenthetical "(Bat telling Harry)". Yet, despite all these signals that this is a narrative from direct speech, it is not framed by quotation marks. The ballad ends with another row of asterisks and the next chapter begins, "That was the ballad that Bat give Harry about Fitz, killing himself with laugh as he say it."[24] This overlap between the narrative in direct speech and the flow of narration in the novel suggests that all of the chapters in *The Housing Lark* are representations of the various ballads that the West Indian immigrants share.

This relationship between the ballads of direct speech and the episodes which unfold between each set of asterisks is further reinforced when a later ballad is introduced in direct speech and then given its own chapter outside the quotation marks. The ballad is set up when Nobby's friends ask him about his dog:

> "Jesus Christ Nobby," Bat say, "you ain't get rid of that dog yet?"
> "Yes," Nobby say.
> "And who is that outside scratching and barking?"
> "That is another one."
> "Another one! You get another one?"
> "Yes man," Nobby say as if he embarrass, "and the damn thing following me about."[25]

Presumably, Nobby tells Bat about how he came to have a second dog, but the ballad is not presented from Nobby's point of view because first the main narrator has to provide the main narratee (and the reader) with the background of how Nobby obtained the first dog as the result of trying to please his animal-loving landlady. To this end, the ballad is actually introduced again this time by the narrator in a metanarrative comment to the narratee: "The episode of how Nobby get that dog could pass time before we go on the excursion to Hamdon Court."[26] This comment is remarkable because it reveals the level of communication occurring between the narrator and the narratee. The main narrator speaks directly to the main narratee in a gesture similar to Battersby's "Let me give you the ballad . . . "[27] Here again, as with the initial rant about weather forecasts, the narrator as a West Indian addresses the narratee as a West Indian, and in the context of exchanging ballads for entertainment and solidarity, a communicative context Selvon calls "old-talk": "he grab the chance to mingle with OUR PEOPLE, to hear the old-talk and to see how in spite of all the miseries and hardships they could still laugh skiff-skiff and have a good time."[28]

The Lonely Londoners also weaves together individual stories about the different West Indian characters in an old-talk format. The sense that both narrator and narratee eavesdrop on the conversations and lives of the characters makes these two novels similar to traditional frame stories. However, the narrators in *The Lonely Londoners* and *The Housing Lark* do not exercise the control over the characters they represent which is commonly found in frame narratives. They do step in to provide background information for what the narratee is hearing, and they do make subjective and evaluative comments about the characters. Yet at the same time, the narrators remain closely allied with the characters in their narration, especially the central characters Moses and Battersby. Ramchand suggests that the consciousnesses of Moses, the narrator, and Selvon "fuse into one" at the point when Moses begins to contemplate writing a book which might be *The Lonely Londoners*.[29] Yet, the dominant metanarrative trope in *The Lonely Londoners* and *The Housing Lark* is not the idea of the central characters writing a book about their experiences in London. Rather, the main metanarrative trope is the sharing of ballads between immigrants in sessions of old-talk when multiple narrators address multiple narratees, a trope which ultimately determines the structural framework of the novels.

The qualities of old-talk can be seen in Selvon's descriptions of this style of communication between the West Indian immigrants. For example, in *The Lonely Londoners*, the exchange of stories about Brackley between Moses and Galahad occurs because "The pigeon and rice have Moses feeling good and he in the mood for a oldtalk."[30] Toward the end of the novel, the narrator reveals that the various immigrants ritually gather in Moses' room to talk:

> Nearly every Sunday morning, like if they going to church, the boys liming in Moses' room, coming together for a oldtalk, to find out the latest gen, what happening, when is the next fete, Bart asking if anybody see his girl anywhere, Cap recounting a episode he had with a woman by the tube station the night before, Big City want to know why the arse he can't win a pool, Galahad recounting a clash with the colour problem in a restaurant in Piccadilly, Harris saying he hope the weather turns, Five saying he have to drive a truck to Glasgow tomorrow.[31]

This passage reinforces the idea of Moses as the central consciousness in the novel, a consciousness which assembles the different characters' stories into a book. Yet elements of *The Lonely Londoners*, such as Galahad's initial reactions to being alone in the tube station and the "p.s. episode with the pigeons what happen to Cap, and he never tell any of the boys because he fraid they laugh at him,"[32] are outside of Moses' consciousness and not available to him as a narrator. Instead, the group of West Indians narrates, and, like traditional frame narrators, they are also narratees, who listen to the different ballads the group tells.

The Housing Lark has a passage that describes the possibility of multiple personae participating as narrators and narratees in the same conversation:

> If you ever want to hear old-talk no other time better than one like this when men belly full, four crates of beer and eight bottle rum finish, and a summer sun blazing in the sky. Out of the blue, old-talk does start up. You couldn't, or shouldn't, differentiate between the voices, because men only talking, throwing in a few words here, butting in there, making a comment, arguing a point, stating a view. Nobody care who listen or who talk.[33]

With old-talk meandering freely between the different voices, the most comprehensive understanding of Selvon's narrative style is that of different narrators contributing their words, comments, views, and stories to a composite audience that is decidedly West Indian. In contrast to Ramchand's sense of central consciousness, different perspectives meld into one narrative structure, a narrative structure which is free-flowing and not dominated by a single voice.

In portraying a discourse being conducted between West Indians, Samuel Selvon actually inverts the frame of European perspectives. The British cannot frame the West Indian discourse in *The Housing Lark*: "It like a game, all of them throwing words in the air like a ball, now and then some scandalous laugh making sedate Englishers wonder what the arse them black people talking about."[34] However, the West Indians can imagine what British people are saying and can frame their discourse: "You could imagine the talk that going on on the boat: 'Look dear, come and see, there's a party of Jamaicans on the bank.' And big excitement on the boat, everybody rushing to the gunnels (is a pity some of them don't break their arse and fall in the Thames) to see."[35] In this way, Selvon manages to create novels which break free from the frames of European perspectives by allowing West Indian speakers and listeners to discourse directly—old-talking as narrators and narratees.

Criticisms which assert that Selvon's novels are "episodic in structure" or "minimal in plot" overlook how the direct speech provides a framework for organizing the different ballads into a cohesive whole. This structure allows various voices and the perspectives and linguistic codes associated with them to be heard in *The Lonely Londoners* and *The Housing Lark*. Most importantly of all these voices speak directly, rather than being subjected to representation by the overarching frame narrators of the European tradition. Rather than being weak in comparison to British works, the narrative structures found in Selvon's London novels are a remarkable development in form.

Bibliography

Brontë, Emily. *Wuthering Heights*. Edited by Pauline Nestor. 1847. Reprint, London: Penguin, 1995.

Conrad, Joseph. *Heart of Darkness*. In *Norton Anthology of English Literature,* vol. 2, edited by M. H. Abrams et. al., 1957-2016. 1902. Reprint, New York: W. W. Norton, 2000.

Hagood, Taylor. "'Prodjickin', or mekin' a present to yo' family': Rereading Empowerment in Thomas Nelson Page's Frame Narratives." *Mississippi Quarterly* 57 (2004): 423-440.

Harris, Joel Chandler. *Uncle Remus: His Songs and Sayings*. 2003. <http://www.gutenberg.org/dirs/etext00/remus11.txt/> (accessed February 14, 2007), Project Gutenberg.

James, C.L.R. *Minty Alley*. 1936. Reprint, London: New Beacon, 1971.

Lalla, Barbara. *Virtual Realism: Constraints on Validity in Textual Evidence of Caribbean Language History*. St. Augustine, Trinidad and Tobago: Society for Caribbean Linguistics, 2005.

Lodge, David. *After Bakhtin: Essays on Fiction and Criticism*. London: Routledge, 1990.

Ong, Walter J. *Orality and Literacy: The Technologizing of the Word*. London: Routledge, 2002.

Prince, Gerald. *Narratology: The Form and Functioning of Narrative*. Berlin: Mouton Publishers, 1982.

Ramchand, Kenneth. Introduction to *The Lonely Londoners* by Samuel Selvon, 3-21. London: Longman, 1985.

Salik, Roydon. *The Novels of Samuel Selvon: A Critical Study*. Westport, Connecticut: Greenwood Press, 2001.

Selvon, Samuel. *The Housing Lark*. 1965. Reprint, Washington D.C.: Three Continents Press, 1990.

—. *The Lonely Londoners*. 1956. Reprint, London: Longman, 2004.

Spivak, Gayatri Chakravorty. "Can the Subaltern Speak?" In *Colonial Discourse and Post-Colonial Theory: A Reader*, edited by Patrick Williams and Laura Chrisman, 66-111. Hertfordshire: Prentice Hall, 1993.

—. *A Critique of Postcolonial Reason: Toward a History of the Vanishing Present*. Cambridge, MA: Harvard University Press, 1999.

Notes

[1] Roydon Salik, *The Novels of Samuel Selvon: A Critical Study* (Westport, Connecticut: Greenwood Press, 2001), 120.
[2] Kenneth Ramchand, Introduction to *The Lonely Londoners*, by Samuel Selvon (London: Longman, 1985), 10.
[3] Samuel Selvon, *The Housing Lark* (1965; reprint, Washington D.C.: Three Continents Press,1990), 10.
[4] Gerald Prince, *Narratology: The Form and Functioning of Narrative* (Berlin: Mouton Publishers, 1982), 7-10, 16-20.
[5] Ibid., 16.
[6] Joseph Conrad, *Heart of Darkness* in *Norton Anthology of English Literature*, vol. 2, ed. M. H. Abrams et. al (1902; reprint, New York: W. W. Norton, 2000), 2011.
[7] Emily Brontë, *Wuthering Heights*, ed. Pauline Nestor (1847; reprint, London: Penguin, 1995), 155.
[8] Barbara Lalla, *Virtual Realism: Constraints on Validity in Textual Evidence of Caribbean Language History* (St. Augustine, Trinidad and Tobago: Society for Caribbean Linguistics, 2005), 11.
[9] Joel Chandler Harris, *Uncle Remus: His Songs and Sayings*, 2003, <http://www.gutenberg.org/dirs/etext00/remus11.txt/> (accessed February 14, 2007) Project Gutenberg.
[10] David Lodge, *After Bakhtin: Essays on Fiction and Criticism* (London: Routledge, 1990), 30.
[11] Walter J. Ong, *Orality and Literacy: The Technologizing of the Word* (London: Routledge, 2002), 146.
[12] Taylor Hagood, "'Prodjickin', or mekin' a present to yo' family': Rereading Empowerment in Thomas Nelson Page's Frame Narratives," *Mississippi Quarterly* 57 (2004): 423-440.
[13] Gayatri Chakravorty Spivak, "Can the Subaltern Speak?" in *Colonial Discourse and Post-Colonial Theory: A Reader*, ed. Patrick Williams and Laura Chrisman (Hertfordshire: Prentice Hall, 1993), 70.
[14] Gayatri Chakravorty Spivak, *A Critique of Postcolonial Reason: Toward a History of the Vanishing Present* (Cambridge, MA: Harvard University Press, 1999), 112-97.
[15] Samuel Selvon, *The Lonely Londoners* (1956; reprint, London: Longman, 2004), 127.
[16] Ibid., 128.
[17] Ibid.
[18] Ibid., 127.
[19] Ibid., 128.
[20] Ibid.
[21] Ibid.

[22] Ibid., 37.
[23] Selvon, *Lark*, 40.
[24] Ibid., 45.
[25] Ibid., 81.
[26] Ibid.
[27] Ibid., 40.
[28] Selvon, *Lark*, 110-11.
[29] Ramchand, 20.
[30] Selvon, *Lonely*, 127.
[31] Ibid., 138.
[32] Ibid., 134.
[33] Selvon, *Lark*, 123.
[34] Ibid., 126.
[35] Ibid., 126-27.

Ghost Know No Borders: A Look at the Functions of Ghosts in Wilson Harris' Fiction in General and the Ghost of Memory in Particular

Suzanna Engman

> "Language is deeper than 'frames,' it transgresses against the frames that would make us prisoners of eternity in the name of one creed or dogma or ideology."[1]

This paper focuses on the Caribbean writer Wilson Harris and on the ghost characters he invokes to move beyond physical, literary, and linguistic borders or "frames." Ghosts recur in most, if not all, of Harris' fictional works. By disregarding the borders between life and death, and between past, present, and future, the ghosts in Harris' literature symbolize hope for life beyond death. His literary ghosts also embody cross-cultural beliefs of four continents that meet in Guyana. European, Amerindian, African, and possibly East Indian ancestors seem to have been seminal in the formation of Harris' views of death, afterlife, and spirits. This analysis of Harris' *The Ghost of Memory* explores why Harris includes ghosts and shows how they disregard borders of time, space, and logic by making these constructs permeable, fluid, and impermanent.

A brief survey of the history of the spiritual beliefs of the Guyanese and of ghosts in literature provide a context for the discussion of ghosts in Harris' latest and—according to him—last novel. French psychoanalyst Nicholas Abraham in "Notes on the Phantom" in *The Shell and the Kernel* asserts that "The belief that the spirits of the dead can return to haunt the living exists either as an accepted tenet or as a marginal conviction in all civilizations, ancient or modern."[2] In *Religion and the Decline of Magic*, historian Keith Thomas observes that before the Enlightenment, Western ghosts would often appear to "denounce some specific injustice."[3] They also returned to Earth to instruct the living about the price to be paid for sinning and to urge them to offer restitution for misbegotten gains. Ghosts provided hope that the border between life and death was imaginary and impermanent.

Ghosts were sanctioned by Catholic doctrine as part of the Trinity and as spirits of Purgatory, a place where those who were not good enough to go to Heaven, but who were not evil enough to be punished in Hell were interned and where, paradoxically, their bodiless spirits suffered extreme physical agony. Often the spirits of the dead, or ghosts, consigned to Purgatory returned to Earth to request prayers from loved ones petitioning for their admission into Heaven. The ghosts ensured that the dead would not be forgotten. Purgatory empowered the living over the finality of death and gave them hope that they could ease the suffering of the ghosts. The offerings to ease the suffering of those in Purgatory, "suffrages," could be purchased from the Catholic Church. Literary critic Stephen Greenblatt in *Hamlet in Purgatory* says that suffrages "gave mourners something constructive to do with their feelings of grief and confirmed those feelings of reciprocity that survived, at least for a limited time, the shock of death."[4] Ultimately, ghosts offer "a ghost of a chance" and hope. It is a sacral hope of life beyond death that requires faith and imagination.

Ghosts were imported by Europeans to the Americas, but they also existed *a priori* in the cultures of the Amerindians. Anthropologist Åke Hultkrantz in *Native Religions of North America* says, "Four prominent features in North America Indian religions are a similar worldviews, a shared notion of cosmic harmony, emphasis on experiencing directly powers and visions, and a common view of the cycle of life and death."[5] Physical death in indigenous populations, says religion scholar Paul V. A. Williams does not involve total annihilation:

> Death rites serve to prove this. Death is no more than a return to Mother Earth hence the dead are so often buried in embryonic position. To die means to ensure that the eternal life cycle will not be interrupted. Death, therefore, is regarded as a supreme initiation and, like all initiations, it is the beginning of a new sacred existence. The "primitive" therefore, does taste immortality but not necessarily in the sense of a life after death. Immortality is a state Man tries to achieve by constant death and resurrection.[6]

Hultkrantz notes that to Native Americans, the afterlife is really a life after death: "The Manacia believe that immediately following the funeral ceremonies the dead person sets out on his journey to the land of death with the medicine man as his guide."[7] The Amerindian belief of death as part of the eternal life cycle is hopeful because it does not see death as the end of life, but as a rebirth or continuation of life.

When Africans were forcibly imported to the Americas for their labor, they brought along their own ghosts, which were often associated with ancestors. Ghosts carry collective memory, and ancestral ghosts link people to their lost families. For Africans, as well as Amerindians, death is not an end to life—life continues on in another realm, the realm of the "living dead." "The concepts of 'life' and 'death' are not mutually exclusive concepts, and there are no clear dividing lines between them," writes theologian Allan Anderson in *The Encyclopedia of Death and Dying* (*EDD*).[8] In many parts of Africa, people believe in a kind of parallel afterworld, invisible but close to the living world. Although the living cannot see spirits, Africans believe that the spirits, "a cloud of witnesses," can see what they are doing.[9] Africans employ mediums who can call back the dead for help in the diagnosis and cure of diseases. Family members may also employ mediums in séances to call back the dead in order to consult them about major family decisions, notes African religion scholar, John S. Mbiti in *Introduction to African Religions*.[10] These spirits of the dead are believed capable of possessing living persons by speaking and acting through them. In the Caribbean and Brazil, the Vodou/Vodoun religion is most noted for retaining possession phenomena.[11] The dead are also remembered by family members in prayers and through the ritual of sharing food and drink with them, by leaving a morsel of food and a drink near their graves. As with Amerindian cultures, funeral practices are important to ensure that the dead rest in peace.

Funeral rites are also important to East Indians. Hindu ritual cremation returns the physical remains of the dead to nature as smoke and ashes. After burning the body, which occurs as soon as possible after death, rituals are performed to complete the transition to the ancestral world, "the world of the fathers."[12]

Recently, ghosts have been proliferating in literature and films of the Americas.[13] Scholars explain this phenomenon, frequently observed in the genre of magical realism, as an aspect of postcolonialism, the work of memorializing and mourning cultures that people have been severed from by diasporas or genocide. Literary critic Kathleen Brogan in *Cultural Haunting* notes that ghosts are increasingly present in ethnic literature of North America and argues that the spectral presence of ghosts signals "an attempt to recover and make social use of a poorly documented, partially erased cultural history."[14] In *The National Uncanny,* author Renée Bergland views the representation of ghostly Native Americans in American literature as a reflection of the collective national imaginary. She concludes that the specteralization of the Indian is a result of repressed guilt for stealing their land: "Ghosts are the things that we try to bury, but that refuse to stay buried. They are our fears and our horrors, disembodied, but made inescapable by their very bodilessness."[15] Bergland presents a model of ghosts as public, political entities in which "family ghosts became less important, while communal ghosts grew more significant" in American literature.[16]

Ghosts embody the baroqueness and lack of closure that characterize novels of the Americas.[17] They dwell in the *in-between* spaces, in liminal space, in Limbo, which is closely associated with Purgatory.[18] They are no longer living, yet neither are they quite dead. They embody the past in a disembodied form. They materialize and disappear, unbidden, move through physical barriers, defy the laws of gravity, and disregard the distinctions between past, present, and future. Postcolonial theorist Stephen Slemon interprets the indeterminacy of ghosts as the source of their discursive power of conversion: "Being caught between presence and absence . . . is also a way of mediating between binary terms, of crossing the borders between them and thus beginning the process of breaking them down."[19] By crossing borders of time and space, ghosts mock the construct of binaries: they are presence in absence, spirit and body, material and nonmaterial. Hence, ghosts know no borders.

Most, if not all of Harris' novels, beginning with *Palace of the Peacock*, have included ghosts. The ghosts achieve transcendence beyond death-in-life to life-in-death in a fictional world where the categories of life and death are fused together and appear to be in flux, where there is no sense of distinction between sleeping and waking states, and where the consciousnesses of the characters seem to meld together. The cultural creolization that occurred in language, art, and religions also occurred in the ghosts of the Americas, and they are represented as creolized ghosts in Harris' novels. For example, the ghosts in his novels often denounce the sins of slavery and cultural dominance. This embodies the European idea of the ghost as emblematic of conscience. The journeys embarked upon by Harris' ghosts call to mind the journeys that Amerindian ghosts embark upon after death. Moreover, African ghost characteristics emerge when the ghosts possess others with their thoughts and actively participate in the lives of the living.

Harris' more recent novels give greater and greater prominence to ghost characters. In *Jonestown*, the main character, Francisco Bone, is a ghostly character who escapes the Jonestown massacre. He interacts with the apparitional teacher, Mr. Mageye, and with those killed in the massacre. *The Dark Jester* depicts a narrator/dreamer's dialogue between the ghostly forms of the Inca emperor Atahualpa and the conquistadors Cortéz and Pizarro. And in *The Mask of the Beggar*, with the exception of the unnamed sculptor the characters are all "solid ghosts," including the ghosts of Odysseus, Lazarus, Montezuma, Cortéz, Quetzalcoatl, and the sculptor's mother.

In *The Ghost of Memory*, "The Author's Note" begins by introducing this narrative of no absolutes: *"The Ghost of Memory* is a novel about life and death or rather—to put it somewhat differently—about the close, almost indefinable cross-culturalities between moments of life and death."[20] The Ghost of Memory, who the author tells the reader should not be taken literally and remains unnamed throughout the novel, describes to the reader his life after death, of "returning across centuries and generations to the end of my age." He explains the paradox of simultaneously returning from the future to the past and returning from the past to the future with another paradox: "[Death] was an end, it was a new beginning one was called upon to probe and discover."[21]

The Ghost of Memory had been accused of being a terrorist and was shot and killed. He falls through space and time into a painting displayed in an art museum in a great city and finds himself to be a beggar in the painting. As a ghost, he is not bound to the paining, but has the ability to step out and assume an apparitional form. The ghost is visible to one patron in an art museum, a man who has changed his name to Christopher Columbus, and invisible to two others, George and Andy. During interludes, the ghost travels with another ghost, Tiresias, through the hinterland of Guyana, muses on eclipsed cultures, and meets yet another ghost, the Wanderer or the ghost of fire, who has also fallen into the painting. The novel closes after Columbus attacks the painting with a knife, slashing it to shreds. Although he was initially fascinated with the painting, he comes to loathe it because, as Harris explains in "The Author's Note," "it brings his unconscious into acute tension with his hard-and-fast-convictions."[22] At the end of the novel, Columbus is led away from the museum in chains, an allusion to the historical accounts of Christopher Columbus the navigator returning to Spain in chains after his fourth voyage.

At the literary level, Harris' ghosts function in several ways. They serve as a medium for the author's thoughts, for example, his thoughts about ghosts and the nature of consciousness. The blind Greek seer, Tiresias, a recurring ghost character in Harris' *oeuvre*, articulates the author's views about the function of an apparition in *The Four Banks of the River of Space*:

> I illume the seed of fire to enhance the regeneration of wheat. I illume the shifting plates within the globe to engage civilizations in movements and migrations of threatened peoples and species upon an earth that is still the

nursery of hope. In the fire of spirit, let us wrest a therapy of the heart and mind. Let us steep every inch of the resurrection in a capacity to weigh a reversed sail that arises and moves above the seas of chaos.[23]

Thus, it seems that the ghost's primary function is to provide hope for reversal of what Harris calls "victor/victim stasis." *The Ghost of Memory* expresses Harris' thoughts about the nature of consciousness, unconsciousness, and Limbo. What Harris calls "the Art of Limbo" in literature is expressed or written through the ghost, who unites the conscious with the unconscious. The Ghost of Memory says that "Limbo fuses contradictory spaces."[24] Limbo is the place in which ghosts dwell, an indeterminate space that fuses the conscious with unconscious and defies the boundaries between the states of living and dead.

Ghosts also act as guides in Harris' fiction. The Ghost of Memory communicates with art museum patrons to guide their thoughts. With the patron who has changed his name to Christopher Columbus and to whom he is visible, the Ghost of Memory engages in heated arguments in an attempt to persuade him to reflect more deeply about his assumptions. On the other hand, the ghost speaks silently to George, to whom he is invisible, and unbeknownst to George, influences his thoughts. This unconscious influence from the ghost onto George can be interpreted as a kind of possession or what Harris in "Profiles of Myth and the New World" calls "ventriloquism of spirit."[25] The ghost had "inserted words akin to what he had said into the depth of his consciousness and [George] listened. It was a habitual way of communicating across an abyss of fact and fiction but few paid any attention to what was happening to them."[26] Afterward, when George begins to speak, it is with a bestowed awareness of pathos.

The Ghost of Memory has his own ghost guide. Tiresias returns during interludes from the ghost's interactions with museum patrons to answer questions about eclipsed cities and cultures buried in the soil of the New World. The questions posed throughout *The Ghost of Memory* are articulated in "The Author's Note:" "What is spirit? What is the New World? What is art? What is truth? What is evolution—how does it bear on the *leaps* that Man has made—without knowing for certain how they were made—and may still be drawn into making in the present or future?"[27] These questions are not answered definitively. However, it is suggested that new ways of seeing, made possible by creolization of cultures, are erasures of delimiting boundaries. Instead of providing answers to the questions, Harris urges readers to consider possibilities and envision potentialities.

Ghosts in Harris' fiction serve as an acknowledgement of, a reverence for, and a memory of subterranean and eclipsed cultures of the New World. It is through memory and through ghosts that the dead live on. The Ghost of Memory acknowledges that "all things break and leave traces that never die in the rapids of history. . . . Nothing dies entirely as it is a compass of traces of the past in the present and the future that seen absolutely new."[28] The ghost reminds readers that "There were Cities beneath the Amazon and the Orinoco basins. Abandoned and long forgotten."[29] And he wonders if the self-named Columbus sees the significance of being haunted: "Did he see that I embodied, in visionary attire, thousands, millions, who had been shot, bombed, broken in the marketplace of history as enemies or terrorists of established states which terrorized in turn those they pursued?"[30] Memory, like dream, is a re-creative act that blurs the boundary between the past and present.

Landscape itself is a metaphoric ghost in Harris' fiction. The landscape of Guyana's interior is both the womb and the grave of past presences; repressed or forgotten Amerindian mythic symbols erupt from the land and even the rocks themselves, the fossils, preserve and give (re)birth to the past. Hauntings, Judith Richardson points out in *Possessions: The History and Uses of Haunting in the Hudson*, arise from the land itself. Her observations and conclusions about the Hudson Valley can be applied to Guyana. She notes, for example, that hauntings result from territorial conflicts about the land—possession and dispossession, rootedness and restlessness. Guyana is still being haunted by border disputes with Suriname and Venezuela. The untamed hinterland of jungles, web of waterways, spectacular waterfalls, and *tepuis* (flat topped mountains) of Guyana's landscape is seen as strange, mysterious, fearsome, and mystical to non-natives. The animals of the region, jaguars, giant river otters, black caimans, anacondas also inspire fear. And animals that produce eerie sounds, such as howler monkeys, make the region seem to be inhabited by ghostly presences. The proximity of various cultures—after multiple, contending colonizations and migrations beginning with Amerindians and including various Europeans (Spanish, Portuguese, Dutch, and English), Africans, East Indians, and Chinese—causes fear of others that is often sublimated into fear of the land itself. Displaced ghosts haunt the land, rise, and make their presence felt.

Harris believes that quantum or parallel realities are embodied in the landscape. His multiple-perspective quantum view of place unites extinct cultures with the environment, and this is witnessed by the Ghost of Memory as he climbs out of a river bank:

> Suddenly there emerged from behind the mound a group of naked people. They were painted in the colours of Nature, so much so they could have been the flakes from trees. Each flake came from the ancient Forest which had been demolished in places. In this spirit they brought traces of the past on their naked bodies. They held in their flaked hands what may have been the thinnest, most slender embodiment of the mother of their tribe.[31]

The scene illustrates "quantum immediacy," a concept that Harris explains in an interview: "A quantum physicist would describe 'Quantum Immediacy' by saying that parts of ourselves are embedded everywhere—in the rock, in the tree, in the star, in the river, in the earth, everywhere. Those parts are very frail. But they are enduring."[32] The idea of quantum immediacy is closely aligned with Amerindian and African beliefs that humans are not separate entities from animals, trees, water; and as such, humans never really disappear when they die. Ghosts are a part of the landscape.

Both Amerindians and Africans believe in a communal relationship between humans and all living plants and animals. The Ghost of Memory reflects this belief when he exclaims, "*We are related to every creature in the tree of life and death!*"[33] The concept of community also extends to include those already dead. Their presence, "a cloud of witnesses," forms an "*essence* [that] cannot be stolen or captured. It leans on 'vacancies' as a measure of the reinterpretation of form, of substance, beyond the million and more individual bodies which perish each year."[34]

Harris' ghosts also operate on a linguistic level. They deconstruct the accepted texts of what Westerners commonly refer to as reality by denying binary opposition and uniting opposites. A reading of the world through the lens of binary opposites (day/night, man/woman, white/black) invites the corollary of binary judgments (good/bad) with one of the binary categories being privileged over the other. Thus, Westerners may see, often unconsciously, objects and ideas with an added overlapped layer of meaning or bias appended to them. A linguistic analysis of Harris' ghosts reveals that Harris makes extensive use of paradox, oxymoron, duality, and images of metamorphosis to abolish binary opposites in order to move beyond their boundaries.

By erasing the boundary between life and death, ghosts alter the relationships of inclusion/exclusion. Another effect of boundary erasure is that it allows contrary interpretations. Harris' fictions simultaneously support different and even opposing interpretations. For example, his use of paradox, a seeming contradiction, does not allow for certainty or stasis. The image of river rapids appearing as still waters brings together a contradiction, and the observation by the Ghost of Memory that

"[Constellations] were surrounded by me—even as they surrounded me," is indeterminate.[35] Throughout *The Ghost of Memory*, the contradictory image of "dying into creativity," is repeated, suggesting that the ghost is an image of hope and rebirth, and this may be incongruous to prevalent representations of death and ghosts as fearsome phenomenon.

Closely related to the contradiction inherent in paradox, oxymoron juxtaposes opposites, which forces, simultaneously, both binaries to apply. The ghost muses that, "One looks into the rapids from beneath above. 'Beneath above' established cultural/psychical links with Nature. Thus one is not merely describing what one sees. One is within, beneath, above what one sees."[36] In other words, one is *both* beneath *and* above the rapids at the same time. This simultaneity of being, of experiencing parallel realities, is another way of breaching the boundaries of binaries. If something is simultaneously *both/and,* it fuses the binary boundary of the *either/or* categorization.

Closely related to parallel realities is duality of consciousness, another way of fusing binary opposites. Beginning with *Palace,* Harris makes extensive use of ghostly doubling, a paradox that unites self and Other. A.J.M. Bundy, editor of *Selected Essays of Wilson Harris,* describes this paradoxical condition:

> The known self occupies an intermediate position between chaos and creation, like the soul placed between two symmetries. In this way pairs of opposites create the phenomenology of a paradoxical self, man's totality. And the coming together of pairs of opposites creates a new conjunction whose character is neither the one known thing, nor the other, *but a third unassimilable or in-between thing.* . . . Twinship can be defined as the unrealized synchrony between two or more cultures which, at first sight, seem remote in time and circumstance.[37]

Doubling also reveals to the reader simultaneous or parallel realities in which the dead and the living to co-exist. In an argument with Columbus, when the ghost tries to illustrate that a painting brings life and death together, he states that "Myth bears on the *two lives we both liv*e. I am quoting your remark! It bears as well on legend *and* reality, masquerade *and* the inexplicable, ancient *and* modern, life *and* death."[38]

Metamorphosis is another way of moving beyond binaries and by turning an object into an action. In the process of becoming, the object is what it *was* in the past, what it *is* at this moment, and what it *will be* in the future. The object is, therefore, *neither* and *both* simultaneously. As the Ghost of Memory stands on an ancient river beside a great forest, he describes an image of metamorphosis: "A stem or broken leaf became a finger on my hand. It pointed to traces of infinity within itself, within other leaves on a tree."[39] The ghost's bones, which broke apart when he fell into the painting then reemerged from a ditch, is another image of metamorphosis. The ghost says that the bones, "came into me with diamonds that turned into a shining fish (imagine a diamond-fish!) *drowning in air.*"[40] Metamorphosis is also illustrated by the metamorphosis of the fusing of individual consciousness with the universal unconsciousness. This happens when George sees himself as part of the whole "celestial unconscious."

Ultimately, Harris' ghosts engender hope. George's life is positively influenced by his unconscious apprehension of the Ghost of Memory's wisdom. "He had been empowered [to embark upon the immense journey of life] by the celestial unconscious. It is real and unreal, and it inspires us to make of illusion a shape which represents an eternity of riddles, a shape brooding upon ruin and unknown fulfillment and origin," concludes *The Ghost of Memory.*[41] The emphasis is not on changing reality but on apprehending it in a different way, made possible by different world views in the process of creolization and through the potential offered by the boundary erasure.

Bibliography

Abraham, Nicholas. "Notes on the Phantom." In *The Shell and the Kernel*, edited and translated by Nicholas Rand, 171-76. Chicago: University Chicago Press, 1994.

Anderson, Allan. "African Religions." *Encyclopedia of Death and Dying.* <http://www.deathreference.com> (accessed April 7, 2007).

Bergland, Renée L. *The National Uncanny: Indian Ghosts and American Subjects.* Hanover and London: University Press of New England, 2000.

Brogan, Kathleen. *Cultural Haunting: Ghosts and Ethnicity in Recent American Literature.* Charlottesville and London: University Press of Virginia, 1998.

Bundy, A.J.M, ed. *Selected Essays of Wilson Harris: The Unfinished Genesis of the Imagination.* London and New York: Routledge, 1999.

Greenblatt, Stephen. *Hamlet in Purgatory.* Princeton and Oxford: Princeton University Press, 2001.

Harris, Wilson. "The Absent Presence: The Caribbean Central and South America." In *The Radical Imagination: Lectures and Talks Wilson Harris,* edited by Alan Riach and Mark Williams, 81-92. Liège, Belgium: Liège Language and Literature, 1992.

—. *The Dark Jester*. London: Faber and Faber, 2001.
—. *The Four Banks of the River of Space*. London: Farber and Farber, 1990.
—. *The Ghost of Memory*. London: Faber and Faber, 2006.
—. *Jonestown*. London: Faber and Faber, 1996.
—. *The Mask of the Beggar*. London: Faber and Faber, 2003.
—. "Profiles of Myth and the New World." In *Selected Essays of Wilson Harris: The Unfinished Genesis of the Imagination*, edited by A.J.M. Bundy, 201-11. London and New York: Routledge, 1999.
Hultkrantz, Åke. *Native Religions of North America*. San Francisco: HarperCollins, 1987.
Kramer, Kenneth P. "Hinduism." *Encyclopedia of Death and Dying*. <http://www.deathreference.com> (accessed April 7, 2007).
Mbiti, John S. *Introduction to African Religions*. Chicago: Heinemann International, 1975.
Parrinder, Geoffrey. *African Traditional Religions*. Westport, Connecticut: Greeenwood, 1976.
Riach, Alan, and Mark Williams, ed. *Radical Imagination: Lectures and Talks Wilson Harris,* 81-92. Liège, Belgium: Liège Language and Literature, 1992.
Richardson, Judith. *Possessions: The History and Uses of Haunting in the Hudson Valley*. Cambridge, Massachusetts and London: Harvard University Press, 2003.
Slemon, Stephen. "Magical Realism as Postcolonial Discourse." In *Magical Realism: Theory, History, Community*, edited by Lois Parkinson Zamora and Wendy B. Faris, 407-26. Durham and London: Duke University Press, 1995.
Thomas, Keith. *Religion and the Decline of Magic: Studies in Popular Beliefs in Sixteenth and Seventeenth Century England*. New York: Simon and Schuster, 1986.
Williams, Paul V.A. "Myths, Symbols and the Concept of Immortality among Some Amerindian Societies." *Folklore* 84 (1973): 327-38.

Notes

[1] Wilson Harris, *Jonestown* (London: Faber and Faber, 1996), 6.
[2] Nicholas Abraham, "Notes on the Phantom" in *The Shell and the Kernel*, ed. and trans.
[3] Keith Thomas, *Religion and the Decline of Magic: Studies in Popular Beliefs in*

Sixteenth and Seventeenth Century England (New York: Simon and Schuster, 1986), 597.

[4] Stephen Greenblatt, *Hamlet in Purgatory* (Princeton and Oxford: Princeton University Press, 2001), 102-3.

[5] Åke Hultkrantz, *Native Religions of North America (*San Francisco: HarperCollins, 1987), 20.

[6] Paul V.A. Williams, "Myths, Symbols and the Concept of Immortality Among Some Amerindian Societies," *Folklore* 84 (1973): 337.

[7] Hultkrantz, *Native Religions*, 133.

[8] Allan Anderson, "African Religion," *Encyclopedia of Death and Dying*. <http://www.deathreference.com> (7 April 2007).

[9] Geoffrey Parrinder, *African Traditional Religions* (Westport, Connecticut: Greenwood, 1976), 58.

[10] John S. Mbiti, *Introduction to African Religions* (Chicago: Heinemann International, 1975), 130.

[11] The spelling of Vodou/Vodoun religion, a religion with West African origin, is also spelled as Voudoun, Vodu, Vodun, Vudu, Hoodu, Voodoo, Voudoux. Scholars often contest the spellings.

[12] Kenneth P. Kramer, "Hinduism," *Encyclopedia of Death and Dying*. <http://www.deathreference.com> (7 April 2007).

[13] Fiction examples with the ghost as a major or central character include Rudolfo Anaya's *Bless Me, Ultima* (1972); William Kennedy's *Ironweed* (1983); Maryse Condé's *I, Tituba, Black Witch of Salem (*1986); Louise Erdrich's *Tracks (*1988) and *The Bingo Palace*, (1994); Leslie Marmon Silko's *Almanac of the Dead* (1991); Erna Brodber's *Louisiana* (1994); Toni Morrison's *Beloved* (1994); Julia Alvarez's *In the Time of the Butterflies* (1995); Pauline Melville's *The Ventriloquist's Tale* (1997); and Dionne Brand's *At the Full and Change of the Moon* (1999). Significant films include *Daughters of the Dust (1991), Sankofa* (1993), and *The House of the Spirits* (1993). Poets such as Derek Walcott (*Omeros*, for example) and Kamau Brathwaite (*Ancestors*, for example), and playwrights such as Derek Walcott (*Dream on Monkey Mountain*, 1970; *The Ghost Dance*, 2002)*;* Dennis Scott (*Echo in the Bone*, 1974) and August Wilson (*Piano Lesson*, 1990) include ghosts in a central way.

[14] Kathleen Brogan, *Cultural Haunting: Ghosts and Ethnicity in Recent American Literature* (Charlottesville and London: University Press of Virginia, 1998), 2.

[15] Renée L. Bergland, *The National Uncanny: Indian Ghosts and American Subjects* (Hanover and London: University Press of New England, 2000), 5.

[16] Ibid., 9.

[17] Alejo Carpentier says that baroque means something multiple, diverse, and enormous. It does not signify decadence, but is at times represented as culmination—the richest moment of a given civilization. The baroque is a constant of the human spirit that is horrified by the vacuum, the harmony of linear geometry. In the baroque, the decorative elements fill every space, motifs contain their own energy, and art moves outward, away from its center, breaking through its own borders. For a more complete discussion of the baroque in Caribbean

literature, see Alejo Carpentier, "The Baroque and the Marvelous Real," rpt. in *Magical Realism: Theory, History, Community,* ed. Lois Parkinson Zamora and Wendy B. Faris (Durham & London: Duke University Press, 1995), 89-108.

[18] Often Limbo and Purgatory were used interchangeably, but technically Limbo is where all the unbaptized dead, including babies and those who lived before Christ, are consigned; and Purgatory is the place where those who weren't good enough to go to Heaven but weren't evil enough to go to Hell landed.

[19] Stephen Slemon, "Magical Realism as Postcolonial Discourse," in *Magical Realism: Theory, History, Community,* ed. Lois Parkinson Zamora and Wendy B. Faris (Durham and London:Duke University Press, 1995), 419.

[20] Wilson Harris, *The Ghost of Memory* (London: Faber and Faber, 2006), vii.

[21] Ibid., 1.

[22] Ibid., viii.

[23] Wilson Harris, *The Four Banks of the River of Space* (London: Faber and Faber, 1990), 81.

[24] Harris, *The Ghost of Memory*, 11.

[25] Wilson Harris, "Profiles of Myth and the New World," in *Selected Essays of Wilson Harris: The Unfinished Genesis of the Imagination*, ed. A.J.M. Bundy (London and New York: Routledge, 1999), 207.

[26] Harris, *The Ghost of Memory*, 61.

[27] Ibid., viii-ix.

[28] Ibid., 20, 22.

[29] Ibid., 21.

[30] Ibid., 27.

[31] Ibid., 24.

[32] Wilson Harris, "The Absent Presence: The Caribbean Central and South America," in *TheRadical Imagination: Lectures and Talks Wilson Harris,* ed. Alan Riach and Mark Williams (Liège, Belgium: Liège Language and Literature, 1992), 81.

[33] Harris, *The Ghost of Memory*, 34.

[34] Ibid., 75.

[35] Ibid., 23.

[36] Ibid., 19.

[37] A.J.M Bundy, ed., *Selected Essays of Wilson Harris: The Unfinished Genesis of the Imagination* (London and New York: Routledge, 1999), 73.

[38] Harris, *The Ghost of Memory*, 32.

[39] Ibid., 1.

[40] Ibid., 1-2.

[41] Ibid., 100.

DRENCHED: WET POETRIES OF LORNA GOODISON AND OLIVE SENIOR

YASMINE SHAMMA

"By the waters of Leman I sat down and wept"
—T.S. Eliot, "The Fire Sermon"[1]

". . . leach the humitidites out, the things that will insist on making meaning"
—Jorie Graham, "The Visible World"[2]

In exploring dislocation, poems by subjects of Diasporas offer a place to stay still in, and tend to encourage in the reader—more than anger, frustration or bewilderment—the very essential and primitive feeling of thirst. Though water in its bodily form (as a sea or river or ocean), and fluidity—which reconsiders its bodily form (as a shoreline simultaneously marking the points of departure and arrival)—, are often considered, Olive Senior and Lorna Goodison's poems imply the fresh notion that being wet means being quenched. Though images of water pervade poetry, Goodison and Senior's almost obsessive employments of water imagery are particular trademarks of poetry that deals with displacement.

In Senior and Goodison's poems, the subjects are repeatedly described as wet, like water, or in water. The actual affect of inviting water into the poem so persistently is one of delay—the poet banks her subject on a shore, while coating and recoating words and ideas; not actually moving at all, but staying still awhile. This way of waiting (the subject waits, and also the reader waits) seems to encircle diaspsoric poetries: The writer arms the subject with natural qualities, so that the subject may take root in something universal, earthly, romantic, and completely free of state-hood. The subject is rooted not in place, but rather in biological and natural rhythm.

Caribbean writer Edouard Glissant predicts this turn towards rooting in rhythm, in his essay "Earth":

> The poet chooses, elects in the world mass what he needs to preserve, what his song accords with. And the rhythm is ritual force, lever of consciousness.

It leads to these powers: Prosodic richness (rigor), guarantor of choice, guardian of conquests; the knowledge of the world in its thickness and in its Spreads . . . That is to say poetry rebegins in the domains of the Epic.[3]

The poetries of Senior and Goodison will be examined accordingly, with particular attention to the "ritual force" of locating oneself in the particular world mass which also has force: water. That Glissant calls the force of nature's rhythm "ritual" suggests that the rhythm of the earth, when heeded, is divine—in the sense that it harks to something above and beyond us, and in that it answers to something within us ("lever of consciousness"). The poems of Goodison and Senior choose or "elect" to take root in the rhythm of water, reimagining it as holy and mythical, a place to reside and a space crucially, in its "thickness and its spread" of delay.

As the effects of oppression on a culture may be, at very least, erosive, water becomes an armor behind which the subject is strong and safe for awhile. The divine quality of wetness reverts to the mythical, as water, like the spiritual, is something one cannot hold. Yet, there is an attempt to clarify wetness as an image and claim it for the poem. Saturation relates to delay—for being wet comes with the implication that time is measured by drying.

The mythical qualities of water necessitate reflection. Water is celebrated as essentially held by the subjects of Goodison and Senior, and in being held it offers a locale (to the displaced) of purity and life (generation). Life and myth beget wetness as well. This is difficult to ascertain, for if one were to candidly consider the quality of something so ephemeral as myth, one would find feelings of remains, such as memory, "penguin dust," depletion, a puff, smoke, void, wind; these are images which accompany myth and are also dry. In feeling parched, the imperative to find relief is both the cause and effect of mythmaking. T.S. Eliot reflects upon the connection of myth and water in "The Waste Land":

> If there were the sound of water only
> Not the cicada
> And the dry grass singing
> But the sound of water over a rock
>
> . . .
>
> Drip drop drip drop drop drop drop drop[4]

So, in being dry, the reader is also offered the sound of water: "drop drop drop." After these lines, Eliot's speaker becomes thirsty on a journey: "To Carthage then I came. / Burning" and, crucially, "O Lord thou pluckest me out / O Lord thou pluckest . . ."[5] The speaker is dry, displaced, essentially near disintegration, and needs relief in the form of moisture. Eliot moves the speaker to a place of religion and myth, which is reached through the evocation of water ("drip drop drop").

Antonio Benítez-Rojo notes in *The Repeating Island* that water myths have been adapted in Caribbean stories with the Demeter and Persephone dynamic uniquely adopted and refigured.[6] He writes of Gabriel García Márquez's tale of Eréndira and claims that the tale "subverts" and so collapses the figuration of Demeter as representative of the colonizer, and Persephone as representative of the dead mother tongue of Africa. Benítez-Rojo also claims that this classical myth is destroyed by Marquez "to construct a new foundational myth, that is, a Caribbean myth."[7] The poems of Senior and Goodison, too, are heavily entrenched in reevaluating the connection between ancestry and self and that between culture and subject.

As Senior's subject explores life on the water's edge in "Cockpit County Dreams," parallels to Persephone's journey through Hades[8] prevail. Senior's poem encourages the reader to consider whether this aimless wandering is punishment for not obeying a foreign imposed rule:

Now my disorder of ancestry
Proves as stable as the many rivers
Flowing round me. Undocumented
I drown in the other's history.[9]

In this struggle with water, a myth is made of water, as history becomes a place to drown. Moreover, this myth is needed, as "documentation" has been lost to "disorder." Thus, water—more a place of smoothing over than synthetic construct—becomes a pleasingly ever-available annexation to the idea of spiritual home. Glissant's glorification of the "ritual force" of the earth and the rebirth of Caribbean poetry in the epic are connected to this construction of water. In *The Fourth Century*, Glissant continuously ties the primordial to the displaced and desert land: "the drought had dried hard into sharp ridges—yes it was all burnt to a cinder."[10] Yet, he inserts the pursuit of wetness parenthetically: "(whenever one of two people there turned . . . and tried to catch a breath, to catch the secret of this half-rotting, half consumed wealth that, even more than the passions of the sap, made the vegetation proliferate)."[11] Sensual moisture then, springs from dryness. Glissant makes this wetness inclusive, for its springing occurs in parenthesis, a figurative and literal enclosure—a place of intimacy on the page, where secrets are told under the guise of tangents. Throughout his tangent filled work, Glissant depicts the place of origin as dry, and the place's silent offspring as full, vibrant, and generative despite the dryness asserted explicitly at the novel's end when "the Longoués had run dry."[12]

Water is recognized as a mythical being and thing of moving magnitude by Jamaican-American poet Thomas Glave:

> And larger and larger and ever larger than me, O sea: water: waves and foam . . . How the sea would take I and wrap I deep in it. How it would drown I, mash I up, wash I into bits . . . And so I does say now that I know the sea this same sea like I does know the back of me hand, says I: these currents, these waves, these foams . . . Let this sea not take I, but let it talk to I. Let it sing. The sea, the sea. Yes, water. Waves. Wetness, poundsurf, that I does love.[13]

Illusive, large, uncontainable (slippery), and anti-erosive in its potential to saturate, water can stand against the self without threatening it with the possibility of being further "othered." If Arthur Rimbaud's claim rings true to these poets, if subjects of French colonial rule feel "je est un autre" (translation: "I is an other"), then the notion of being *même encore un autre* (exhaustingly: yet an other as other) is absolutely devastating. To imagine this in terms of water, one might consider the shell that arrives on a French shore from Africa being picked up by tide and swept in the ebb to arrive again in a holding pattern on a Miami beach. Pre-empting this othering then, Caribbean poetess Norbese Philip's notion of "i-magining" spins a tapestry to begin a truer story in artistry. The process Philip explores avoids compromising the imagination, as such compromises might lead to exponential alienation.[14] She claims that the I, must be centered in the creative and natural process, which for Caribbean poets might mean centering the I in water. Refreshingly, the attempt matriculates out of the context of the marginalized. The move implicitly suggests that the new direction is towards a center.

Writers of diasporas particularly seem to employ images of inundation to the effect of myth, eluding to something at once as essential, natural, and uncontainable, as they as movable humans are, and so subtly defend the fact of their moving. For example, facing potential Diaspora, Palestinian poet Mahmoud Darwish molds his world where, "The sea is walking in the streets. The sea is dangling from the windows and the branches of shriveled trees. The sea drops from the sky and comes into the room."[15] This links the self to something at once selfless and unattached to the desire for public self-hood.

Yet such socially unattached living feels at best a perpetual delay. This feeling of delay is most delicately offered by Goodison's poem, "The Mulatta as Penelope," in which soaking oneself is suggested to be a way of anchoring oneself in time. "You're my anchor awhile now / and that holds deep," writes Goodison, playing on the slip of myth, as she explores and satirizes the colonial construct of the mulatta under the classical construct of the female (Penelope).[16] Crucially, the wanton is conflated with the waiting. The poem incorporates the rhythms of spinning, loving, wanting, waiting, and stopping into the woven storyline, so suggesting that these constructions lyrically sound nice, but do not fit—or that their time has passed. Now, instead of pulling string through a loom, Goodison's Penelope pulls "your limbs / through small soft garments / your head will part my breasts."[17] The patriarchy collapses with the material base, and the female body becomes at once sea-like and loom-like. This is doubly crucial, as the place of illustration, message, and memory—the tapestry—also becomes the body of the writer/weaver who is sea-like as her breasts are parted by a masculine thing (whether religious, earthly, colonial or phallic), and as she is equated to the sea through rhyme: "Till the sailor finally weary of the sea / returns with tin souvenirs and a claim to me."[18] It is further interesting that this character chooses to *pass* as the ultimate figure of delay, and so she at once reconfigures the myths of passing and delay. This complex appropriation of myth is done through the active art and imagined projection of writing: interweaving self, place, context, and myth. Lamming claims that such interwoven constructions are explicitly Caribbean:

> There is a Caribbean sensibility whose undiscovered history resides in its fiction, whose narrative achieves authenticity through the intricacies of metaphor. What the imagination implies achieves a greater force of persuasion for truth than the statistical evidence, which measures this evasive and mesmerizing reality, which history records.[19]

As Goodison offers a new form of passing in her poem, she achieves this "greater force of persuasion for truth" than could ever be so sensitively offered by a look at dates and facts of colonization. Most importantly, Goodison's poems, and poems like hers, are on this path traced by Lamming: seeking the authentic, and forcing, through the flow of their lines, the evasive away—whether it be Aeneus (the man Penelope waits for in the myth Goodison's poem is after), a myth that does not hold right, or a story that is too dry.

Recognizing the need for buoyancy, Lamming's writing feels like a weaving wave, as the hypotaxis offers a layering of words which artistically mimics the sort of layering that "history records." He leaves as heavy and unnecessary the idea of an active historical character: writing and ordaining. So one thought surfaces: History is alive in the abstract. The subsequent impulse is to emerge from history's recording through "the intricacies of metaphor." Caribbean poet Mervyn Morris responds in his poem entitled "Riding Pillion with the Poet": "Trying to see the emerging shape / I whittle away until what remains is what I feel to be essential, as story, as metaphor."[20] History, then, is not only alive, but emergent. If nature does not, as Glissant argues, mend with culture, then maybe what is being constructed is a natural culture: one of water through which emergence out of troublesome dichotomies is possible. Starting anew or "beginning here again" allows for the i-mage, the metaphor, or creative force, to be untangled from history.

Feeling the tangle of history and ancestry, Olive Senior's "Cockpit Country Dreams," begins with an immediately wet simile: "the hours . . . like stalagmites," so that time takes the form of dripping water.[21] In the exploration of the male/female dichotomy, and, simultaneously, the culture/nature dichotomy, Senior invokes water as an adjective, a noun, a pronoun and a verb: "I . . . plunged," "river/ . . . nurtured me," "Our river, undocumented . . . "[22] The poem approaches its relative climax when both the place of writing and the place of the self are set in water, as the mother's voice rises:

> Listen child, said my mother
> whose hands plundered photo albums
> of all black ancestors: Herein
> Your ancestry, your imagery, your pride.
> Choose *this* river, *this* rhythm, *this* road
> Walk good in the footsteps of these fathers.[23]

The photo album, the thing "plundered" by the plain-in-sight Demeter, and rhythm, road, ancestry, imagery, and pride are all wet by associations, italic, and otherwise. A mother, depicted as not collecting, but almost raiding seems also to represent a sort of desperate fishing in a mirroring place. She offers, explicitly, advice—actually, the imperative—to "choose." Though she orders a distinct choosing, the freedom of the act's thought is "plundered" too, so that there appears the very distinctness of the non-distinct: river, rhythm, and road, offered, yet all essentially vague and overwhelming, like an ocean. They are also myth like in their all-encompassing, all-inclusive, universal, un-plottable locations, and in their alliteration take on the form of song, like the lyric myth. Making them less tangible is that they can be tied to the three non-distinct things in the photo-album: ancestry may be linked to river to flow, imagery to rhythm in ephemeral quality, and pride to road in linear potential. So the things plundered are for the plundering, are unquantifiable, and are qualifiable as linked to poetic images. And the quality of self is advocated in "Cockpit Country Dream", an unitalicized thought stands for the stressing in the line of "Walk good." The rhythm of the lines, set beating with the invocation of "your ancestry, your imagery . . . ," makes the stress fall on "good," which also makes goodness a firm thing. These roots so become routes, and the "good" is in the following secured.

Yet Senior does not depict a good or sequential walking, but a back and forth ebbing of thinking. A significant and pivotal shift in parenthetical speakers occurs, as it becomes the place for narrative secret in contrast to the earlier motherly commentary:

(Yet she could no more stop my mind slipping
those well-worn grooves of piety, work, praise
than rivers cease flowing). [24]

A slip from the mother's advice in rhyme and rhythm to the narrator's thought in less rhyme and more elusive rhythm takes place. Slipping away from the traditional, the move is towards a remodeling of "river," "rhythm," and "road." They become instead "grooves of piety, work, praise." The river, tied then to goodness and divinity,[25] anchors the motion of slipping, as the unstoppable slip of the speaker's mind is equated to the unstoppable flowing of the natural and timeless water. Structurally, these lines command a different sort of attention as they are enclosed in parenthesis, noticeably longer, and come to halt by their iambs when they near overflowing, so that they mimic water. Moreover, these lines offer one of the poem's longest parenthetical statements. Earlier, "eyes wide open" is contrasted inwardly with "(dreaming so)," and the parental disagreement is suggested as foreshadowing, "(Portents of a split future)." It is clear here that the author and the parenthetical voice are inward and escapist, confronting the undesirableness of these specifics in their recesses. Specifically here, the author/reader plight is tied to the mother/child plight, and the dynamic is particularly relevant with regards to the earlier discussed Demeter/Persephone situation these writers may be located within.

The father appears last in "Cockpit Country Dreams" and speaks only after being called upon by the mother ("Walk good in the footsteps of these fathers"). Post allusion to flowing, his speech flows:

> Listen child, said my father
> From the quicksand of his life:
> Study rivers. Learn everything.
> Rivers may find beginnings in the clefts of separate mountains
> Yet all find their true homes
> In the salt of one sea. [26]

Senior depicts the mother speaking from an act, and the father inactively from an active place (the "quicksand of his life"). Hence, the notion of place as created vs. place as plotted (active vs. passive) comes into view. Furthermore, where the mother points to the particular ("this river"), the father points to the universal ("rivers"). As such, the father entrenches this child in his quicksand, giving assess to nature through "study," and not "choosing." The father also chooses to be all-inclusive, as to locate the unity offered by the minute and readily available particles of salt. And this unity is requested against the backdrop of familial disunity, subtly undermining the request. There is here an incredibly complex formulation: salt—the resource a land was once qualified by (consider the expression: "salt of the earth" and the fact that salt was once the most valuable thing a plot could offer) is, in all its usefulness, disparate and like the father / Father / traditionally ruling force.

The father's advice sounds like a lullaby, as his first two lines enjoy the sing-song trochaic tetrameter. The rhythms, though, halts, with the advice given in a blunt and uneven caesura: "Study rivers. Learn everything." The contrast is stark, as is the demand. The heavy advice does not ease but troubles, as the imperative to locate a unified field through the physical and abstract at once (and in this respect similar to the mother's imperative) leaves both reader and writer out of the earlier "slipping" into unstable not ground but universal disorder. Senior reflects in the next (and earlier quoted) section: "Now my disorder of ancestry / Proves as stable as the many rivers / flowing round me."[27] Though uniting the mother and father, these lines do not feel comfortably unified. The line break after "river" is particularly destabilizing, so that the "flowing" that starts the line feels deliberately powerful, active, and overwhelming. The clause that precedes this inundation, "proves as stable," furthermore implies a deceit, and the only relief is in the flowing "round" her and not "around" her. That is she is not shown as resilient but rather as a creation, as formed by the natural and continuous—the tide-like force of her imagery.

Senior completely renders the formation transcendental in her conclusion of the poem. She considers delaying the public moment:

> I had thought of walking far from the terrible

> Knowledge
> Of flames. Spathodea . . .
> . . . from personal
> disaster. God's blinding judgment.
> Drunken mystery . . . [28]

The move is away from knowing, and into feeling, and is again towards the wet and newly divine: "Drunken mystery." Senior leaves her reader then, perpetually beatified, in the "cockpits crying lonely / lonely."[29] Then, as Senior attempts to leave the terribleness of her situation, she is met by confusion, hell and damnation. Total unfixing of thought and place results, so that there is a delayed moment of action in the space of thought.

"Created illusions," as opposed to frameworks of history, appear repeatedly in these poetries of the displaced, and rightfully so, as Glissant writes in response to the idea of a specific construction informing "us": "In what you call History, between the pits where our heroes went to earth nameless, I see only this trace of our feet."[30] Glissant highlights the unbearable disconnect which Senior explores. And preceding these lines Glissant warns, parenthetically, "(Our poem interweaves in your reticences, complicates itself by your conquests; but our scream is clear beneath the entanglements)" that though weighted by history, authentic feeling surfaces with unweightable buoyancy and un-taintable clarity.[31] Perhaps, this is the reason water appears and reappears; it is clear in contrast to the murky inherited, "nameless" past.

But it seems too that the notion of delay deserves contemplation, as the idea of feet tracings, history as considered—as a deliberation, metaphor—poetically open constructs, and prohibition all relate to saturation and delay at once. Markham helpfully confesses: "I wait and wait for all the drowned things to surface." Markham, Goodison, Senior, Walcott, Morris, Glave, and Glissant—these poets are all involved in this sort of waiting, but refuse to falling into a state of victim-hood. This form of patience embodies the duality of light and heavy, and offers agency—finally and forcefully. "I am struck by the fate of flowers" Glissant writes, "The shapeless yielding to the shapely."[32] Picturing wave and shoreline helps envision Glissant's thought, as the shapeless (water) yields by sheer fact of natural rhythm, to the shapely (the shore, the moment of contact). Goodison's poem "The Mulatta as Penelope" also expounds on a few metaphoric notions related to water (such as saturation, bathing in myth, and banking water as defense). However, her poem also arrives at a crucial point: Penelope is waiting in the sun for her hair to dry, in the greatest and most unconventional calm—waiting for the wet to leave and take with it the waiting for the hero to wake up, and for the night to call on the colonizer's day. Yet in its eighteen lines, "The Mulatta as Penelope" offers something that Senior's "Cockpit County Dreams" avoids: the notion of a live reconstruction in process: "this time will not sit and spin and spin / the door to let the madness in."[33] Goodison not only then reconsiders myth; she re-appropriates waiting and takes on the large and all encompassing notion of "passing" as a way towards victory.

Something vitally not passive echoes throughout Goodison and Senior's poems, and it is anchored "awhile now / and that holds deep."[34] The anchoring explored is not purely aesthetic—it is a source of endurance both for the poetic image at work and also the imagining. Glissant completes his consideration of the fragrance-less flower—the natural void of essence due to some outside power fating upon it by writing: "We dream of what we cultivate in the future, and we wonder vaguely what the new hybrid that is already being prepared for us will look like . . ."[35] While Senior and Goodison's poems are cultivations of futures and pasts alike, they prepare their own hybrids, as opposed wondering vaguely what might be given to them. The dreamings offered by Goodison and Senior in their poetry pursue unrestrained and organic hybrids, drenching, soaking, and nurturing their subjects. So the personal and public locals which give these poets voice are displaced, in this vague and large way, by a body of water. And the water filled poem serves as a place, like the cup of water to the plant, for finding portable root.

Bibliography

Benítez-Rojo, Antonio. *The Repeating Island.* Raleigh: Duke University Press, 1996.

Berry, James. "Faces Around My Father." In *Hinterland: Caribbean Poetry from the West Indies and Britain*, edited by E.A. Markham, 185-8. Newcastle upon Tyne: Bloodaxe, 1989.

Braithwaite, Edward Kamau. "Kingston in the kingdom of this world." In *Hinterland: Caribbean Poetry from the West Indies and Britain*, edited by E.A. Markham, 128-30. Newcastle upon Tyne: Bloodaxe, 1989.

Darwish, Mahmoud. *Memory For Forgetfulness: August, Beirut, 1982.* Berkeley, California: University of California Press, 1995.

Eliot, T.S. *Prufrock and Other Poems.* New York: Dover Publications, 1998.

Glissant, Edouard. *Caribbean Discourse: Selected Essays*. Translated by J. Michael Dash. 1989. Reprint, with an introduction by J. Michael Dash, Charlottesville: University of Virginia Press, 1999.

—."Earth." In *Poems for the Millennium: The University of California Book of Modern and Postmodern Poetry Volume Two: From Postwar to Millennium*, edited by Jerme Rothenberg and Pierre Joris, 416. Berkeley, California: University of California Press, 1998.

—. *The Fourth Century*. Lincoln: University of Nebraska Press, 1997.

Goodison, Lorna. "The Mulatta as Penelope." In *Hinterland: Caribbean Poetry from the West Indies and Britain*, edited by E.A. Markham, 238. Newcastle upon Tyne: Bloodaxe, 1989.

Graham, Jorie. *The Dream of the Unified Field*. New York: Ecco, 1997.

Lamming, George. "Myths in the Caribbean." Center for Caribbean Studies in Casa de las Américas. <http://www.casa.cult.cu/revistanales/2003lamming.htm> (29 April 2006).

Morris, Mervyn. "Riding Pillion with the Poet." In *Hinterland: Caribbean Poetry from the West Indies and Britain*, edited by E.A. Markham, 157-9. Newcastle upon Tyne: Bloodaxe, 1989.

Philip, Nourbese Marlene. "The Absence of Writing of Writing or How I Almost Became a Spy." In *Grammar of Dissent: Poetry and Prose by Claire Harris, M. Nourbese Philip and Dionne Brand*, edited by Carol Morrell, 37-9. Fredericton, New Brunswick: Goose Lane, 1994.

Senior, Olive. "Cockpit Country Dreams." In *Hinterland: Caribbean Poetry from the West Indies and Britain*, edited by E.A. Markham, 217-9. Newcastle upon Tyne: Bloodaxe, 1989.

Notes

[1] T.S. Eliot. "The Waste Land," *Prufrock and Other Poems* (New York: Dover Publications, 1998).

[2] Jorie Graham, *The Dream of the Unified Field* (New York: Ecco, 1997).

[3] Edouard Glissant, *Poems for the Millennium: The University of California Book of Modern and Postmodern Poetry Volume Two: From Postwar to Millennium*, ed. Jerme Rothenberg and Pierre Joris (California: University of California Press, 1998), 416.

[4] Eliot, 39.

[5] Ibid.

[6] Antonio Benítez-Rojo, *The Repeating Island* (Raleigh: Duke University Press, 1996), 280.

[7] Ibid., 287.

[8] Persephone's journey calls for a crossing of the River Styx while obeying a ritual of carrying penance.

[9] Olive Senior, "Cockpit Country Dreams" in *Hinterland: Caribbean Poetry from the West Indies and Britain*, ed. E.A. Markham (Newcastle upon Tyne: Bloodaxe, 1989), 217.

[10] Edouard Glissant, *The Fourth Century*, (Lincoln: University of Nebraska Press 1997), 4.
[11] Ibid., 1, 4.
[12] Ibid., 293.
[13] Thomas Glave, "Sea." John Hopkins University Library, *Callaloo*. <http://muse.jhu.edu/login?uri=/journals/callaloo/v030/30.2glave02.html> (4 April 2006).
[14] Marlene Nourbese Philip, "The Absence of Writing of Writing or How I Almost Became a Spy" in *Grammar of Dissent: Poetry and Prose by Claire Harris, M. Nourbese Philip and Dionne Brand*, ed. Carol Morrell (Fredericton, New Brunswick: Goose Lane, 1994), 37.
[15] Darwish, Mahmoud. *Memory for Forgetfulness: August, Beirut, 1982.* (California: University of California Press, 1995), 6.
[16] Lorna Goodison, "The Mulatta as Penelope" in *Hinterland: Caribbean Poetry from the West Indies and Britain*, ed. E.A. Markham (Newcastle upon Tyne: Bloodaxe, 1989), 238.
[17] Ibid.
[18] Ibid.
[19] George Lamming, "Myths in the Caribbean." Center for Caribbean Studies in Casa de las Américas. <http://www.casa.cult.cu/revistanales/2003lamming.htm> (29 April 2006).
[20] Mervyn Morris, "Riding Pillion with the Poet" in *Hinterland: Caribbean Poetry from the West Indies and Britain*, ed. E.A. Markham (Newcastle upon Tyne: Bloodaxe, 1989), 157.
[21] Senior, "Cockpit Country Dreams." 217.
[22] Ibid.
[23] Ibid.
[24] Ibid.
[25] It is worth also noting that "piety" comes from the Latin, *pietas*, which more specifically means goodness as articulated through a respect for parents.
[26] Ibid.
[27] Ibid., 218.
[28] Ibid.
[29] Ibid.
[30] Glissant, *Poems,* 417.
[31] Ibid.
[32] Edouard Glissant, *Caribbean Discourse: Selected Essays*, trans. J. Michael Dash (1989; reprint with an introduction by J. Michael Dash, Charlottesville: University of Virginia Press, 1999), 52.
[33] Goodison, 238.
[34] Ibid.
[35] Glissant, *Caribbean*, 52.

THE USE OF ENGLISH LEXIFIED CREOLE IN ANGLOPHONE CARIBBEAN LITERATURE

MARTA VIADA BELLIDO DE LUNA

Caribbean societies have been shaped by many elements. Among the most important elements are their common history, especially the initiation and development of slavery and slave trade, colonization and growth after independence, and the emergence of a Creole language and culture. Language has definitely played a significant role in the Caribbean; moreover, the use of Creole in Caribbean literature has become one of the most heated debates regarding whether or not Creole is a distinguishing feature of Caribbean literature. This debate is rooted in colonial era where many racist and ethnocentric European ideologies and discourses were explicitly invented and propagated with the purpose of colonial domination promoting the development of certain attitudes toward the "self" vs. the "other." Colonial ideologies toward Caribbean languages perpetuated prejudice and negative evaluation of the "other" for power and control. The inequalities created by these ideologies were clearly evident in the way that languages were considered in colonial era and are still considered today even after independence. Creoles were labeled as broken, simplified, lazy, and uncivilized languages spoken by people who were clearly inferior and uncivilized as well. This constructed discourse imposed a notion of inferiority upon these Creole languages. When people start feeling negatively toward their language, they will more easily justify replacing it. Both Mervyn Alleyne[1] and Peter Roberts[2] posit that the people of the Caribbean have yielded to the naming systems imposed on their Creole languages by the ruling colonial power. They have accepted the idea that their Creole languages are corrupted and simplified versions of European languages. Feeling that one's language is deviant from a standard-form may lead to the acceptance that indeed one's native tongue is inferior, broken, or corrupt. It is this kind of linguistic imperialism that is being challenged by modern Caribbean writers. The foreign language is losing its power to enclose the mind of the native population; it can no longer rule domains such as education, government, or literacy. The native Creole populations are no longer blind to the potential of their native

Creole language. This realization of the power of one's mother tongue is what Caribbean writers who are using Creole in Caribbean literature are addressing.

The cosmopolitan nature of Caribbean Creoles has developed from a mixture of European and African languages and indigenous languages of the Caribbean such as Arawakan and Carib may have also influenced the very complex process of Creole genesis. John Holm states:

> Creole has a jargon or pidgin in its ancestry; it is spoken natively by an entire speech community, often one whose ancestors were displaced geographically so that their ties with their original language and sociocultural identity were partly broken."[3]

The majority of Creole languages are based on English, Portuguese, French, Spanish, Dutch, and other European superstrate languages. Superstrate languages were the languages spoken by the ruling colonial powers and which provided the lexica for Creoles. This definition is common knowledge among Creolists, with local or immigrant languages that have served as substrate languages, which were the languages of those who had less power and were in marginalized or dominated positions. Pidgins are rudimentary languages improvised by non-native speakers. When pidgins creolize they develop fully formed and stable grammars, usually as the result of being learned natively by children and adults. Stated very simply, a Creole is a language descended from a pidgin that has become the native language of a group of people.

Jamaican linguistic scholar Mervin Alleyne explains that Creole languages are thought to have risen from a mixture of European, African, and other non-European languages.[4] He states that these contact zones between radically different linguistic groups first gave way to a "contact language" known as pidgin.[5] Enslaved people who were removed from their communities of origin suffered a radical break in transmission of the native language and began to rely exclusively on the pidgin. When the pidgin became extensive enough that a generation of children started speaking it as a mother tongue, it began a process of complexification and became an elaborate fully ledged Creole language.

According to Alleyne[6] the English and French speaking territories became fertile ground for the development of Creoles and dialects that represented blends of European and mainly West African languages. These territories had more than one colonial master and their indigenous populations were destroyed not only through enslavement, but also through the denial of their identities, by forcing them to replace their names with European names, to speak European languages, and to become

Christianized. In Pre-Columbian times indigenous peoples highly valorized their languages. These languages linked the physical environment with indigenous cultural knowledge; they transmitted an awareness of flora and fauna, and balanced nature and spirit.[7] This scenario started changing as soon as colonization began. The Europeans, because of their feelings of linguistic superiority and their designs for imperialistic conquest, constructed a set of discourses that brought about the devaluation of indigenous languages and cultures. As stated by Crystal[8] a kind of "linguistic suicide" took place. Colonial governments and missionaries used their beliefs about the inferiority of indigenous languages to justify replacing them with European languages such as English or French. In fact, Jalil Sued Badillo,[9] posits that the negative vision of indigenous peoples created by the conquistadors lied within a broader European configuration where both indigenous and African-descended people were held responsible for the weaknesses and flaws in the characters of Creoles while all the positive traits were inherited from the "virtuous and civilized" colonizers. Colonization became the optimal environment for the death of first, indigenous languages, and later, African languages by forcing these languages into becoming socially and economically disadvantaged under the heavy pressure of colonial invasion.

The binary opposition between European languages vs. Creole gave way to the negative perception of Creole by the colonized for many years. Alleyne posits the following about the colonized and Creole:

> Caribbean peoples have largely accepted Europeans' views of their language behavior as part of a more general self-depreciation and negative evaluation of their cultural behavior. The general feeling is that Creole languages and dialects are defective—that they may be suitable for the expression of "folklore" (folktales, folk music, proverbs, swearing, etc,), but they are quite inadequate for the expression of complex and abstract thought.[10]

Creole speakers have often referred to their native language as having patois, broken language, corrupted language, or bad and lazy English. Those who advocate the use of English Creole (as well as other Creoles) contend that Creole differs from English in its phonetic and grammatical system. Most of the words in English Caribbean Creoles are English words filtered through a distinct phonetic system with fewer vowels and different consonant sounds.[11] Creole is written phonetically to approximate these differences. Thus, English "girl" becomes Creole "gyal." For non-linguists who are unaware of the structured phonological changes that take place as part of linguistic variation this may seem as a corruption of an English

Standard form; thus, creating a negative perception about the Anglophone Creole language.

A small amount of Creole lexicon derives from African origin (e.g. "nyam – to eat; or "duppy" which means ghost).[12] However, Creole's greatest divergence from English is in its grammar, which has been influenced by the languages of West Africa. Because of this influence, English speakers cannot easily understand deeper basilectal or mesolectal forms of Creole speech. The influence of the grammars of both West-African languages and indigenous languages of the Caribbean upon the grammatical structures of Caribbean Creoles thus becomes a significant reason attesting to the complexity of Creoles and the difficulty that English speakers have in understanding them. Essentially, a Creole is a natural language of contact with African and European roots and possibly with Indigenous roots as well.

An example of West African influence on Creole grammar is evidenced in Jamaican Creole. Instead of using a suffix like "ed" as in "walked," a Creole speaker puts a word before a verb like "deh." The English sentence "I walked" becomes in Creole "Me deh wak." The same is done in Haitian Creole by adding "te" before a verb to indicate the past tense. In Nigerian Pidgin, "bin" becomes a past tense marker and "A bin waka" means " I walked." This is called tense marking and it is a common feature of West African languages. My research on indigenous languages of the Caribbean has revealed that tense marking is also a characteristic of these languages, especially of Arawakan.[13] If I said, "Bring me some shrimp" in Jamaican Creole, I would say "Kyai com gimmi a janga." Such a sentence reveals other African grammatical features in Creoles such as "verb serialization." Verb serialization or the use of serial verbs is a frequent feature of most Creoles in which two or more verbs are stringed together without being joined by a conjunction and both having the same subject. In the example above the serialized verb construction consists of three verbs: "kyai" meaning carry; "com" meaning come; and "gimmi" meaning give me.

Some of the general features of English lexified Creoles (and other Creoles as well) are the following: serialized verb constructions, word compounding, the use of reduplication, lack of inflectional morphemes, drop of final consonant clusters, use of particles for tense marking, stative verbs are considered in present; whereas, active verbs are considered in past where there is no other special marking, special forms of pronouns different from English, use of double negatives, lack of copula, no copula before adjectives, cross-over between grammatical categories (multi-functionality), no required marker for definiteness or indefiniteness, and extended meanings of words such as prepositions. These are among the many features one may consider in a grammatical analysis of Creoles; however, a detailed analysis of the structure of Creole is beyond the scope of this paper. Nonetheless, being able to recognize these features in the Creole language spoken by the many fictional characters created by Caribbean writers results is fascinating to any one who is interested in the study and development of Creole languages and cultures. The use of Creole in Caribbean literature attests to the new vision and the new roles of Creole languages in the Caribbean basin and throughout the world. Creole languages are well developed and full-fletched languages capable of expressing literary complexity.

According to Mimi Sheller, who attempts to provide non-Caribbean readers with an overview of Creole language and literature, Creoles are "new languages, evolutionarily younger than non- Creole languages, which have developed gradually and organically over centuries without any radical breaks in transmission from one generation to the next."[14] Similarly, Michel DeGraff states: "Creoles are linguistic neonates whose morphologies lack the features that characterize older more mature languages."[15] DeGraff contends that there is a preconception that Creoles are somehow exceptional languages because of their emergence due to catastrophic conditions or because they were born out of an attempt of "inferior" beings trying to acquire superior languages. The notion that Creoles are simplified or exceptional languages has perpetuated the negative perception of Creoles. This linguistic interpretation tends to perpetuate a negative perception of Creole languages because labeling them as exceptional places them outside the realm of natural languages.

The theories of Creole genesis have had far-reaching effects upon the construction of Caribbean culture and literature. Caribbean literature has taken a prominent role in metropolitan literary studies since the 1980's when post-colonial and non-western literatures became more read.[16] The development of Caribbean literature is based on the belief that this literature has something native and unique, something that is Creole about it. Caribbean writer and scholar Antonio Benítez-Rojo stated that Caribbean literature is a mixture:

> The literature of the Caribbean can be read as a mestizo text, but also as a stream of texts in flight . . . The Caribbean poem and novel are projects that communicate their own turbulence, their own clash, and their own void, the swirling black hole of social violence produced by the encomienda and the plantation, that is, their otherness, their peripheral asymmetry with regard to the West. Thus Caribbean literature cannot free itself totally from the

multiethnic society upon which it floats, and it tells us of its fragmentation and instability.[17]

These hybrid texts are contrasted to the West, just as Creole languages are compared to the older Western languages. For Benítez-Rojo, part of the beauty of Caribbean language and literature is that it is seen as more dynamic, chaotic, impure, less structured than the older forms. The rawness, chaos, and impurity mentioned by Benítez-Rojo translates into a literature that is capable of portraying the reality, the beauty, and the life-force of the Caribbean "criollo" not only of his/her culture and identity, but also of the Creole language as well.

The use of Creole in literature transports the narrator to the center, giving the narrator a central rather than marginal voice, and thus allowing the author to valorize discourse in its Creole form of expression. Moreover, this sense of valorization of Creole discourse portrays Creole as an effective tool for identity construction. Thus, Creole becomes a major indicator of defining Caribbean identity. There has been a significant expansion in the functions of Creole in Caribbean literature, as well as a positive adjustment in language attitudes. For example, contrary to the use of Standard English in the educational and governmental systems, the use of Creole has become increasingly common in popular dramas and lyrics for popular songs and in radio and television. The use of Creole in story telling celebrates life in the Caribbean. Through the use of Creole in Caribbean literature, the voices that had been silenced in the past come to life in the present; the burden of an imposed language is relieved; the female voice rises to a new dimension; and both sexual and social identity are defined and redefined by Creole.

The inclusion of Creole has been pivotal to the development of a Caribbean literary discourse. The use of Creole has followed a series of developmental stages. First, it was used as a distorted, broken language that interfered with the European language; it was a representation of the voice of "the other" as exemplified in the works of V.S. Naipaul and Samuel Selvon. Second, it followed a kind of censorship. For instance, Caribbean authors such as Derek Walcott were torn between expressing the richness of their native Creole in their writing versus using the standard written form of the lexifier language. Third, (likely where Caribbean authors stand today), Caribbean literature utilizes a creative, more open form of expression by using a dual or hybrid form of expression, and by alternating or code-switching between the standard and the vernacular dialect. This duality gains significance because it reinforces the importance of two linguistic codes in the Caribbean, each with its distinct functions, the Standard and the Creole, not in competition with each other, but complementing each other in an attempt to describe more truthfully the realities of the languages and cultures of Caribbean people.

Caribbean writers such as Patrick Chamoiseau, Oonya Kempadoo, Merle Hodge, and Jean Buffong are resisting assimilation, preferring to write in Creole or write in English with Creole phrases or words woven into their work. This incorporation of Creole idioms and rhythms into literature written in English changes and enriches the language so that it reflects "the other's" experiences. Creole language is much more effective to render Caribbean cultural experiences than English because it is used as a form of resisting assimilation to the 'metropolis' and as a subtle weapon of resistance. Likewise, when a narrator speaks in Creole in Caribbean texts, he/she shows the reader the feelings and images that arise out of lived experiences. Books that include Creole and push the reader away from the standard are challenging; they make the reader stop and pay attention to the language, which contributes to understanding the rhythms of life in the islands, hence forcing the reader to pay attention to his/her cultural roots as well. As such, the reader is forced to notice the language; it is impossible to overlook its significance and cultural and social messages.

Caribbean writers, some of whom have been previously mentioned are experimenting with the use of Creole either by using standard and non-standard registers, or by using Creole only in their dialogues while the narrator uses standard forms of language. Both strategies allow the reader to see experiences differently through the use of Creole. Roslin Kahn asserts that Creole has also been used to mimic the European patterns evident among the upper classes and a Creole culture with non-European elements peculiar to a region.[18]

Creole is used in various Anglophone Caribbean texts. In particular, the character of Anasi, the notorious Spider in Caribbean folktales, masters Creole to perfection. Sharlene May Poliner states that "Ananse's language mimics that of corrupt slave traders, masters and missionaries who promised food, adventure and salvation, and who delivered betrayal and death."[19] Language has become a powerful tool for Anansi. He can use language to control and submit; nevertheless, he has the power to mark African culture and identity. His powerful verbal strategies become a symbol of authentification of Creole languages providing confidence to speakers of Creole who have been constantly looked down on, ridiculed, and punished for speaking a so called "broken or corrupt" Creole.

Anansi tales such as "How Stories Came to Earth," "Anansi Proves He Is the Oldest," "Anansi Plays Dead," "Anansi Borrows Money," and "Anansi Owns All Tales That are Told" as well as most Anansi folktales are especially appealing due to the way the spider speaks. He uses language both metaphorically and deceptively. Anansi is indeed a brilliant linguist who is very much aware of the semiotics of language for he is a master of communication. For example, Anansi usually gets the best of his opponents by tricking them into doing what he wants. The spider is sometimes a culture hero or one who is responsible for the way certain things are (i.e. "How the Sky God Stories Became Ananse Stories.") On the other hand, the spider is sometimes a cunning trickster, a greedy person who must pay for his actions with shame and punishment (i.e. "Kwaku Ananse and the Capful of Hot Beans.") He skillfully uses all sensory modes to structure a pattern of communication that meets his physical and emotional needs. Therefore, Anansi is master of rhetoric because his word play and sweet talk usually gets him what he wants. This is exemplified in the Anasi stories that deal with the problem of hunger and famine. While others starve to death, Anansi manages to have a full belly. He has an extraordinary power for convincing others into doing what will satisfy his greedy nature.

Characters in Anansi stories are core vernacular figures, exemplars of folk culture who speak in a consistently basilectal way. Peter Patrick provides an example of a mesolectal and basilectal variation in "Anansi Mek Grong":

> Mesolectal: Let me tell you some'pn bout Bredda Anansi. Him is a very smart man you know! I goin' tell what happen to him to the end.
> Basilectal: Mek mi tel yu som?n boot Breda Anansi. Im iz a veri smaat man yu noo. A gwain tel wa hapm tu him tu en.
> Mesolectal: Now him form a law in him country once that everybody that meddles in another one business mus' get hurt. But accordin' to him, him supposed to get them fi eat. So him go up on a rock-top once an say, well then, 'im goin grow crops because him know people mus' fass with him.
> Basilectal: Noo in a faam a laa ina in konchri wans dat evribadi dat faas in anada wan biznis mos get hort. Bot akaadin tu im him supuos tu get dem fi iit . So him go op an a rak tap wans an se wel den im gwain mek grong bika im nuo piipl mos faas wid im.
> Mesolectal: By she reach round the corner, him forget the law. Him say, "Eh! A whe' that-there dry-head something a go?" Him can' go a met, too? Same time Bredda Anansi drop off o'the rock an come down. Sista Guineahen jus' come back come pick hin up. And that was the end of Bredda Anansi. Him too smart.
> Basilectal: Bai shi rich roon di kaana hin figet di laa. Hin se ee A we dat de drai ed sinting a go. Im kyaan ga a met tu. Siem taim Breda Anasi jrap aaf a di rak an kom dong. Sista Gini En jos kom bak kom pik im op. An dat was di hen av Breda Anansi. Him tuu smaat.[20]

The richness of Trinidadian dialect, of what many call a broken or corrupt patois, is brilliantly used by Trinidadian writer V.S. Naipaul to give life to the characters in *Miguel Street*. One of the many interesting uses of Creole in *Miguel Street* is evidenced in the Calypso verses that occur throughout the novel. These verses become a living culture in themselves. They reflect the popular beliefs of a lower and marginalized class in Trinidad and reveal sexist ideas about women. For example, "Man centipede bad, Woman centipede more than bad," means that women are worse than men by far.[21] Later in the text, Naipaul writes, "Matilda, Matilda yu tief my money and gone Venezuela" to explain the relationship between two characters in the novel, Hat and Dolly.[22] Dolly ran away with another man taking off with all the gifts that Hat had given her. Hat finds her and beats her up so badly that he remorsefully confesses to the police, "I kill a woman."[23] Dolly does not die, but the lawyer "dis sort of lawyer who does get man hang, you know"[24] sees that Hat is put away in prison for four years. The interaction among "the boys" flows easily against the backdrop of a Creole language that serves as a unifying force among the men who live and strive along Miguel Street.

Under the Silk Cotton Tree by Jean Buffong is a jewel for linguists who wish to explore the use of Creole language in Anglophone Caribbean literature. Buffong masterfully blends acrolectal and basilectal forms of Grenadian English Creole by moving smoothly through the continuum and allowing the reader to accept and understand the language. Not only does Buffong provide a huge array of Creole terms and phrases (e.g. babalay, wooye, oyoye, pappy show, liming, lajabless, beat mouth, dough hair, box brains, marrieding, vex vex, rush rush, tight tight, bad john she playing, getting into bacanal, pougate in the skin, take my farseness, be passing blood, funny in the head, is we walk we walk, was making baby, catch woman malady), but she also depicts many of the typical grammatical features of Creole. For instance, she employs the use of reduplication (e.g. I get vex, vex); absence of copula (e.g. I thirteen); different usages of pronouns (e.g. was making she baby); verb serialization (e.g. I rimemba. We go kom); and multifunctionality (e.g. Is wak we wak). Definitely, as a linguist, I consider Buffong's work a jewel for scholars who wish to explore the use of Creole in Caribbean literature and the controversies that it has unleashed. It raises important questions that need to be considered by Creolists and Caribbean writers: How far can language deviate from the standard at a scholarly level? What language should be accepted as the norm in Creole societies? Should children be taught in their native Creole before they master the standard form of European languages? Buffong portrays the constant clash between the colonial world and the Creole world. The duality that one sees in the people of Grenada responds to the colonial ideologies that were deeply enclosed in the minds of Caribbean peoples, and which continued to exist even after independence.

Samuel Selvon is a pioneer in the use of dialect in narration. He depicts the features of Trinidadian English Creole by presenting this language as a tool in the hands of a great novelist who lures readers into the reality of people and cultures, which had long been ignored in colonial discourse. Moreover, these Creoles had been considered as lacking identity, an issue that is also addressed by Selvon in *A Brighter Sun*. For example, when Tiger tells Joe, "I never grow up as Indian, you know,"[25] he is expressing a conflictive personal reality of many Caribbean people who embark in a quest for identity torn between two (or perhaps more) languages and cultures.

A few examples of Creole features used by Selvon in this text are the following: (1) Mainly nominative pronouns are used even where English would utilize objective or possessive pronouns (i.e. "so wat de arse we have to do wid dat? Dem Indian people does have plenty money hide away. Why Tiger don't buy a bed for he wife;"[26] (2) Lack of inflection on verbs;[27] (i.e. "Yuh too! Could have gettam plenty more ting! Yu eatam too quick! Stupid boy");[28] (3) Double negatives (i.e. "She lie Joe, she ain't have no cuckoo;"[29] and (4) Innovative use of words (i.e. "Come an'see sugar pie, come dou-dou."[30] Selvon brilliantly portrays the differences among ethnic (Creoles, East-Indians, Chinese, British) and social classes (poor, peasants, rich) in Trinidad within a specific historical and socio-economic context. He explores the significance of ethnicity and how it leads to tension among different groups. Because of the close relationship between language and ethnicity, Selvon masterfully employs the use of Creole to highlight and exploit these differences through the use of language. In general, Caribbean authors (as is the case of Selvon) employ Creole language "to educate" the English reader in the language and ways of Caribbean people.

Oonya Kempadoo is one of the younger Caribbean writers who has become a master of poetic prose and Creole language in her novels. One cannot deny that one of the most striking elements in both of her novels is the originality in the use of language. *Buxton Spice*, her first novel, is a series of semi-autobiographical vignettes, which offer an erotic tale of the coming of age of Lula, her twelve-year-old narrator. It is a story of sexual awakening, a passage from innocence to experience where language becomes overpowering in the narrative. Kempadoo uses language with an openness that might shock the more conservative reader. Her prose is very sensuous and explicit when referring to female sexuality. In one part of the text, Kempadoo uses the voice of Lula to explain how a young girl experiments with sexuality through masturbation:

> The flowing musn't stop . . . hammering on the top of the Tip while the bomb i me was growing making my heart beat faster, muscles tighter. Bomb getting bigger. Oh Shit! Somebody going to realize I running the tap so long. The flowing lolo can't stop. I should have turned on the shower too. The Tip going to blow off. Oh me Lawd! My legs shot down from the wall and I clamped my thighs together. Heart bombing up inside me and trembles jerking running up and down my arms and body, twisting me up so . . .[31]

When compared to her text entitled *Tide Running*, Kempadoo is more conservative with the use of Creole in *Buxton Spice* although she does use some innovative Creole expressions such as "broughtupsy" meaning "refined,"[32] "putagee" meaning "Portuguese,"[33] "bestest" meaning "the best,"[34] "t'iefed," meaning "thieved" or "stolen;"[35] "taking man" meaning "having sexual intercourse with a man;"[36] "easy snake does bite hot" meaning "beware of people who seem to be very kind or good; they may be the worst or most evil of all."[37] The freshness and sensuality of Kempadoo's writing results from the use of Creole with which she is able to capture the "everydayness" of the Guyanese childhood of Lula (the protagonist) and her coming of age.

In *Tide Running* Kempadoo captures the native dialect of Tobago especially through Cliff, a young and beautiful black man who is exploited by Bella and Peter to indulge in their sexual fantasies, but also through the use of rich poetic prose overflowing with sensory images, innovative similes and personifications, as well as a highly sexually charged language. Kempadoo shows a glimpse of her mastery of poetry and prose when she describes the weather: "In this cold whiteness the sea come like a dead body. Dark, grey, and swoll'n . . . "[38] and when Cliff says to himself:

> [How] can a man do dat boy. He own wife. Me an another fella sex girl same time already, we was just ketching a ting but this is the man own woman. And is not to say he don't love she you could see it in he eye. He ain' shame to tell she he love she right in front'a me. I never see people so. Sexing up and down and loving each other too[.][39]

The passages about the sea are important throughout the novel since the sea become a major character in the development of the plot. The sea lures both Bella and Cliff as some kind of primitive instinct. When Cliff is put in jail, he says "the sea stop today"[40] meaning that he can no longer enjoy the freedom and carelessness of his youth. The scenes that have strong sexual connotations are narrated with explicitness, but with great taste that is achieved through the use of powerful and sensuous Creole.

In *Tide Running,* the shift in narrative voice from Cliff to Bella, the beautiful, rich Creole wife of Peter who seduces Cliff corrupting him into doing things that he does not like, is accompanied by a shift in dialectal narration. Cliff's heavy Creole dialect mixes with Bella's more standardized use of the English language. For example, the following dialogue illustrates the differences between the Creole spoken by Bella and by Cliff:

> Bella: "Oh shit? Cliff? What the you doing?"
> Cliff: "I sorry! Sorry. Oh shit."
> Bella: "So why you run? You jumped further than me. You scared me!"
> Cliff: "I jump when I see allyou, I ain' lie! I didn' expec' you to be sitting here with the lights turn-off. I jumo, no joke. All me blood beating. True, feel my heart."[41]

It is also through language that Bella becomes more closely identified with Cliff; whereas, Peter, Bella's rich husband who together with his wife use Cliff as "a black dollie" for sexual pleasure, who had a father/son, boy/man closeness with Cliff, becomes equally excluded through difference in language.

Mimi Sheller states that one way in which Creole has resisted assimilation is through its 'rawness', "if language is raw enough, deep on the Creole continuum, vulgar, rough, crude, sexual, violent, harsh on the ear, it will repel any who might potentially eat it."[42] Perhaps, Kempadoo has tried to use Creole in this manner to achieve an "erotic autonomy" through the use of language in her novels.

Language is a carrier and conveyer of culture and is far from being static or fixed. Likewise, through language, literature achieves a similar role. The Caribbean has become an area of heated debate, especially after the 1960s regarding both issues of language and literature. The issue still remains about which language Anglophone Caribbean writers should use. One side, those who advocate the use of native Creoles, argues that English is the language of colonial domination and Western Imperialism and therefore should be shunned in favor of Native Creole languages. The other side, those who favor a less radical position, contends that "one must not throw the baby out with the bath water" meaning that English might have been the language of colonial conquest, but it is also the global "lingua franca" and as such needs to be valorized in the light of the 21st century and the social, economic, cultural, political, and linguistic implications that its mastery entails. Even though English is related to colonial roots, it is not necessarily evil and contains some good within. In fact, English is the most important global language, a fact that is widely discussed by David Crystal in his book *English as a Global Language*. It is spoken in most countries around the world, especially in postcolonial societies. It has also become a cross-cultural world language, which allows dialogue between various ethno-linguistic groups—a feat that would have not happened if writers restricted themselves only to their regional languages.

Caribbean writers have reached a stage where the English language has become strengthened by the Creole language. Creoles add depth and vigor to the language as they reflect the culture and experiences of its speakers. An excellent example of this eclectic approach embracing the language mix typical of the Caribbean is beautifully depicted by the case of Papiamento in Aruba. Papiamento is the native Creole language. It was first an anti-colonial phenomenon, but it is now an accepted language in its own right. Moreover, it has become the language of instruction in primary schools and an official language in Aruba; children are first taught in their mother tongue, and later learn to speak fluently in English, Spanish, and other languages as well. This attitude toward the learning languages has made a difference in the educational system in Aruba. The linguistic situation in Aruba exemplifies successful language learning policies. Moreover, it might offer an alternative to help solve the linguistic controversy of other Caribbean islands.

Changes in attitudes towards Creole are evidenced in Caribbean literature. More and more Caribbean writers such as Walcott are using both English and Creole in their works as a way of asserting their Caribbean identity.

Bibliography

Alleyne, Mervin. *Comparative Afro-American: A Historical Comparative Study of English Based Afro-American Dialects*. Ann Arbor: Karoma Publishers, 1980.

—. "Acculturation and the Cultural Matrix of Creolization." In *Pidginization and Creolization of Languages*, edited by Dell Hymes, 169-86. Cambridge: Cambridge University Press, 1971.

—. "A Linguistic Perspective on the Caribbean." In *Caribbean Contours* edited by Wilfred Mintz, Sidney and Sally Price 155-179. Baltimore: John Hopkins, 1985.

—. "Indigenous Languages of the Caribbean." *SCL Popular Series*. Paper No.3. June 2004. Society for Caribbean Linguistics Publishers.

Badillo, Jalil Sued. *Los Caribes: ¿Realidad o Fábula?* Río Piedras, PR: Editorial Antillana, 1978.

Benítez-Rojo, Antonio. *The Repeating Island: The Caribbean and the Postmodern Perspective*. Raleigh: Duke University Press, 1996.

Buffong, Jean. *Under the Silk Cotton Tree*. New York: Interlink Books, 1993.

Cobham, Rhonda. "Impact on Caribbean Literature and Culture." *Women Crossing* (2002) <http://womencrossing.org/cobham.html> (accessed December 1, 2005).

DeGraff, Michael. "Morphology in Creole Genesis: Linguistics and Ideology." In Ken Hale: *A Life in Language*. Edited by Michael Kenstowicz, 53-121. Cambridge, MA: MIT Press, 2001.

Holm, John. *An Introduction to Pidgins and Creoles*. Cambridge, Cambridge University Press, 2000.

Kempadoo, Oonya. *Buxton Spice*. New York: Beacon Press, 1998.

—. *Tide Running*. London: Picador Publishing, 2001.

Khan, Roslin. "Impact on Caribbean literature and Culture." *Caribbean Impact* 3 (2004). <http://caribimpact.net/v3_24_feature_10.html> (accessed December 1, 2005).

Naipaul, V. S. *Miguel Street*. New York: Penguin Books, 1971.

Patrick, Peter. *Jamaican Creole Transcription*. <http://courses.essex.ac.uk/LG/LG449/Shots.html> (accessed October 7, 2004)

Poliner, Sharlene May. "The Exiled Creature: Ananse and the Search for Afro-Caribbean Identity." *Studies in the Humanities*. 11.1 (June 1984): 13-22.

Roberts, Peter. *Language, Race, and Ecology: The Shaping of Identity in the Caribbean*. Unpublished manuscript.

Selvon, Samuel. *A Brighter Sun*. London: Longman, 1952.

Sheller, Mimi. "Oraliteracy and Opacity: Resisting Metropolitan Consumption of Caribbean Creole." Paper presented at the Franklin College Conference: The Caribbean Unbound, 9th–11th. April 2003. <http://www.lancs.ac.uk/fass/sociology/papers/sheller-oraliteracy-and-opacity.pdf> (accessed November 3, 2008).

Notes

[1] Mervyn Alleyne, "Indigenous Languages of the Caribbean," *SCL Popular Series*. Paper No.3. June 2004. Society for Caribbean Linguistics Publishers.
[2] Peter Roberts, *Language, Race, and Ecology: The Shaping of Identity in the Caribbean*. Unpublished manuscript.
[3] John Holm, *An Introduction to Pidgins and Creoles*, (Cambridge: Cambridge University Press, 2000), 6.
[4] The possibility of the influence of the grammatical structures of indigenous languages upon the grammars of Caribbean Creoles has been explored in Marta Viada's recent doctoral dissertation titled "Matelots, Metis, and Maroons Meet Mass Comparison and the Matrix: Possible Influences From the Indigenous Languages of the Caribbean on the Grammars of Caribbean Creole."
[5] Mervyn Alleyne, *Acculturation and the Cultural Matrix of Creolization*" in *Pidginization and Creolization of Languages*, ed. by Dell Hymes (Cambridge, Cambridge University Press, 1971), 169-186.
[6] Mervyn Alleyne, "A Linguistic Perspective on the Caribbean" in *Caribbean Contours*, ed. by Sidney Wilfred Mintz and Sally Price (Baltimore: John Hopkins, 1985), 155-79.
[7] David Crystal addresses the issue of indigenous language valorization upon the arrival of Columbus in his book *Language Death*, (Cambridge: Cambridge University Press, 2000).
[8] Ibid.
[9] Jalil Sued Badillo, *Los Caribes: ¿Realidad o Fábula?* (Río Piedras, PR: Editorial Antillana, 1978).
[10] Alleyne, "A Linguistic Perspective on the Caribbean," 160.
[11] Some scholars who have addressed the study of the phonological variation in Anglophone lexifier Creoles are Winford Donald, Hubert Devonish, Walter Seoler, and Edwarda Walter.
[12] The origin of the term can be found in Leach MacEdward's, "Jamaican Duppy Lore." *The Journal of American Folklore* 74 (293): 207-15.
[13] Arawakan together with its dialectal variations was the native language spoken by the indigenous peoples of the Antilles upon the arrival of Columbus.
[14] Mimi Sheller, "Oraliteracy and Opacity: Resisting Metropolitan Consumption of Caribbean Creole." Paper presented at the Franklin College Conference: The Caribbean Unbound, 9th-11th. April 2003.<http://www.lancs.ac.uk/fass/sociology/papers/sheller-oraliteracy-and-opacity.pdf> (accessed November 3, 2008), 3.
[15] Michel DeGraff, "Morphology in Creole Genesis: Linguistics and Ideology" in *Ken Hale: A Life in Language*, ed. by Michael Kenstowicz (Cambridge: Cambridge University Press, 2001), 54.
[16] Sheller, 12.
[17] Antonio Benítez-Rojo, *The Repeating Island: The Caribbean and the Postmodern Perspective* (Raleigh: Duke University Press, 1996), 27.

[18] Roslin Khan, "Impact on Caribbean literature and Culture," *Caribbean Impact* 3 (2004). <http://caribimpact.net/v3_24_feature_9.html> (accessed December 1, 2005).
[19] Sharlene May Poliner, "The Exiled Creature: Ananse and the Search for Afro-Caribbean Identity," *Studies in Humanities* 11.1 (June 1984): 17.
[20] Peter Patrick, *Jamaican Creole Transcription*, <http://courses.essex.ac.uk/LG/LG449/Shots.html> (accessed October 7, 2004), 2-3.
[21] V.S. Naipaul, (New York: Penguin Books, 1971) *Miguel Street*, 98.
[22] Ibid., 162.
[23] Ibid., 163.
[24] Ibid., 164.
[25] Samuel Selvon, *A Brighter Sun* (London: Longman, 1952), 197.
[26] Ibid., 39.
[27] The lack of inflection on verbs is a major inflectional form attached to action verbs used indiscriminately with different tenses.
[28] Selvon, 6.
[29] Ibid., 24.
[30] Ibid.
[31] Oonya Kempadoo, *Buxton Spice* (New York: Beacon Press, 1998), 99.
[32] Ibid., 63.
[33] Ibid., 53.
[34] Ibid., 14.
[35] Ibid., 39.
[36] Ibid, 166.
[37] Ibid., 148.
[38] Ibid., 150.
[39] Ibid., 7.
[40] Ibid., 201.
[41] Oonya Kempadoo, *Tide Running* (London: Picador Publishing, 2001), 130.
[42] Sheller, 10.

SI-DIEU-VEUT:
VODOU AS CATALYTIC AND FATALISTIC RELIGION IN *MASTERS OF THE DEW*

DARA GREEN

"... Si mwê mérité, pini mwê" ("If I deserve it, punish me").
Praisesong for the Widow[1]

In his novel *Masters of the Dew*, Haitian writer Jacques Roumain succinctly captures the essence of religious fatalism within the vodou religion through his characters' usage of the words "si-dieu-veut" or "if God wills." The French phrase has an interchangeable use for both the God of Roman Catholicism and the Afro-Haitian *lwas*—or spirit deities— due to the syncretism of Christianity and Pan-African religions in Haiti. Fatalism is not, by any means, singular to vodou; elements of fatalism appear in many major religions such as Islam, as well as with Catholic and Protestant Christianity.[2] For example, the common Arabic phrase "in'shallah," which means "God willing," parallels the aforementioned French Christian saying in many Arabic cultures. Decisions executed through like theodicean philosophies attempt to reconcile a belief in higher deities with the presence of evil, and one's own capacity to perform actions perceived as contrary to that deity (i.e. evil). Based upon the presupposition that the higher deity's will should be accomplished, all other human philosophical impulses become secondary and even undesirable.

Within the context of a text replete with Marxist ideology, this religious fatalism stands in stark opposition to the formation of an organic community. In her examination of Roumain's novel, critic Celia Britton notes, "While the refusal of religious fatalism is in no way specific to Marxism (it is in fact just as characteristic of a modernizing capitalist agriculture), it does mean that the confrontation between Manuel's Marxism and Christianity is entirely coherent within its own limits."[3] Scholars such as Britton, Carolyn Fowler, Valerie Kaussen, and Michael Dash have critically examined the various roles that Marxism plays in the novel, but few have broached the complex relationship between religious fatalism in vodou and revolutionary action in the novel. Furthermore, *Masters of the Dew*, through its portrayal of peasant belief in vodou and communist practices, insinuates that there is a space for compromise where these two ideologies meet.

At the beginning of the novel, the protagonist Manuel Jean-Joseph returns from sugar-cane farming in Cuba to his native village of Fonds Rouge, Haiti, and finds it is caught in the midst of both a drought and a decade-long feud. He successfully finds a source of water to save the village, but it requires the effort of all the townspeople to dig a canal to force the water down the mountain. When Manuel proposes to end the feud, another peasant murders him. His subsequent assassination, purposely disguised as an illness, reunites the village and serves as the impetus for reconciliation and progress. The object of this paper is to examine how, for the peasants of Fonds Rouge, the principles of vodou are paradoxically the initial hindrance to and the catalyst for social change. The paper systematically demonstrates vodou-related instances of fatalism in *Masters of the Dew*, and then shifts its focus to study how those same instances theoretically lend themselves to the novel's dynamic conclusion.

In the novel, only Manuel determines to act without uttering "if it's God's will" out of respect and fear. Conversely, his fellow citizens seem to be paralyzed by their beliefs in the *lwas*. This fatalistic ideology would ostensibly make any sort of rebellious action impossible. Within the framework of the text, however, vodou plays the dual roles of being both fatalistic and catalytic in that Voudouisants (or believers) initially do not take action because they feel themselves to be merely pawns to the *lwas*. Although, as Fowler suggests, the novel seeks to "recognize and correct weaknesses . . . such as the passivity fostered by the religious heritage of vodun," the peasants subsequently act based upon the perceived wishes of the *lwas*.[4] This duality causes *Masters of the Dew* to successfully and logically adopt the characteristics of a text that mutually privileges Marxist revolution and fatalistic vodou beliefs.

Several autobiographical details correspond to occurrences in *Masters of the Dew*. Roumain, a Marxist who went into exile because of his publications, advocated a Marxist approach to Haitian peasantry. He was a proponent of the African-based *coumbite* (collective agricultural effort) that his central character died attempting to implement. At the beginning of the novel, before Manuel appears, his father, Bienaimé, dreams of days past where the then-thriving community engaged in such a practice. Valerie Kaussen astutely notes that the concept of the coumbite applies to both African practice and a local praxis of communist theory.[5] Roumain at least partially gleaned his concept of communal farming from now-communist Cuba, as he lived in Cuba during his exile. He was very much a proponent of formal education for rural Haitian peasants, asserting that a change of mindset was necessary for progress. In the story, Manuel also expounds on the virtues of establishing schools for his fellow townspeople upon his return. Throughout the novel, the protagonist partly becomes the intersection between Roumain's politics and his fictional vision of Haitian cultural unification.

This paper will provide a brief overview of the major *lwas* and Haitian vodou principles immediately relevant to this text. This framework is significant because Roumain employs the *lwas* themselves as characters in the novel, remaining true to their attributes. Furthermore, some of the fictional characters adopt traits inherent to certain *lwa,* which I will outline later in the paper. Above all, vodouism is spirit worship; those who practice vodou in Haiti do not name "vodou" as their religion—they say that they "serve the spirits" and call themselves *serviteurs* (servants).[6] Another apt term for the *lwas* is found in the French word *anciens*, also translated as the Old People. These spirits are believed to be those of the African ancestors left behind because of the slave trade. Claudine Michel describes Haiti as a land where the "cult of ancestors guards peasant traditional values and is largely linked to family life and the land."[7] However, a distinction does exist between dead ancestors and the *lwas.* The *lwas* are a pantheon of divine spirit "ancestors" not related to the individual. As in Africa, vodou is composed of several different *nasyons* (nations or sects); the two most common sects are Rada and Petwo. Vodouisants believe the *lwas* reside in *Guinen*, or Guinea, in Africa. Thus, during a ceremony, they must call the divinities to the place of worship through a series of ordered invocations. First, in the procession or hierarchy is Papa Legba, who stands at the crossroads between good and evil. The title of "Papa" denotes his good nature and benevolence. As leader of the *lwas*, he must be invoked first before communication with any other *lwas* can take place. He is usually depicted as a stooped old man with a sack and a hat.[8] Other deities include Dambala, the compassionate father and snake figure; Agwe, the sovereign of the sea; Ogoun, the traditional Nigerian god of fire; Marassa, the divine twins, which symbolize balance; and Erzulie, also known as Ezili Freda, the *lwa* of beauty.[9]

These deities do not play a detached role in the lives of their people; they have physical traits and manifestations that distinguish them. Possession, an integral element of a vodou ceremony, occurs when the spirit of a god "mounts" an attendee. This attendee becomes the god's *chual* (horse) and proceeds to adopt the traits of the god, including the sex, deportment, and specific traits ascribed the god in vodou lore.[10] The *lwas* act and speak through the *chual*; therefore, when an individual becomes possessed, the congregation addresses this person by the name of the god that has mounted. The divinities also have jealous natures that require animal sacrifice in order to avoid retribution that may range from loss of financial income to sudden death. Any misfortune could indicate a slight from a *lwa*. Thus, believers call the *houngan* or *manbo* (vodou priest or priestess) to perform ceremonies that either thank—as occurs in *Masters of the Dew*—and/ or implore the divinities, then wait until the *lwas* send a sign.

Vodou plays a two-fold role in *Masters of the Dew*, but its primary role is fatalistic. As a whole, the inhabitants of Fonds Rouge see themselves at the mercy of the *lwas*, who do not dispense hope. Old Délira, Manuel's mother, is perfectly ready to die, but this preparedness has less to do with her age than with her belief system. She speaks the first words of the novel: "We're all going to die."[11] This sentiment echoes resoundingly. When Destine, a neighbor, informs her that she will also be leaving Délira for literally greener pastures in a different village, the narrator (most likely appropriating Destine's thoughts) sighs, "Oh *loas*, my *loas* of Guinea, you don't weigh the work of our hands according to our share of misery. Your scales are false. That's why we're dying with no help and with no hope."[12]

Note this divergence from the promise of "peace that passeth all understanding" in Christianity.[13] Traditional African vodou's syncretism with Roman Catholicism in Haiti appears most prominently in the alignment of African *lwas* with Catholic theology to produce a religious view that includes both cosmologies. Délira's belief in vodou does not conflict with her belief in the Christian God; in fact, she names both the triune God and the pantheistic *lwa* in a hierarchy that places *Bondye* (the Good Lord) as Master over the spirits. She tells Manuel, "He [God] *is* the Lord of all things! He controls the spirits of the springs, the sea, and of the trees. 'Papa Loko,' he says, 'Master Agoué,' he says 'do you hear me?' Loko-atisou answers, 'Thy will be done.' And Agoueta-woyo answers, 'Amen'."[14] This apparent inconsistency is common in many Haitian peasants, who nominally list Catholicism as their religion on census forms, but still serve the spirits on a daily basis.[15] According to her system of beliefs, she may call upon either *Bondye* or the *lwas* to help her, but will most likely blame the *lwas* for any misfortune in her life. At the crossroads of the decision to remain feuding or reconcile, Larivoire, the patriarch of Manuel's rivals, tells his men that they will meet the following day and decide, "if-God-wills."[16]

Not only does the older generation within the novel espouse the principles of fatalism, but the younger people believe it as well. Manuel's fiancée, Annaïse, first reacts with a despondent air to his ideas of rebellion. "But what can we do?" she cries. "Aren't we helpless and with nobody to turn to when misfortune comes? It's just *fate*, that's all" (emphasis added).[17] In the original novel, Roumain employs the French word *fatalité*, which, although it translates accurately in English to "fate," demonstrates the author's intention to transmit the denotation of fatalism. He could have easily substituted the words *sort*, *destin*, or *hasard*, as they all imply uncontrollable destiny; therefore it is significant that he chooses a word that resembles, etymologically, the French cognate *fatalisme*. After Manuel's slaying, although his comrade Laurélien believed in the rebellion, the latter still expresses a twinge of fatalism in a colorful allegory. He laments, "But death made its choice like a blind man who selects mangoes at the mart, groping until he finds a good one and leaving the bad."[18] While he does not question the gods or God by name—as Annaïse does upon learning of her lover's demise—his statement still reflects the prevalence of fatalism throughout the novel.

Although Roumain ostensibly privileges peasant belief in vodou by inscribing a perceived lower class religion into Haitian literature, the text is still laden with critiques of its fatalism. The author makes use of a third person narrator of ambiguous convictions.[19] Throughout the text, the narrator primarily remains neutral; in certain cases, it seems to express an opinion. For example, as stated previously, the narrator makes use of Destine's voice in the lament to the unjust *lwas*. A second, more ominous, authorial intrusion occurs at the end of the vodou ceremony: "Dancing and drinking anesthetized them—swept away their shipwrecked souls to drown in *those regions of unreality and danger where the fierce forces of the African gods lay in wait*" (emphasis added).[20] Even though a vodou ceremony of thanks has just taken place, the tone leaves the reader with a boding sense of doom.

In the passage about ceremonial revels, some of Roumain's original meaning (within the italicized portion) becomes lost in translation. In Roumain's "Governeurs," the original French text reads: " . . . ces régions iréelles et louches où les guettait *la déraison farouche* des dieux africains" (87; emphasis mine). The Larousse dictionary defines the French word *déraison* as "manque de bon sens"[21], or "lack of good sense" (translation mine). Webster's Concise French Dictionary translates it as "folly."[22] Thus, the "fierce forces" become the "fierce folly" of the *lwas*, which changes, if only slightly, the perception the author transmits about the gods. They are not yet fierce, but they are capricious; they "lack good sense." In addition to this default, the phrase "lay in wait" indicates a predatory attribute of the *lwas*. Finally, the seemingly innocuous word "unreality" provokes a thought that completely undermines the vodou belief system. As vodou's foundation stands on the principle that the spirits are real and involved in human affairs, the concept of a "region of unreality" runs opposite to that line of thinking. Readers may not safely assume that, since this statement belongs to no apparent character, these sentiments necessarily belong to Roumain; however, the term does align with the trend of opinionated narrative intrusion within the text.

A second, more direct, example of the novel's critique of fatalism materializes in Manuel Jean-Joseph, who is at times a mouthpiece for the author's communist ideologies. Manuel is not a "partisan of the resignation" characteristic of the spirit worship; in fact, he renounces outright the belief of the *lwas*' direct involvement in *human* activities. Upon his arrival, when his mother thanks God and the *lwas*, he counters her, saying, "There's heavenly business and there's earthly business. The sky's the pasture-land of the angels."[23] In his personal belief system, he attributes a spirit to the earth, rather than attributing an earthly characteristic to a spirit. While the older peasants attend the vodou ceremony, he sits inside the house and drinks a bottle of rum with a friend. By rote, he possesses a cognizance of the vodou rituals; but just as the peasants live their belief, he demonstrates his disbelief through his actions. One particularly striking illustration unfolds when he encounters the *lwa* Ogoun during the vodou ceremony. After the *lwa* asks the location of Manuel, Manuel commences to challenge him as no other individual dares.

> "Here I am, *oui*," said Manuel.
> "Answer me, '*Oui*, papa . . . .One would say you're impertinent, isn't that so?"
> "No."
> "Answer me, 'No, papa!'"[24]

The prodigal son refuses to bestow any semblance of genuine respect upon the old god by denying him the affectionate term "papa." He only repeats the god's words after each second request. Indeed, since Manuel holds to the idea that the *lwas* of Guinea are capricious and therefore not benevolent, his uttering the expression constitutes mockery rather than obedience. He also expresses his dissatisfaction to Annaïse, who changes her fatalistic views after listening to him extemporize. Almost sacrilegiously, he declares that the people's entreaty to the *lwas* for rain amount to "so much silly monkeyshines," that the "blood of a chicken or goat can't . . . alter the course of the clouds and fill them with water like bladders."[25] Yet, immediately after uttering those words, Manuel still professes a respect for his parents' belief in the traditional gods of Africa.

Manuel's simultaneous respect and ambivalence is not unlike Roumain's own position on vodou as a traditional religion in Haiti. When the Haitian government began their anti-superstition campaign against vodou in 1942, he wrote an essay titled *Autour de la campagne anti-superstitieuse* ("About the anti-superstition campaign") in defense of the peasants' right to retain their religion. In it, Roumain demonstrates his profound comprehension of the life-consuming worship typical of vodou. J. Michael Dash quotes him as writing, "The essential is not to make the peasant renounce his belief in Ogoun. It is rather a question of completely changing his *conception of the world* . . . If one really wishes to change the *archaic religious mentality* of our peasants, we must educate them" (emphasis added).[26] Three points in this quote are crucial: that of world perception, of archaic mentality, and of education. Firstly, the world perception of a Voudouisant, like that of one who ascribes to an African philosophy, does not necessarily accept the ideals of the Western linear system of belief. Regarding African epistemological principles, African religionist Mambo Ama Mazama writes, "Because Life is one, there can be no dichotomy between so-called natural and supernatural worlds . . . life and death . . . are complimentary."[27] For that reason, Roumain is precisely correct; just as Christianity hinges on the linear timeline of birth, death and afterlife, vodou governs through the principle of cyclical life. The ancestors are not dead in the sense that they no longer have agency. On the contrary, they simply pass into an alternate phase of living, with a remaining ability to effect change among the living. As Roumain indicated, this world perception would be impervious to a verbal renunciation of vodou. Secondly, Roumain, like Manuel, supports the right of the peasants to worship the spirits. However, he also uses a more pejorative term to describe their beliefs—an archaic mentality—which betrays his own thoughts in terms of vodou. Finally, the author imprints the desire for education onto his character, further making Manuel Jean-Joseph nearly parallel with his creator. Once again, snippets of Roumain's biography emerge from the fabric of the novel. Manuel also prescribes education both for himself and for all the inhabitants of Fonds Rouge: "He [Manuel] had always regretted, . . . not knowing how to write. But when, thanks to irrigation, existence became easier, they'd ask the Communal Magistrate in town to set up a school in Fonds Rouge. . . . Instruction was a necessary thing; it helped you understand life."[28]

Another indication of the novel's condemnation of fatalism appears in the name of the last remaining source of water in Fonds Rouge, called the

Zombi Pool, which is a stagnant breeding ground for mosquitoes and "rotten as a dead adder."[29] Zombification is primarily practiced in Petwo, the occasionally malevolent *nasyon* of vodou, which has its roots directly in the island of Hispaniola.[30] Although it has been widely popularized by movies, the zombi of Haitian vodou refers primarily to a body without a soul, or as folklorists Hans W. Ackermann and Jeanine Gauthier attest, "a body buried in sight of all and resurrected by unknown means."[31] A sorcerer does so by stealing the *Ti Bon Ange*—the second part of the dual soul—either before or after digging up a previously poisoned body. The purpose of this resurrection is to transform an individual into a type of slave that works mindlessly for its creator. Here, it differs from the zombi present in American horror films, which exists primarily to eat living people and change them into zombies (as in the classic horror film *Night of the Living Dead*). Zombies created through Haitian vodou do not know they are dead unless someone gives them salt, at which point they awaken and at times revenge themselves against the sorcerer.[32]

Hence, the presence of the word "zombi" in the Zombi Pool provides an interesting symbolic connotation for the characters in the novel. This pool cannot plausibly serve as a source of water for Fonds Rouge simply because a zombi, in itself, does not possess the essence of life. Roumain has rightfully made the Zombi Pool a hotbed for mosquitoes, the living carriers of death, because the zombi is the veritable living dead. Metaphorically, the pool symbolizes the people of Fonds Rouge, who have been stagnant for ten years waiting for the *lwas* to effect a change in their lives. Their inactivity serves as a breeding ground for those who seek to work evil upon them. The blood-sucking, corrupt rural policeman Hilarion Hilarius, his wife, and the greedy Magistrate have stolen the *Ti Bon Ange* of the peasants, and the people work tirelessly without reaping any significant profit for themselves. In line with this allegory, Manuel, who repudiates the influence of vodou principles, represents the salt that awakens the people from their trance. Hitherto, they are not aware of their zombified state. When discussing the literal effects of salt deprivation on the human body, Professor of Medicine Thomas G. Orr states that in cases of severe imbalance, "Death can be delayed by administering water and sodium chloride [salt]."[33] He may be referring to biological functions, but his words inadvertently apply to the situation in *Masters of the Dew*. The people are prepared to die, but salt (Manuel) and water do save them from the death they passively await. Certainly, without Manuel, they would not have the means to assume agency and take revenge on Hilarion with their communal industry. The final image of the novel reinforces the metaphor that salt awakens the zombi to new life; Manuel's intended, Annaïse, feels his child stirring within her womb.

At this part in this paper, there will be an analysis of the connections between fatalistic and catalytic substantiations by discussing a popular dancing activity in vodou. Vodou practice acts as a catalyst for the trope of dancing in *Masters of the Dew*. The group of *serviteurs* present at a ceremony does not merely amount to a passive congregation; they allow the service to happen with them, as opposed to happening to them. In short, they enjoy dancing. At one instance during the ceremony, the narrator discloses that the dance the peasants are performing is the *yanvalou*, which belongs to Papa Legba, but not solely to Legba. Anthropologist Yvonne Daniel explains that some dances in Haitian vodou are singular within the context of African-based religions in that they may manifest several different *lwas*, rather than just one.[34] In an almost comical fashion, even Manuel recounts the compulsion—and his subsequent obedience—to dance:

> The other night, at the Legba ceremonies, I danced and sang to my heart's content. I'm Negro, no? And I enjoyed myself like a real Negro. When the drums beat, I feel it in the pit of my stomach. I feel an itch in my loins and an electric current in my legs, and I've got to join the dance.[35]

His admission contains both agency and impulse; he joins in the dance. Furthermore, he is a primary example of vodou as catalyst for dance because he does not ascribe to the belief system. Thus for him, more so than for the *serviteurs* who partake, this truly constitutes an act of his will versus the will of the *lwas*.

Belief in vodou also works as a catalyst for the actions of the people. Voudouisants cannot act on their own accord to make major decisions for fear of affronting the *lwas*. Paradoxically, in times of adversity, the fatalistic vodou convictions serve as the catalyst for the sole course of action: calling the *houngan or manbo* for a ceremony. These measures are not circumstantially proactive, but rather prescriptive or preventive. Hence, vodou belief presides especially over small details, even for everyday actions, such as eating. Indeed, the feasting of the gods, called *mangé lwa*, is a prominent practice in both the vodou ceremony and in quotidian life. Renowned Swiss anthropologist Alfred Métraux explains that this "restor[es] to the gods the energy which is constantly drawn from them by their worshippers."[36] Depending on which *lwa* the people invoke, they will place different items at the *poto mitan*, the sacred central pole, for the divinity to make himself at home with his favorite things. During the ceremony depicted in the novel, the *houngan* sets a sack, an ear of roasted corn soaked in syrup and olive oil, salt fish, cakes, and liquor at the *poto mitan* for Papa Legba. Through the personage of Fleurimond, Papa Legba graciously accepts his gifts and blesses the people.

Ancestral reverence goes far beyond the reach of the *poto mitan*. Before any person eats or drinks, each person must set aside a portion to quench the hunger and thirst of the *anciens*. For example, upon Manuel's return, their neighborhood throws a feast. Before taking a swig from the bottle of clairin[37], his father, Bienaimé, pours a couple of droplets on the ground for the dead (gods), and says, "They, too, are thirsty."[38] This practice does not originate in the syncretized vodou of Haiti; rather, it is traditionally African. Thus, Mazama explicates African libatory practices: " . . . so that they [the ancestors] may continue to play a part in their family's affairs . . . we offer food and libations to them as gestures of appreciation, hospitality, and respect.[39] The physical execution of this belief appears throughout the Caribbean in various rituals, such as the Big Drum Ritual in Carriacou, Grenada. Caribbean writer Paule Marshall centers her novel *Praisesong for the Widow* on this remembrance of African nations and gods. Carriacouan Lebert Joseph, an old man who represents Papa Legba in the text, explains his personal devotion to the "Long-time People":

> I tell you, you best remember them! If not they'll get vex . . . everything start gon' wrong and you don' know the reason . . . That's why . . . the first thing I do the minute I reach home is to roast an ear of corn just pick out from the ground and put it on a plate for them . . . Next thing I sprinkles a little rum outside the house. They likes that.[40]

Lebert clearly believes in the power of the *lwas*, whom he calls the Long-time People, and preemptively does what he must to avoid their vexation with him. In an action that replenishes the food supply and gives honor to the *lwas*, Délira in *Masters of the Dew* also invokes their presence before sowing corn. Like the *houngan*, she scatters corn grains to the four sacred directions and prays, "Jesus Christ, angels, spirits of the dead, saints, here's the corn that I give you."[41] Notably, she, Bienaimé, and Lebert do not require a priest or priestess to perform these libations toward the gods; they do so of their own impetus.

An additional symbolic catalyst can be found in the Ogoun trope within the text. The *lwa* Ogoun's presence in Haiti stems from the colonial period.[42] Author Leslie Desmangles, in his book *The Faces of the Gods*, states that Ogoun originates from Nigeria, while Roumain's text describes Ogoun as a Dahomey god.[43] Since Nigeria borders the ancestral Dahomehan land, now the modern day nation-state of Benin, and colonialism decimated ancient African tribal boundaries, both explanations of the *lwa's* derivation are plausible. Originally, Ogoun is the god of artisans, farmers, and those who work with fire—and by consequence, those who make and wield weapons. In his creolized position in Haitian vodou, Ogoun is the fierce warrior divinity that fights on behalf of the people, and his material symbol is the machete. He has three slightly distinctive manifestations: Ogoun Feray, the warrior general and national hero; Ogoun Batala, the healer; and Ogoun Badagri, the magic healer (in conjunction with the *houngan*). According to Desmangles, Ogoun Feray historically "is a political leader who is said to have generated the violent spirit of the maroon raids . . . of the Haitian revolution."[44] Through his novel, Roumain bestows upon Ogoun once more this traditional role and a new character, Manuel, for him to mount.

In the ceremony portrayed in *Masters of the Dew,* Ogoun appears uninvited, but he has a message seemingly tailor-made for Manuel. When the possessed mount bumps into a townsperson, Simidor Antoine, the latter is terrified with recognition of the war god. Although Dorméus, the *houngan*, gently tells Ogoun that the ceremony belongs to Legba, the Nigerian *lwa* insistently stays within the *chual* he has mounted and continues to assert his presence. Finally, the priest marks the sacred circle to welcome him and brings the *lwa* a cigar and a bottle of rum. The possessed Simidor Antoine under the influence of Ogoun, rises and sings, "We'll dig the canal, I say! Ago yé! / The vein is open, the blood flows."[45] Manuel's mother, Délira, is right to have concern about the presence of Ogoun at Legba's ceremony. In one sense, it reinforces the belief that the gods know the affairs of the peasants (the canal); on the other hand, it raises the question of whose blood flows. The symbol of blood in conjunction with Ogoun is no accident. The night Gervilen fatally attacks Manuel, the narrator expounds on a picture near Manuel's bed; "It was a picture of Saint James there, who is at the same time Ogoun, the Dahomey god. He had a fierce air, with his bristly beard, his brandished saber. As the flame licked the dappled red of his clothing, it looked like fresh blood."[46] That prescient image also echoes Délira's worry because of whose blood will flow. The most likely answer reveals itself some pages later. When Manuel lays on his deathbed, the narrator's view again sweeps to the picture of Ogoun. However, this time his "crimson cloak wrapped him in a cloud of blood."[47] Manuel's death fulfills the Ogoun-related prophecies hidden in the text. At the completion of the novel, the men dig the canal, which flows like Manuel's blood.

Two conceivable reasons for Manuel's death exist within the framework of vodou philosophy. The first provides a logical complement to the respect and fear inherent in the phrase "si-dieu-veut." As a disobedient subject, Manuel has offended the old gods of Guinea with his impertinence, and they have exacted their punishment upon him. In a 1940 study of Haitian peasants, anthropologist George Eaton Simpson remarks, "The few who are bold enough to defy the gods have nothing but misfortune for the rest of their lives."[48] Within the context of Roumain's 1920's and 1930's setting, Simpson's remarks are valid.[49] Manuel rebels against the status quo—passivity—without so much as imploring any god. He declares, "Well, I swear I'll find water and I'll bring it to the plains with the rope of a canal around my neck. I'm telling you, I, Manuel Jean-Joseph!"[50] In keeping with vodou philosophy, as a living human, Manuel lacks the fatalism necessary to exercise complete faith in the *lwas*. He, much like the divinities he refuses to honor, inspires other men (such as Laurélien) to have faith in him. In addition, if the gods allowed him to escape punishment, it would be tantamount to undermining their own authority, as he impudently flaunts his disbelief. This transgression is a serious one; therefore, according to the ideology of vodou, he must die. More specifically, he crosses Ogoun himself during the ceremony; all ensuing passages involving Ogoun refer to blood (i.e. death). In fact, the word "death" appears, again as an ironic warning. Even within the sunlight of Annaïse's happiness about her impending marriage, the shadow of death yet lingers in the narration. She daydreams on the morning before his murder, "But it's a tale that ends happily . . . Because, oh God! some are full of death and disaster."[51] Oblivious to the forces in play, she unconsciously foresees the preliminary end to own her happiness.

The second explanation for Manuel's death is that he represents an actual Ogoun figure in the text. Within the Christian tradition, his name means "God with us." This name is also a derivative of the Hebrew name "Emmanuel," which is one of the names of Jesus Christ. In fact, a popular depiction of Ogoun consists of a pose reminiscent of the crucifix: outstretched arms and a slumped, injured body. Also like a Christ figure, Manuel suffers a sacrificial death at the hands of one of his own people; he bears the wounds on his side. In death, he is well aware of his position. He tells his mother, ". . . what counts is the sacrifice of a man. The blood of a man . . . Tell [Larivoire] the will of the blood that's been shed."[52] Mazama states that "death is . . . a rite of passage that allows one to gain another existential status, that of ancestor."[53] Thus it is only as an ancestor, a dead familial spirit, that the people can truly execute Manuel's wish for reconciliation. As a dead, yet cognizant, spirit, Manuel deserves the honor of having his wishes carried out; the peasants do so without hesitation. As he now exists in the ancestral realm, he becomes *ley mo*, or an undeified "living dead."[54]

Parallel to the figure of Ogoun as a wounded General, the men fashion a chant for their rebel leader even before his death: "General Manuel! / Salute! Ho!"[55] Rightfully, they position him at his wake with a machete by his side; not only does it symbolize the warrior Ogoun, but it also confirms the narrator's prophetic description of Saint James. They call him a true peasant, and since Ogoun also identified with the farmer, Manuel fully embodies both the historic and creolized form of the Dahomehan *lwa*. Finally, in what arguably counts as Roumain's greatest message in the novel, the previously fatalist Laurélien articulates one final, significant statement about Manuel. He muses, "Now you're dead, Chief, dead and buried. But your words we won't forget. And, if, one day on the hard road of this life, weariness should tempt us with, 'What's the use?' and 'It's not worth the trouble,' we'll hear your voice and we'll be of good courage."[56] In conjunction with the water, Manuel's last true gift was to divest his people of the fatalism that held them captive. He does not, in the process, strip them of their belief in the *lwas*; he merely provides them with the knowledge that they also have hope in each other. Thus, as the Ogoun figure, it is fitting that Manuel propels his people to action, machete in hand, and serves as the catalyst that will ensure his people live to honor his memory for generations to come. Both interpretations of Manuel's death make use of the cyclical quality of vodou philosophy in that they mutually return to the image of living, involved ancestors.

As a whole, *Masters of the Dew* presents a close rendering that allows the reader to glimpse the mindset of the then-contemporary peasant who more than practiced, but also lived the vodou religion. The fatalism discussed in this essay demonstrates the deep-seated convictions the Vodouisants of Fonds Rouge possess; in truth, even their submissiveness is an act of faith. At the same time, as is shown by the Ogoun trope, vodou can serve as a powerful catalyst for social action. Despite Roumain's critique of fatalism, he yet succeeds in portraying both viewpoints in a balanced manner. This parallelism between Manuel Jean-Joseph and his village exemplifies a final vodou trope in the novel: the Marassa.

The *lwas* called Marassa, the divine twins, originate from an Ibeyi African tradition in which contradictory and complementary oppositions balance—much like the Chinese yin and yang.[57] The twins, believed to have died at birth, are capricious and stand for birth and rebirth. They are invoked, after Papa Legba, at the start of each vodou service. Of the novel, Britton observes, "The text is structured so that almost everything in it recalls or predicts its symmetrical counterpart--parallel or contrast."[58] The most general, encompassing metaphor is contained in the balancing duality between the fatalistic and the catalyst natures of vodou philosophy. For while the *lwas* may apparently manifest, at times, capricious personalities, and seem to give no hope to the Vodouisants, that is not entirely true. Their natures also are dual. Even though Délira agrees with her son that she, too, has not heard from the *lwas,* she continues to offer sacrifices to them in *hope* that they will change her situation. Papa Legba, entreated at the ceremony, controls the crossroads of both good and evil, and his words as presented in the novel are kind: "I'll help my Creole children find the right road," he says. "They will leave behind this road of misery."[59] The country of Haiti embodies fatalist and catalytic ideas, as well as that of the Marassa. The Marassa's colors are red, white, and blue; these are also the colors of the Haitian flag in its current incarnation.[60]

In addition, several of the characters are twinned. For example, Délira and Bienaimé demonstrate the opposite qualities of bitter and sweet. Even when he admits to being a "disagreeable Negro," he avails himself of the anger he is accustomed to and bristles when his wife agrees with him. Gervilen, the murderer, and Manuel are both progeny of the defunct Dorisca and Sauveur; one man is represented as wholly darkness, and the other is anointed in light. Gervilen, described as "a compact shadow, hardly different from the night" stands as the only unequivocally evil character in the novel.[61] Manuel retains a light on his forehead, even in his untimely death. Herein lies the final correspondence between an author and his creation.

Figuratively, had Jacques Roumain not died suddenly at the age of 38, *Master of the Dew* may become the catalyst for a Marxist movement within Haiti. As the founder of the Haitian Communist Party, he would have undoubtedly led his people with the very zeal he imbued into Manuel Jean-Joseph. By proxy, from its author's ideological perspective and wishes for the text, *Masters of the Dew* also serves as a catalyst (Marxist) novel of dissent. Roumain rests as one of the first Haitian novelists to publicize hitherto little known issues, such as the problems that mass deforestation and subsequent soil erosion have caused in Haiti. Additionally, *Masters of the Dew* subverts the breach between the Haitian peasantry and elite, for the novel is neither singularly peasant nor elite—it is *Haitian.* As Manuel stated:

> We're *this country*, and it wouldn't be a thing without us, nothing at all . . . We don't yet know what a force we are, what a single force—all the peasants, all the Negroes of plain and hill, all united. Some day, when we get wise to that, we'll rise up from one end of the country to the other . . . and we'll clear out poverty and plant a new life (emphasis author's).[62]

Michael Dash, a prominent West Indian scholar, asserts in the introduction to the English translation of the novel: "... we can conclude that it is not a matter of forgiving Roumain for his good intentions as is sometimes the case with political art. ...While never neglecting the legacy and resources of the peasant novel, Roumain was able to manipulate this genre even further to produce a parable of universal proportions."[63] The strength of Roumain's novel stems rather from its refusal to solely privilege either the elite intellectual philosophy or the fatalist peasant ideology. It is, instead, a synthesis of the two. Jacques Roumain, in a literary sense, represents Manuel Jean-Joseph to Haiti, in that he employs his knowledge of both vodou and Marxism to offer an awakening salt to his people: hope. Although scholars have written extensively about the politics of Roumain's works, little has been said regarding the intersection of vodou and Marxist belief systems in this particular novel. This paper seeks to contribute to the discourse on contemporary Afro-Caribbean literature. This study also prompts needed discussions on how African-based philosophies collide and coincide with European philosophies in Haitian and other Caribbean literature.

Bibliography

Ackermann, Hans-W. and Jeanine Gauthier. "The Ways and Nature of the Zombi." *Journal of American Folklore* 104, no. 414 (1991):466-494.

Britton, Celia. "'Common being' and Organic Community in Jacques Roumain's *Gouverneurs de la rosee*." *Research in African Literatures* 37, no. 2 (2006): 164-176.

Cosentino, David. "Who Is That Fellow in the Many-Colored Cap? Transformations of Eshu in Old and New World Mythologies." *The Journal of American Folklore* 100, no. 3 (1987):261-275.

Daniel, Yvonne. *Dancing Wisdom*. Urbana: University of Illinois Press, 2005.

Dash, J. Michael. Introduction to *Masters of the Dew* by Jacques Roumain, 5-21. Translated by Langston Hughes and Mercer Cook. London: Heinemann, 1978.

Desmangles, Leslie. *The Faces of the Gods: Vodou and Roman Catholicism in Haiti*. Chapel Hill: University of North Carolina Press, 1992.

Fowler, Carolyn. *A Knot in the Thread: the Life and Work of Jacques Roumain*. Washington: Howard University Press, 1980.

Hill, Donald R. "West African and Haitian Influences on the Ritual and Popular Music of Carriacou, Trinidad, and Cuba." *Black Music Research Journal* 18, no.1/2 (1998): 183-201.

Kaussen, Valerie. "Slaves, Viejos, and the Internationale: Modernity and Global Contact in Jacques Roumain's *Gouverneurs de la rosée*." *Research in African Literatures* 35, no. 4 (2004): 121-141.

Marshall, Paule. *Praisesong for the Widow*. New York: Plume, 1983.

Mazama, Mambo Ama. "Afrocentricity and African Spirituality." *Journal of Black Studies* 33, no. 2 (2002): 218-234.

Michel, Claudine. "Of Worlds Seen and Unseen: The Educational Character of Haitian Vodou."*Comparative Education Review* 40, no. 3 (1996): 280-294.

Orr, Thomas R. "The Romance of Common Salt." *The Scientific Monthly* 39, no. 5: (1934): 449-454.

Rigaud, Odette. "The Feasting of the Gods in Haitian Vodu." *Primitive Man* 19, no. 1/2: (1946) 1-58.

Roumain, Jacques. *Masters of the Dew*. Translated by Langston Hughes and Mercer Cook. London: Heinemann, 1978.

Simpson, George Eaton. "Haitian Magic." *Social Forces* 19 no. 1 (1940): 95-100

Notes

[1] Paule Marshall, *Praisesong for the Widow* (New York: Plume, 1983), 165.

[2] For the purposes of this study, I regard fatalism as the belief that all proceedings are beyond human control; in the text, Afro-Haitian *lwas*—or spirit deities—primarily hold the agency.

[3] Celia Britton, " 'Common Being' and Organic Community in Jacques Roumain's *Gouverneurs de la rosee*," *Research in African Literatures* 37, no. 2 (2006): 172.

[4] Carolyn Fowler, *A Knot in the Thread: the Life and Work of Jacques Roumain* (Washington: Howard University Press, 1980), 247.

[5] Valerie Kaussen, "Slaves, Viejos, and the Internationale: Modernity and Global Contact in Jacques Roumain's Gouverneurs de la rosée," *Research in African Literatures* 35, no. 4 (2004): 135.

[6] Claudine Michel, "Of Worlds Seen and Unseen: The Educational Character of Haitian Vodou," *Comparative Education Review* 40, no. 3 (1996): 284.

[7] Ibid.

[8] David Cosentino, "Who Is That Fellow in the Many-Colored Cap? Transformations of Eshu in Old and New World Mythologies," *The Journal of American Folklore* 100, no. 3 (1987): 265.

[9] Leslie Desmangles, *The Faces of the Gods: Vodou and Roman Catholicism in Haiti* (Chapel Hill: University of North Carolina Press, 1992), 146.

[10] Odette Rigaud, Alfred Métraux, Roda Métraux, "The Feasting of the Gods in Haitian Vodu," *Primitive Man* 19, no. 1/2 (1946): 1-58.
[11] Jacques Roumain, *Masters of the Dew*, trans. Langston Hughes and Mercer Cook (London: Heinemann, 1978), 23.
[12] Ibid., 112.
[13] Philippians 4:7 (King James Version).
[14] Ibid., 54-5.
[15] Desmangles, 52.
[16] Roumain, 136.
[17] Ibid., 88.
[18] Ibid., 165.
[19] I apply the term "ambiguous" because these viewpoints change in accordance with the characters in a given scene.
[20] Ibid., 71-2.
[21] *Larousse de Poche: dictionnaire des noms communs, des noms propres, précis de grammaire*, s.v. "déraison."
[22] *Webster's New World Concise French Dictionary,* 1st ed., (Indianapolis: Wiley, 2004), s.v. "déraison."
[23] Ibid., 44.
[24] Ibid., 70.
[25] Ibid., 87.
[26] Michael J. Dash, introduction to *Masters of the Dew,* by Jacques Roumain, trans. Langston Hughes and Mercer Cook (London: Heinemann, 1978), 8-9.
[27] Mambo Ama Mazama, "Afrocentricity and African Spirituality," *Journal of Black Studies* 33, no. 2 (2002): 222.
[28] Roumain, 147.
[29] Ibid., 53.
[30] Donald R. Hill, "West African and Haitian Influences on the Ritual and Popular Music of Carriacou, Trinidad, and Cuba," *Black Music Research Journal* 18, no. 1/2 (1998): 183.
[31] Hans-W. Ackermann and Jeanine Gauthier, "The Ways and Nature of the Zombi," *Journal of American Folklore* 104, no. 414 (1991):474.
[32] Ibid.
[33] Thomas G. Orr, "The Romance of Common Salt," *The Scientific Monthly* 39, no. 5 (1934): 452.
[34] Yvonne Daniel, *Dancing Wisdom* (Urbana: University of Illinois Press, 2005), 13.
[35] Roumain, 87-8.
[36] Riguad, Métraux, Métraux 7.
[37] Clairin is a Haitian alcoholic beverage made from fermented cane sugar.
[38] Roumain, 43.
[39] Mazama, 221.
[40] Paule Marshall, 165.
[41] Roumain, 60.
[42] Desmangles, 145.

[43] Roumain, 146.
[44] Desmangles, 148.
[45] Roumain, 70.
[46] Ibid., 146.
[47] Ibid., 155.
[48] George Eaton Simpson, "Haitian Magic," *Social Forces* 19, no. 1 (1940): 96.
[49] Valerie Kaussen, "Slaves, Viejos, and the Internationale: Modernity and Global Contact in Jacques Roumain's Gouverneurs de la rosée," *Research in African Literatures* 35, no. 4 (2004): 126.
[50] Roumain, 59.
[51] Ibid., 145.
[52] Ibid., 158.
[53] Mazama, 220.
[54] Daniel, 54.
[55] Roumain, 130.
[56] Ibid., 178.
[57] Desmangles, 146.
[58] Britton, 168.
[59] Roumain, 66.
[60] The Haitian flag was red and black during the Duvalier regimes; the existent design has been in place since 1986.
[61] Ibid., 95.
[62] Ibid., 74-5.
[63] Dash, 18.

CHAPTER TWO

DRUMMING UP THE NATION: REPRESENTATIONS IN CARIBBEAN MUSIC, DRAMA, AND DANCE PERFORMANCE

"Drumming up the Nation: Representations of Caribbean Music, Drama, and Dance Performance" explores the revolutionary ideals embedded in reggae, the music and dance performance in Afro-Puerto Rican culture, and the representations of the Caribbean in North American theater. The essays in this chapter present convergent concepts of the formation of a Caribbean identity that evolves and metamorphoses to accommodate multiple Caribbean realities. In particular, the major issues address the idea of Caribbean music as an instrument of social agency, racial stereotyping in the images of the Caribbean infiltrated in dance and theatrical performances, and the construction of the Caribbean as "other" in the form of biased images in Caribbean music, drama, and dance performance.

Adam Lloyd presents a detailed analysis of the life and revolutionary ideals of reggae legend Bob Marley and how these permeate his music. His essay "Bob Marley: Postcolonial Activist and (R)evolutionary Intellectual" offers a chronological review of Marley's music trajectory that is juxtaposed to the transformation of his political and social ideals from "blind acceptance of negritude and the need for armed rebellion to a transnational, transracial belief in the unity and brotherhood of men and women." Marley's music has a universal appeal beyond Caribbean reality; it conveys quintessential trans-cultural ideas such as social reform and freedom. Advocating for the deconstruction of the problematic image of the mammy in the form of the traditional *bomba* costume for dance performances, Melanie A. Maldonado offers a complex study of the development, and transformation of *bomba* from "colonial mimicry" to a more creolized and "transracial" Afro-Puerto Rican *bomba trigueña*. According to Maldonado, "by disavowing the costume women are reappropriating their bodies, reclaiming the agency lost, or covered by the costume, and ironically, moving toward [a liberated] aesthetic and dance vocabulary." Following Maldonado's critical approach, Juan A. Recondo examines the image of the Caribbean in J. Robinson's play *The Yorker's Stratagem, or, Banana's Wedding*. In the essay, he analyzes elements of racial tension, and discrimination, as much as the construction of the Caribbean as "other" which are issues embedded in the very history of slavery in the Caribbean and beyond. Moreover, Recondo contends that, in the play, "the 'othered' discourse becomes a transgressive force that constantly threatens republican virtue and hierarchies of capitalistic power and race in the United States."

Going Bananas on the New York Stage: Representations of the Caribbean as Seen in J. Robinson's *The Yorker's Stratagem; or, Banana's Wedding*

Juan R. Recondo

The Yorker's Stratagem; or, Banana's Wedding was staged for the first time as an afterpiece to the longer production of *Constitutional Follies; or, Life in Demerara* on April 24, 1792. Both plays, which were written by J. Robinson, seemed to have been welcomed by audiences, and the comic afterpiece "was received with universal applause by the public."[1] *The Yorker's Stratagem; or, Banana's Wedding* had a short run in New York, and according to the *Annals of the New York Stage*, "the final curtain fell here in May, 1792."[2] Regardless of its limited yet successful New York run, not much is known about the playwright, whose initial is the last surviving remnant of his first name. In his essay, "The West Indies, Commerce, and a Play for U. S. Empire: Recovering J. Robinson's *The Yorker's Stratagem* (1792)," Sean X. Goudie cites William Dunlap's description of the playwright as "a West Indian immigrant like [Alexander] Hamilton and conspicuous 'in a crowd' for being a 'large-framed young man' and indulging in perhaps too great a fondness for flashy dress, a 'gold-laced collar' and 'three gold hatbands' serving as his fashion trademark (196)."[3] Goudie seems to have misquoted Dunlap, who was not referring to Robinson but to Robins, "a scene-painter, [who would] occasionally . . . sing a song, and join in the choruses."[4] Furthermore, there is no reference of Robinson as being from the West Indies in Dunlap, yet George Seilhamer, in his *History of the American Theatre*, states that "Robinson was probably a West India [sic] actor."[5] The fact that it is probable puts into question Goudie's assertion about Robinson's West Indian background. These minor defects do not affect the significance of Goudie's article for this piece in any way, but unquestionably add to the mystery surrounding the identity of the elusive Mr. J. Robinson. The few references found about Robinson mostly relate to his inability as an actor and his talent as a playwright. Seilhamer states:

"Although Mr. Robinson was a member of the Old American Company when the services of actors were most needed, he seldom appeared. He was a better playwright than player, and even in his own pieces he accepted unimportant roles."[6] Regardless of his mediocre acting abilities, Robinson's talent as a playwright must have been respected amongst his peers since the responsibility of this role was considerable especially if we take into account his theatre company's history in New York during the second half of the 18th century.

According to Mary K. Henderson's *The City and the Theatre: New York Playhouses from Bowling Green to Times Square*, William Hallam's London Company of Comedians arrived to Williamsburg in 1752. They performed in New York for a few months between 1753 and 1754. After an apparently successful tour of the colonies, the troupe left for Jamaica, and later returned to New York under a new manager, David Douglass, and a new name, the American Company of Comedians. Douglass's decision to change the troupe's name was probably due to the tensions between the colonies and British rule. Nevertheless, the company still catered to a colonial aristocracy, thereby earning the antipathy of the North American people. The increasing revolutionary spirit and the corresponding republican dislike of anything British and aristocratic, lead to the Chapel Street Theatre riot in 1766, where a mob of New Yorkers burned down the American Company's playhouse located on Chapel Street. As Bruce McConachie points out in *The Cambridge History of American Theatre*: "Tarred as a symbol of English corruption, Douglass's 'American Company' left for Jamaica in February of 1775."[7] After Douglass passed away in Jamaica, Lewis Hallam, the son of the troupe's founder, took over the company and renamed it as the Old American Company of Comedians. He returned to New York in 1784, facing a young new nation fervently in search of a new identity.

As a playwright, Robinson's work seems to be aimed at forming a new theatre audience and rescuing the stage from the negative portrayal it had gained in the new nation. To this extent, his play had to respond to the predominant issues that permeated the burgeoning society and thus build on a more characteristic North American dramatic expression. This feeling is reflected in the introduction to *The Yorker's Stratagem; or, Banana's Wedding* when he writes: "To the generous Patrons of the Drama, and to the worthy Sons of Columbia who feel an interest in the welfare of the American Stage, the *Yorker's Stratagem* is most respectfully dedicated . . ."[8] This adulatory dedication specifically addresses a people and a theatre linked by a single North American identity. Ironically, identity is a slippery concept that constantly evades any monolithic representation because it is a construct comprised of contradictory definitions. Hence, there is no such thing as a unique North American identity, but is more a conglomeration of diverse factors that may oppose each other and which include race, politics, geography, and historical context, among others. This diversity is seen in Robinson's play in the character of Amant, a business-savvy North American, and his assumed Yankee persona, Jonathan Norrard.

In Robinson's play, Amant arrives at an unidentified West Indian island with the intent of getting married to Sophia, a young West Indian woman whose parents died. She was left under the protection of Fingercash, an avaricious merchant who takes advantage of anybody in order to add to his fortune. Amant's goal is to get the girl and her fortune, the reason why Fingercash does not want to lose his adopted daughter. As a ruse to overcome the thieving merchant, Amant approaches Fingercash as Jonathan Norrard, a Yankee bumpkin who has brought a cargo from the United States to sell in the West Indies. Consequently, Fingercash will be busy trying to steal Jonathan's money without paying attention to Amant's ultimate aim. It is interesting how in the character of Amant/Jonathan, Robinson has combined two very dissimilar ideologies that defined the nation at that time. During the final decades of the 18th century, the strengthening capitalist tendencies and their association to individualistic interests were taken by firm believers of the republican ideal as opposite to the spirit of community championed by the revolution. On one hand, Amant is defined by North American capitalist inclinations. The character represents a significant element of the early North American economy, the U.S. businessman whose power to outsmart the competition is necessary for the subsistence of the country. Goudie explains that this attitude was championed by Alexander Hamilton, the Secretary of the Treasury at the time, who called for an active commerce through which U.S. trade would prevail over any other country hence capitalizing on the cunning North American merchant. Goudie points out:

> Capitalization symbolizes not only the Hamiltonian ideal of empire, but the entrepreneurial "capital" the U.S. *hemispheric man of commerce* [sic] embodies in "spirit" and that the nation might exploit in order to right itself. . . . Finally, active commerce augurs the even greater prosperity the new nation might yet enjoy . . . [9]

Amant is the commercially shrewd hero who stands for the economic future of the nation. McConachie relates the rising capitalism to traditional theatre, hence demonstrating republican prejudice against both. He writes: "Conventional playgoing, seen by many in the mid-1780s as a corrupting luxury of the rich, could only flourish if the strictures of republican communitarianism were loosened and individual capitalist enterprise given more breathing room."[10] This economic system then extends to a cultural dimension creating a discourse that subsumes not only U.S. imperialist ambitions, but also a specific form of traditional theatrical performance.

On the other hand, as Richard M. Dorson explains in his article "The Yankee on the Stage: A Folk Hero of American Drama," Jonathan Norrard "emerges as a generic folk figure capably illustrating cheeky traits of the American temper."[11] In this sense, the Yankee is associated more to the ideals of republicanism and its populist inclinations. The Yankee, who had become a stereotype in American drama, negates any type of fashionable behavior or classic culture, and "even though his naïveté was a subject for ridicule . . . Jonathan admitted inferiority to none and proudly vaunted his American independence."[12] In theatrical terms, it is feasible to say that the Yankee is linked to what McConachie refers to as "republican street theatre," the preferred performative expression more in tune with the republican ideal made up of carnivalesque acts that empowered the common people, such as the aforementioned Chapel Street Theatre riot.[13]

Although to a certain extent capitalism and republicanism rival each other, Robinson combines these two contradicting discourses in one figure, thus making each one contaminate the other. It could be argued that one inclination is given more emphasis than the other, since Jonathan and his country mien is after all a mask that the astute Amant wears to dupe Fingercash, yet Amant is also an assumed persona taken by the actor on stage. Therefore both entities coexist and intermingle in the same performing body producing an intricate system of transgressions. Binary categories come together through Robinson's writing in a plausibly conscious effort to reach different audiences and at the same time inadvertently exposing North American identity as an unstable formation composed of juxtaposing elements. Identity is not only composed of dissimilar elements, but as Jeffrey Richards points out in his book, *Drama, Theatre, and Identity in the American New Republic*: "Identity is only meaningful when placed in opposition to something else."[14] Therefore identity is defined when juxtaposed against an "other" that is constructed for that purpose. Along these lines, I contend that although in J. Robinson's *The Yorker's Stratagem; or, Banana's Wedding* the black West Indian "other" is created as an opposing entity to the dominant North American identity, the "othered" discourse becomes a transgressive force that constantly threatens republican virtue and hierarchies of capitalistic power and race in the United States. I will use Peter Stallybrass and Allon White's interpretation of Mikhail Bakhtin's theory of carnival to understand how the dominant (white North American) and peripheral (black West Indian) discourses come in contact with each other thus perpetuating the unstableness of identity.

In Mikhail Bakhtin's *Rabelais and His World*, carnival is envisioned as a celebratory expression of populist rebellion against high, classical discourses. Stallybrass and White question this idealized vision by calling attention to the fact that carnival also works to reveal those structures of power through which identity is partly created since all discourses, regardless of where they originate, participate in the carnivalesque act. In their book, *The Politics and Poetics of Transgression*, Stallybrass and White state:

> If we treat the carnivalesque as an instance of a wider phenomenon of transgression we move beyond Bakhtin's troublesome *folkloric* approach to a political anthropology of *binary extremism* in class society. This transposition not only moves us beyond the rather unproductive debate over whether carnivals are politically progressive or conservative, it reveals that the underlying structural features of carnival operate far beyond the strict confines of popular festivity and are intrinsic to the dialectics of social classification as such. The 'carnivalesque' mediates between a classical/classificatory body and its negations, its Others, what it excludes to create its identity as such.[15]

The carnival is then the perfect tool to understand how difference is classified through the creation of "otherness" as a significant process in the constitution of identity. It is important to note that the stage becomes the location where the carnivalesque becomes real through performance. The stage represents the West Indian island where the action takes place. Yet the interaction between identities does not remain limited to onstage reality, but transcends to the reality outside situated in the auditorium. Not only are Amant/Jonathan's identities being consolidated and challenged onstage, but also the audience participates in these identity transgressions hence spreading the contamination of "otherness" beyond the confines of the performing space. Stallybrass and White point out:

> Part of the transgressive excitement of the fair for the subordinate classes was *not* its 'otherness' to official discourse, but rather the disruption of provincial habits and local tradition by the introduction of a certain cosmopolitanism, arousing desires and excitements for exotic and strange commodities. The fair 'turned the world inside out' in its mercantilist aspect just as much, if not more, than it 'turned the world upside down' in its popular rituals.[16]

As in the fair, the exoticism of the island becomes real on the stage emphasizing the division between the outside (onstage, West Indies) and inside (auditorium, North America). This relation also foregrounds North American imperialistic desires to take over and commercially colonize that which doubly appears repugnant and desirable because of its difference. Hence, the audience actively participates in the process of identity formation through opposition. At the same time, a space is opened from which the norms that regulate their reality, and all the discourses produced from this site, will be disrupted. To this effect, I am interested in how various carnivalesque elements, such as inversion, the grotesque, and hybridization, which are diversely present in *The Yorker's Stratagem; or, Banana's Wedding*, become disruptions to various markers of North American identity such as republicanism, capitalism, and race. I will begin by analyzing how in the play black West Indian society is constructed as a matriarchy, which is an inversion of the patriarchal structure that dominates white North American discourse. Then I will proceed to discuss how expressions of love and masculinity in Banana, the black West Indian character, are representative of a low discourse that juxtaposes the characteristically high and classical white North American conceptions, represented by Amant and Ledger. Finally, I will consider how the theatrical tradition of blackface becomes a racially hybridizing practice that blurs racial division thus threatening white purity.

In the play, the North American ideal is strategically expressed at the end of the first act by Louisa, the young West Indian girl in need of rescue since she is being forced to marry Banana, a black West Indian planter. She says:

> . . . we may all of us be enabled to set sail for your country [North America], where Virtue gives distinction, Industry wealth; and where, like Majesty Divine, the hand that can deal thunder to usurping foes, distributes the blessings of Liberty and Concord to his fellow citizens, by the justice and wisdom of his laws.[17]

North America is represented as a land where good and truth prevail since virtue is the key to distinction, not money or education. This idea reflects the populist republican posture that champions the goodness of the people. Louisa also refers to the capitalist ideal that sacrifice and work will be financially rewarded in the United States. The system that provides for this is guarded by a powerful entity looking over "*his* fellow citizens" who abide by "*his* laws." This evinces a hierarchy of power dominated by an omnipotent white masculinity in the reality beyond the West Indian island onstage. Interestingly this balance of power is apparent in the theatre as well. McConachie points out that "as in England, theatregoing males treated the actors like servants. Men through the playhouse had the presumed right to shout down, talk over, or ignore the players; patriarchy typically made for noisy performances."[18] The discourse being verbalized onstage clearly echoes the audience's reality further carnivalizing the theatrical experience by intermingling actual reality and onstage reality. This affirmation of national identity must have provoked a discharge of applause and a more direct participation of the spectators in the theatrical experience. At this moment, a classificatory process is enacted onstage that designates the high discourse and its difference from the low.

In the play, the low discourse becomes a deformation of the high as seen in Mrs. Banana. She is the black West Indian matriarch who is forcing Banana, her son, to renounce his feelings for Priscilla, his love interest and the mother of his child, so he can marry into a white family. Mrs. Banana is the character negotiating her son's future, just as Fingercash is doing with his daughter. Fingercash is constructed as a negative patriarchal figure because he is violating moral and racial codes by promising his white daughter to a black man. Yet Mrs. Banana is presented as a further oppositional force since she represents a carnivalesque inversion of what is considered to be the North American balance of power that is admired by Louisa. Stallybrass and White define inversion and its assault against hierarchy in the following excerpt:

> Inversion addresses the social classification of values, distinctions and judgements which underpin practical reason and systematically inverts the relations of subject and object, agent and instrument, husband and wife, old and young, animal and human, master and slave. Although it re-orders the terms of a binary pair, it cannot alter the terms themselves. It is commonly found in popular woodcuts and prints and its most frequent representation is 'the world turned upside down'.... In these ... relations of power and dominance are reversed and ... the woman stands with a gun in her arms whilst the husband sits spinning; the wife holds her husband down and beats him, the daughter feeds her mother, the son rocks his father in the cradle.[19]

The quote asserts the emphasis of inversion on gender and paternal-filial relations of power. Inversion is manifest in the play through the mother's act of taking away the prerogative of the male to decide his future. If this authority would have been exercised by the father, his patriarchal decision would have not been questioned since this would have been consonant with the male hierarchy of power. However, in Banana's case, Mrs. Banana is the one making the decision, hence symbolically castrating the black West Indian representation of masculinity. This is made clear in the way she scolds Banana when he announces that he loves Priscilla. Mrs. Banana says: " . . . you no hab no more amminition in you than one hog."[20] The mother declares that the son does not have any power whatsoever. By referring to Banana's lack of ammunition, which could be interpreted as a reference to the metaphor of the gun as a phallic symbol, Mrs. Banana squashes any resistance emanating from her son's already weakened masculinity that has been sacrificed to his mother's control over him. Mrs. Banana's matriarchy is further strengthened through her capital power, since she is the owner of a plantation and possesses financial wealth.

Having a black West Indian woman in charge of a plantation also represents an inversion of U. S. racial and economic hierarchies. In the play, there is an instance where Mrs. Banana exercises power over what could be interpreted as a white character. Mrs. Banana received a letter from Fingercash, and since she does not know how to read, she asks her overseer to read it for her. When he starts reading the letter in the text, the dialogue follows the English used by the white characters, rather than the theatrical language construction used by the black characters. Therefore it is plausible that this character was white in performance. Even though there is a certain consideration to racial hierarchy, since Mrs. Banana refers to the white overseer as "massa" or "master," he is still a white male who works for a black West Indian woman in power. The U.S. power structure that determines the supremacy of the wealthy white master over his dispossessed black slave is thus inversed when a white man is positioned as an underling to a wealthy black woman. In relation to this, Goudie writes: " . . . Mrs. Banana is sensitive to white dominance on the island, and although leery of Fingercash's double-dealings, she seeks to capitalize on her status as a plantation owner and infiltrate white society by marrying her son to Louisa."[21] Mrs. Banana is conscious of the power structure and yet defies it not only by marrying her son into a white family, but also as a landowner with white men at her command. As a representative of an inferior discourse, Mrs. Banana is a carnivalesque agent that constantly threatens to transgress the division between identities marked by race, gender, and capital.

In Robinson's play, black West Indian femininity and masculinity are constructed as deformations of the corresponding North American ideals. McConachie explains how the 18th century conception of gentility, a cultural system that worked in combination with patriarchy, defined the European and American concept of "taste." He states:

> The primary stage for genteel performance was the town mansion or plantation house, where the rituals of dining, conversing, and dancing separated the truly refined from the pretenders. The successful performance

required a clean, white body, emphasized through smooth clothes, an erect posture, and behavior that mixed decorous formality with casual ease. If the central image of patriarchy was a powerful male on horseback, porcelain figures of a man and woman dancing the minuet might stand as the essence of gentility.[22]

The patriarchal and the genteel models are expressed visually through the white body, the locus from which the high discourse is formed. In *The Yorker's Stratagem; or, Banana's Wedding*, Amant and Sophia verbalize their love in ways that correspond to classical tradition and to the norms of North American gentility as seen in the following dialogue:

> Amant: My Sophia (kneeling and kissing her hand) how blest am I to press this hand unseen by other eyes than those of friendship. Can you forgive, my love, this premature discovery, that has so ruffled this dear form?
> Miss Bellange: And can you, Amant, ask me that question? (Looking tenderly.)
> Amant: No, my angel, I read my welcome in those beauteous eyes, true to the dictates of a heart where love and candour only dwell.
> Miss Bellange: Oh, my Amant! What have I not suffered since the sad event that drew me from you!
> Amant: My soul felt all your anguish; by the strong power of sympathetic love I shared in all your sorrows, and now am come to sooth the sad remembrance, to be your friend, your father, and your -----------[23]

The exchange between Amant and Sophia implies a love savored from a distance because of its lack of carnality. It is a love perceived through both lovers' eyes, since Amant refers to the eyes that see the hand and to Sophia's visual perception at his arrival. Given that this love is not expressed through any concrete onstage action, the encounter points towards a more spiritual kind of love dominated by the heart and the soul. Its purity stands as a symbol of white cleanliness that befits the norms of gentility unlike Banana and Priscilla's love. In Amant and Sophia's love there is no possibility of any impure physical contact that would result in an exchange of fluids.

While Amant and Sophia's love is sensed through the eyes, and felt in the heart and the soul, Banana and Priscilla's love has already created a baby. Consequently, the black West Indian couple has broken the norms of white gentility dictated by the high discourse. Banana and Priscilla stand for the locus from which the lower discourse originates and where difference is set through the classification of the grotesque. Stallybrass and

White discuss the difference between the grotesque and the classical ideal in the following excerpt:

> The classical statue has no openings or orifices whereas grotesque costume and masks emphasize the gaping mouth, the protuberant belly and buttocks, the feet and the genitals. In this way the grotesque body stands in opposition to the bourgeois individualist conception of the body, which finds its image and legitimation in the classical. . . . The 'grotesque' here designates the marginal, the low and the outside from the perspective of a classical body situated as high, inside and central by virtue of its very exclusions.[24]

Opposite to the heart and the soul, Banana and Priscilla's love is associated with the genitals, the lower strata of the body. Their "grotesque" expression of love is more consonant with a lower discourse based on race since it is juxtaposed to the North American conception of white gentility. Even when Mrs. Banana is trying to teach her son how to act "white" in front of Louisa, the symbols of "white" love are taken over by a love that originates in the orifice. This is evident in the following dialogue:

> Mrs. Banana: Dere, dere for you! Go in your chamber, make yourself Mackey beau, for go marry wid de lady.
> Banana: Lard, mumma, I no hab de heart. . . . When de lady put he yi upon me, I will shame so.
> Mrs. Banana: . . . come let a me see how you will berave yourself when you come before company. . . . You must gib he sweet mout, tell him you love he better dan all the world.[25]

In contrast to Amant and Sophia's relationship, for Banana the heart does not represent the organ from which love for Louisa originates, since he admits that his heart is not in it. In this case, Mrs. Banana identifies the "sweet mout" as the origin of love. This not only points to the fact that Banana's words of love for Louisa would be empty since he only feels for Priscilla, but it also displays his inability to feel pure love because it would only emanate from the mouth. This idea can also be interpreted as a sexual allusion since the production of love from a point located on the physical body changes the classification from a high and pure love, emanating from the heart, to a low and grotesque form of love. In this case, love is expressed through the mouth that is described as sweet, an adjective commonly used in relation to the sexual experience. Therefore, in the character of Banana two contradictory perceptions converge. On one hand, Banana is a symbol of weakened masculinity due to the emasculation to which he has being subjected by his mother. On the other hand, Banana is also portrayed as a highly sexual being, not only through his relationship with Priscilla, but also through the advice Mrs. Banana gives him. Both juxtaposed sexual identities respond to "othering" practices that are an essential component in identity formation. In the theatre, the practice of blackface is another instance of classifying the "other" and where also two very distinct identities converge in one body.

A significant component of 19th century North American popular culture was blackface as specifically used in minstrel shows. However blackface was already in practice in North America during the 18th century, and tensions with African stage representations occurred from the beginning. Goudie explains that in Charleston blackface was prohibited and so black characters were done in whiteface. White men in Charleston thought that theatrical representation would only make the enslaved black community feel that they were important. However Goudie asserts that "whites were not banishing blacks from the stage in Charleston. They were newly banishing representations of themselves representing the black other."[26] Evidently there are certain racial tensions uncovered by blackface. These tensions have to do with the fact that a peripheral discourse marked by race threatens the purity of the high official discourse associated with whiteness. It is undeniable that blackface is a racist practice that works through the appropriation and deformation of racial identity to legitimize slavery and white supremacy. Yet there is also another side to blackface which I would like to consider and it is the way that two different racial markers are mixed together in one location. In his book, *Love and Theft: Blackface Minstrelsy and the American Working Class*, Eric Lott explains the "racial desire" involved in blackface that challenges the traditional theory of "racial aversion" championed by critics. He writes:

> It was cross-racial desire that coupled a nearly insupportable fascination and a self-protective derision with respect to black people and their cultural practices, and that made blackface minstrelsy less a sign of absolute white power and control than of panic, anxiety, terror, and pleasure. As it turned out, the minstrel show worked for over a hundred years to facilitate safely an exchange of energies between two otherwise rigidly bound and policed cultures, a shape-shifting middle term in racial conflict which began to disappear (in the 1920s) once its historical function had been performed.[27]

Blackface then reveals the ambiguous relation of white attraction and repugnance towards blackness and how both racial identities intermingle in the liminal performing body.

The mixing of discourses in one location is intrinsic to carnival and to a practice that Stallybrass and White refer to as hybridization. They define the term in the following way:

> Hybridization, a second and more complex form of the grotesque than the simply excluded 'outside' and 'low' to a given grid, produces new combinations and strange instabilities in a given semiotic system. It therefore generates the possibility of shifting the very terms of the system itself by erasing and interrogating the relationship which constitute it.[28]

Hence the performing body becomes the location where the low discourse marked by race threatens to overpower and/or contaminate the high. In *The Yorker's Stratagem; or, Banana's Wedding*, blackface is obviously used to portray the black characters. However, I would like to focus on an instance in the play where blackface is enacted by Ledger, the white North American interested in marrying Louisa.

Forced by his mother to confront Louisa, Banana starts wooing her by using words that resemble a classical expression of love. Nevertheless, these declarations become a deformation of a high discourse through Banana's use of language:

> Banana: (Timidly approaching Louisa) Suppose you no bex, I will tell you one tory; I lobe a you, I lobe a you, like peppa pot my heart da burn, a burn a like a fire coal, put you yi sweet upon me, sorry fo'me, sorry fo'me, sorry fo'me do, or I da go dead like a one pig.[29]

Banana uses the heart as an identifiable source of a classical conception of love. However, not only does his characteristically black theatrical language already deforms the high expression of love, but also the grotesque element of the pig, representing the low discourse, finds its way into his romantic words. It is interesting how the mixing of these two very distinct discourses would probably have been a successful comic scene if performed appropriately. Yet the reaction it provokes on the character of Ledger, who has been hiding and overhearing Banana's conversation with Louisa, is one of violent outrage. Ledger jumps out from his hiding place with a gun in his hand and threatens Banana. This reaction is not only provoked by the fact that Ledger and Louisa are in love, but also by the appropriation of white identity by a black man, a violation not taken lightly by pure-blooded white North Americans. Ledger then forces Banana into a room and he proceeds to appropriate his racial identity. Impersonating Banana is the only way Ledger will be able to marry Louisa. In order to assume the black West Indian persona, Ledger must not only appropriate Banana's clothes, but also his color. At that moment,

Ledger seizes being white and becomes a black man in order for the ruse to work. Consequently, the person who marries Louisa is no longer a white North American but a black West Indian. Clearly both racial identities are not only mixed in the character of Ledger, but also transcend the performing body resulting in an interracial marriage. Interestingly, the ceremony is conducted offstage because it would have really tested the North American audience's moral standards if a black man and a white woman were married in a holy ceremony. This union defiantly blurs racial divisions just as blackface does. In Banana and Ledger's racial appropriations there are instabilities being created with the awkward union of two very distinct discourses. In Amant's case, the two personas that coexist in one body, the Yankee and the capitalist, are identified with a purely white North American identity. Yet the mixing of racial identities threatens with a forbidden carnivalesque hibridity that poses a bigger danger, the product of an interracial union.

Identity formation is then a significant aspect of *The Yorker's Stratagem; or, Banana's Wedding*. Richards argues that these conflicts related to identity and nationality were not always as clearly debated in real life as they were in the theatre. He points out:

> Although the American stage was occasionally a testing-ground for questions of nationality, more often the issues it evoked or represented were ones that might have seemed more immediate than the often vague and not entirely coherent notions of citizenship and allegiance then circulating.[30]

The fact that the elements that make up a national identity are not as explicit on the social stage as they are on the theatrical one does not mean that they do not participate as active elements in the formation of the dramatic presentation. Though Jeffrey is correct to an extent in stating that the dramatic text "is influenced primarily by other plays more than by current events,"[31] it is important to see how the theatre responds intentionally or not to the different discourses present at a specific historical context. At the time of the production, the slave revolution in Saint-Domingue must have created various racial tensions in the United States. This overturning of the hierarchies of power in the Caribbean represented a threat to racial supremacy, a distinct element in North American identity. J. Robinson is aware of this and thus portrays the West Indian island in the play as a deformation of the North American system. Nevertheless, Robinson delivers "to the worthy Sons of Columbia" by reaffirming the supremacy of the North American masculinity as the bringer of virtue and harmony over the corrupting West Indian heritage. In this sense, issues that defined the United States in that historical context find their way into Robinson's play and his designation of the "other."

Bibliography

Bakhtin, Mikhail. *Rabelais and His World*. Translated by Hélène Iswolsky. Bloomington: Indiana University Press, 1984.

Dorson, Richard M. "The Yankee on the Stage: A Folk Hero of American Drama." *The New England Quarterly* 13 (1940): 467-497.

Dunlap, William. History of the American Theatre. 1797. New York: Burt Franklin, 1963.

Goudie, Sean X. "The West Indies, Commerce, and a Play for U.S. Empire: Recovering J. Robinson's *The Yorker's Stratagem* (1792)." *Early American Literature* 40 (2005): 1-35.

Henderson, Mary K. *The City and the Theatre: New York Playhouses from Bowling Green to Times Square*. New Jersey: James T. White and Company, 1973.

Lott, Eric. *Love and Theft: Blackface Minstrelsy and the American Working Class*. New York: Oxford University Press, 1993.

Lown, Charles R. "The Businessman in Early American Drama." *Educational Theatre Journal* 15 (1963): 47-54.

McConachie, Bruce. "American Theatre in Context, from the Beginnings to 1870." *The Cambridge History of American Theatre*. Vol. 1, *Beginnings to 1870*. Edited by Don B. Wilmeth and Christopher Bigsby. Cambridge: Cambridge University Press, 1998: 111-181.

Odell, George C. *Annals of the New York Stage*. Vol 1. New York: AMS Press, 1970.

Richards, Jeffrey H. *Drama, Theatre, and Identity in the American New Republic*. New York: Cambridge University Press, 2005.

Roach, Joseph. *Cities of the Dead: Circum-Atlantic Performance*. New York: Columbia University Press, 1996.

Robinson, J. *The Yorker's Stratagem: or, Banana's Wedding*. New York: T & J Swords, 1792.

Seilhamer, George O. *History of the American Theatre*. Vol. 1. New York: Benjamin Blom, 1968.

Stallybrass, Peter and Allon White. *The Politics and Poetics of Transgression*. Ithaca: Cornell University Press, 1986.

Walser, Richard. "Negro Dialect in Eighteenth-Century American Drama." *American Speech* 30 (1955): 269-279.

Williams, Eric. *From Columbus to Castro: The History of the Caribbean 1492-1969*. London: André Deutsch, 1970.

Notes

[1] George O. Seilhamer, *History of the American Theatre*, 345.
[2] George C. Odell, *Annals of the New York Stage*, 307.
[3] Sean X. Goudie, "The West Indies, Commerce, and a Play for U.S. Empire," 1.
[4] William Dunlap, *History of the American Theatre*, 195.
[5] Seilhamer, *History of the American Theatre*, 322.
[6] Ibid., 364.
[7] Bruce McConachie, "American Theatre in Context, from the Beginnings to 1870,"128.
[8] J. Robinson, *The Yorker's Stratagem; or, Banana's Wedding*, 3.
[9] Goudie, "The West Indies, Commerce, and a Play for U.S. Empire: Recovering J. Robinson's The Yorker's Stratagem," 3-4.
[10] McConachie, "American Theatre in Context, from the Beginnings to 1870," 129-130
[11] Richard M. Dorson, "The Yankee on the Stage: A Folk Hero of American Drama," 467.
[12] Ibid, 469.
[13] An example of this type of performance is the Boston Tea Party in 1773, where a group of North American patriots dressed as Indians, boarded ships and destroyed the cargo. The act has a theatrical dimension in its role-playing element since the invaders were dressed as Indians. It is also a carnivalesque defiance to the power structure since it was the North American people's challenge to British rule.
[14] Jeffrey H. Richards, *Drama, Theatre, and Identity in the American New Republic*, 6.
[15] Peter Stallybrass and Allon White, *The Politics and Poetics of Transgression*, 26.
[16] Ibid, 37.
[17] Robinson, *The Yorker's Stratagem: or, Banana's Wedding*, 15.
[18] McConachie, McConachie, "American Theatre in Context, from the Beginnings to 1870," 123.
[19] Stallybrass and White, *The Politics and Poetics of Transgression*, 56-7.
[20] Robinson, McConachie, "American Theatre in Context, from the Beginnings to 1870," 22.
[21] Goudie, "The West Indies, Commerce, and a Play for U.S. Empire: Recovering J. Robinson's The Yorker's Stratagem," 8.
[22] McConachie, "American Theatre in Context, from the Beginnings to 1870," 124.
[23] Robinson, *The Yorker's Stratagem; or, Banana's Wedding*, 13.
[24] Stallybrass and White, *The Politics and Poetics of Transgression*, 22-3.
[25] Robinson, *The Yorker's Stratagem; or, Banana's Wedding*, 19.
[26] Goudie, "The West Indies, Commerce, and a Play for U.S. Empire: Recovering J. Robinson's The Yorker's Stratagem (1792),"12.

[27] Eric Lott, *Love and Theft: Blackface Minstrelsy and the American Working Class*, 6.
[28] Stallybrass and White, *The Politics and Poetics of Transgression*, 58.
[29] Robinson, The Yorker's Stratagem: or, Banana's Wedding, 25.
[30] Richards, *Drama, Theatre, and Identity in the American New Republic*, 5.
[31] Ibid, 5.

BOMBA TRIGUEÑA: DILUTED CULTURE AND (LOSS OF) FEMALE AGENCY IN AFROPUERTO RICAN MUSIC AND DANCE PERFORMANCE

MELANIE A. MALDONADO

Introduction

With a chuckle, a Euro-American woman comments to a Puerto Rican woman dressed in a traditional *bomba*[1] costume for performance, "You look like Aunt Jemima."[2] This imposition of a U.S. trope on a Puerto Rican iconic image both intersects and conflicts this representation of the Island's history with a U.S. based collective memory imbedded in racism. The mid-twentieth century use of the mammy-style *bomba* costume by commercial practitioners performing in Puerto Rico[3] (PR) established a standard by which all presentational groups[4] continue to measure themselves aesthetically. As a signifier for Island based Black culture in the Puerto Rican imaginary, the use of the costume has become a stand-in for representations of Black culture. This paper proposes that the politically ambiguous history between the U.S. and PR compelled the creation of the *bomba* costume for women and has contributed to a Western history of black cultural suppression. In doing so, it connects the introduction of the costume to other acts in Puerto Rico demonstrating a general sentiment of affiliation with the United States throughout the colonial history between the two nations. I will also attempt to analyze the use of the costume as an act of colonial mimicry, study it as a representation of cultural retention, and attempt to theorize it as a tactic of resistance. Through this process, the commercialization and ensuing folklorization of the genre are demonstrated to be directly connected to the professional use of this costume. Finally, this work reveals a "whitening" of the genre both through the established standard of an all-white costume and in the representation of it by a majority of non-Black, costumed performers. Some of the questions driving this analysis include: What were the historical conditions in PR leading to the creation of the *bomba* costume for women? How does the costume silence both female and black bodies? How did Banco Popular's 2001 *Raices* video contributes to costume use in the Diaspora?[5] What are the implications of costume use in PR and in the United States? How does the costume allow eager cultural enthusiasts to pass as practitioners? What is at stake when uninformed and white bodies parade a costume that marks them as Black and becomes a carnivalesque signifier of a racialized history of oppression? How does white privilege complicate the use of the costume? and, How is the costume linked to ideas of authenticity, purity and tradition?

Bomba Trigueña

Puerto Rico was a small Caribbean island populated by Tainos[6] when Columbus arrived on his second voyage to the "New World" on November 19, 1493.[7] For just over 400 years from that time, the Island would remain a Spanish colony until the end of the Spanish-American War when it was ceded to the United States in 1898. Under Spanish control, Tainos, as a homogenous group, were decimated through slavery, disease and intermarriage. Enslaved Africans were brought to Puerto Rico as early as 1510[8] to replace the declining Taino labor force and remained in this status until abolition occurred on March 22, 1873.[9] As is recorded in other parts of the Hispanophone world, the Spanish implemented a color code system in Puerto Rico that categorized colonial subjects according to their ethnic makeup. This resulted in a litany of combinations according to parentage and produced a lengthy list of coded labels that over time came to be associated mostly with color.[10] Through this categorization, colonial laws, and other social values, Spanish racist ideologies pervaded the Island's culture and continue to influence residents' prejudicial treatment of and reference to one another. Below is a contemporary list of identifications still in use:

Item	Approximate Meaning
1. Negro	Black; may be derogatory
2. Trigueño	Literally, wheat colored; intermediate category
3. Jabao	Light-skinned with kinky hair
4. Blanco	White

5. Indio	Literally, Indian; brown-skinned with straight hair
6. Prieto	Black; features equivalent to *negro*
7. Jincho	Pale-skinned; may be derogatory
8. Moreno	Dark-skinned; may refer to African-Americans
9. Colorao	Redheaded; reddish skin with freckles
10. Negrito	Literally, little black; used as a term of endearment
11. De color	Of color; used as a euphemism for *negro*
12. Cano	Blonde, light-skinned
13. Canela	Literally, cinnamon; brown-skinned
14. Cáfe con Leche	Literally, coffee with milk; light brown-skinned
15. Albino	Albino
16. Rubio	Blonde
17. Papujo	Pale-skinned; may be derogatory
18. Mulato	Mix of *blanco* and *negro*
19. Mestizo	Mix of *blanco* and *negro*
20. Carabalí	Very dark-skinned; derogatory

Table 1: Gravlee, Clarence C. "Ethnic Classification in Southeastern Puerto Rico," 956.

Linguist Frances Aparicio borrows from these terms to theorize music forms closely associated with national identity amongst Puerto Ricans. In an attempt to uncover the racialization of these genres, Aparicio provides a gendered construction and positions *danza*[11] as the aristocratic white lady.[12] Similarly, she proposes the mixed classification of *mulata* for *plena*.[13] Unfortunately, a discussion of *bomba* and a position of it along this continuum as *la negra* or "the black woman" are missing. This omission in her work contributes to the elision of blackness in Puerto Rican history and cultural analysis. By inserting *bomba* into a triad of musical investigation, it is clear to see a place for it in discussions of *plena* in connection to other genres. As one of *plena's* ancestral forms, *bomba* has a direct relationship to and is often paired to *plena* as a complimentary genre.[14] Therefore, *bomba*'s position at an end of a Black/White spectrum is a necessary inclusion in a hued analysis of Puerto Rican music. For the purposes of this study, *bomba* is postulated as graduating away from the trope of "*bomba* as black" and moving closer toward a middle ground of classification, in this analysis *trigueña*. While *mulata* might reasonably be the category that describes a half way point between *blanco y negro* (or "black and white,") it has historically been used as a Caribbean (and in many instances U.S.) trope for wanton sexuality.[15] Also, because the color identifier *mulata* is no longer a word possessing the same manner of vernacular circulation as in earlier times, it is not implausible to consider *trigueña* a more appropriate term for the "lightened" *bomba* that is practiced today by costume bearing and other performers.[16] As a form hybridized through a colonial and slave history, professionalization, and diasporic practice, *bomba* can no longer be considered a music and dance tradition exclusive to Black people on the Island.

A Creole Genre

Ethnomusicologist Hector Vega Drouet reports 50,000 – 70,000 Africans were estimated to have been brought to Puerto Rico during the Island's experience of slavery.[17] The majority of this labor force was concentrated in the sugar producing plantations of the coasts where it is surmised two-thirds to three-quarters of all slaves worked.[18] It is in these Puerto Rican plantations where *bomba* – a hybridized expressive art, a fusion of the various African ethnic amalgams present and colonial experiences of the Caribbean – was created.[19]

Puerto Rico's relatively numerically small slave population (by Caribbean standards)[20] might be a contributor to the factors that kept *bomba* from becoming a more mainstream or Island-wide popular music form. Musicologist Luis Manuel Álvarez and sociologist Angel Quintero Rivera posit that the number of free people of color was always greater than the number of slaves on the Island; they note the proportion was ten free to every one enslaved.[21] Given this division of social and class status, *bomba*'s association to slave cultural expression may have prompted free people of color[22] to distance themselves from the practice of the genre in order to divorce their identities from a disempowered, chattel-like existence, confirm upwardly mobile status, and culturally whiten themselves.[23] These social forces may have been compounded by the Island's topographically dense interior that made traversing it (before the advent of motorized vehicles, paved roads and highways) and being connected to other communities difficult, especially for residents with few means.

As a creole genre that was popular primarily amongst African diasporic people in Puerto Rico, *bomba* did not penetrate mainstream practices until the mid-twentieth century. Its relative isolation to the Black population and developing regional styles (along the north coast in the San Juan metropolitan area, along the south coast near the port city of Ponce, and along the west coast – centered in Mayaguez) further contributed to its internal complexities and external difference as an Othered form of Island culture. Although some have argued for its African origins (see Vega Drouet 1979,) *bomba* is widely considered[24] a genre that is inherently African but also the product of influences found throughout Puerto Rico.

Regional Styles

Contemporary practitioners[25] understand *bomba* to be a confluence of West African cultural expressions including the use of floor drums and call-and-response singing; however, Taino, Spanish, Haitian[26] and other international influences may be found within the various regional practices. At the present time, Puerto Rico boasts at least four different regional styles: Southern, West Coast, Northern[27] (also known as *Cangrejera*[28] or "from *Cangrejos*,") and *Loiza*.[29] Each of these may be identified by their singing styles (or *seises*,)[30] the manner in which the drum is slapped, the rhythms[31] that are generated, and the dance interpretations made by individual participants.

Over the last half century, *Bomba* in the area that was once *Cangrejos* has largely been influenced by the work of the commercial family *Los Cepeda*. These longstanding bearers of *bomba* tradition are often referred to as the "patriarchal family" within this music and dance genre. Their performance of *bomba* has become the standard by which all groups with the intention of promoting a folkloric image of the genre have measured themselves. The contributions made by *Los Cepeda* to the history of *bomba* on the Island and abroad is monumental: the composition of reportedly more than 400 songs;[32] the prolific use of a folkloric, Victorian era costume for women (reminiscent of U.S. mammy images;) flamboyant skirt movement that has come to incorporate flamenco postures; and a rhetoric that promotes "*Elegancia*" – a Westernized standard of dance that demands an erect posture, often limiting movements for women to those strictly above the waist.[33] In *bomba cangrejera*, men have traditionally sung lead and chorus, danced, and played the necessary instruments while women have primarily danced and supported the singing through the chorus. In late 2006, these long held gender roles were ruptured by the emergence and ongoing presence of Puerto Rico's first all-female *bomba* group, the *Carolina*-based Nandí. *Cangrejos* is most well known for its *sicá* and *yubá* rhythms; *Santurce* – a section in *Cangrejos* most associated with the *bomba* practice of *Los Cepedas*, specifically for its *gracimá*.[34]

The tradition of *bomba* in *Loíza* is significantly different than it is elsewhere on the Island. The most marked difference is the practice of it by the general population of this community on the north coast of the Island. Unlike the other regions in Puerto Rico, *bomba* in *Loíza* is less often a staged performance and more so one in which residents of both genders and multiple generations participate. As it relates to the dance interpretation in this former maroon community, practitioners from other areas comment[35] that *Loíza* style dance is either a complete fabrication and therefore a *disparate* (or "a ridiculous spectacle") or the most unWesternized and therefore untainted *bomba* in Puerto Rico. Here *bomba* dance is divergent from other regional variations. In *Loíza*, women rarely wear a skirt, often dance barefoot, and employ rigorous shoulder and hip undulations. In all practices of *bomba* throughout the Island, onlookers and other participants laud complicated arrangement of *piquetes*[36] that are made with the skirt, hands, feet, or shoulders. In *Loíza*, dancers enjoy the freedom (and are encouraged) to utilize movements (often read as sensuous) that counter notions of *Elegancia* (or Elegance) practiced elsewhere; in this respect, they interpret *bomba* rhythms in the most unregulated fashion throughout the Island. While men and women enjoy this equal opportunity to dance, present-day women do not sing lead or play instruments. The rhythms most associated with *Loíza* style bomba, *corve* and *rule* (also called *seis corrido* when played quickly,) are almost exclusively played in this town.

In 2001, Banco Popular produced a film celebrating AfroPuerto Rican music entitled *Raíces* (roots.)[37] In this film, an elder practitioner from *Mayaguez* – a western coastal town – reports that women rarely danced (and therefore did not participate much physically given that this is the most common role available for women in all *bomba* practices) in their regional experience. According to his explanation, *bomba* was – in times past – a dance primarily for men. However, this statement is challenged by the many women of the Nadal family of practitioners and their familial and communal predecessors.[38] The most distinguishable quality of the

West Coast tradition is its pervasive AfroFrench influences[39] most easily identifiable in the lyrics of many songs from this part of the Island. Although, there is recognizable Haitian impact throughout the AfroPuerto Rican musical tradition from *Mayaguez*, it is the fastest rhythm of *bomba*, *holandé*,[40] that most identifies this region. Other rhythms such as *cüembe* and *cunyá* are also amongst the most popular here. As the widely identified birthplace of *bomba*, *Mayaguez* plays a significant role in understanding the intricacies of *bomba* practices throughout the Island.

Until the recent work of the Nandí women, women enjoyed the most visibility and activity in the exercise of southern *bomba*. Representations of this regional style position women as lead singers and chorus. Particular to the custom of this area, women almost always begin their dance as part of a couple with a male partner.[41] Although this feature was prominent throughout the Island, it has been retained more strongly in the South and in the West than in other regional representations. The popular rhythms and *seises* of this region (*güembe*,[42] *belén, and leró*) are sometimes played and sung in slower tempos than elsewhere on the Island. The dance of both men and women compensates with deliberate steps, turns and weight shifting that accentuates the music. Men and women approach the lead drummer as a couple and dance together until the man defers to the woman by allowing her to dance before he takes a turn before the drum.[43] Their movements are languid and facilitate a coquettishness that the faster rhythms do not inspire. In female dance, there is markedly less skirt movement than in the northern region of the Island; women do not bring their skirts as high as the *Cangrejo* practice and instead use a greater variety of complex foot accents to draw *repiques* (slaps) from the drummer. Unlike the three other practices identified, women are the primary lead singers and chorus in southern *bomba*. Another important identifier of southern *bomba* is the manner in which (male) drummers position themselves to play the *barril*.[44] According to Álvarez and Quintero Rivera, drums from the North were made of salt pork barrels whereas those from the South were made from rum barrels.[45] Because rum barrels were longer than their northern counterparts, they were too tall to be played while seated on a bench and instead were turned on their side and sat upon.[46] This unique drum position, also works to functionally and aesthetically identify *bomba* from the South.

Bomba Music and Dance

The *barriles de bomba* (*bomba* drums or simply *bombas*)[47] are used to generate the rhythms particular to this genre and the improvisational sounds that complement the steady rhythm. *Bomba* music is created by a host of efforts. Most important to this sound creation is the constant repetition of a regional rhythm on a *buleador* (or second drum;) in concert with this drumming is the improvisation on the *subidor* or *primo* (which is the lead drum;) a pair of sticks called *los cua* are played on the side of the *buleador* (most traditional practice,) on a piece of bamboo (most contemporary practice,) or on another small barrel to keep the time and reinforce the particular rhythm of the music; and a *maraca*[48] (or shaker instrument) is also used to keep time and add dimension to the overall sound. A lead singer will dictate to the community what rhythm will be played by the *seis* or song structure s/he selects. The basic singing practice involves the lead singer "calling" by singing the chorus once, singing one verse of the song to establish the story, and then pause to allow the chorus (or *coro*) to "respond" with the chorus established at the beginning of the song (at which time the instrumentalists will enter in with the already indicated rhythm.) A dancer or a dance couple will emerge, mark the space with a *paseo* (a promenade that defines the dance space,) salute the *primo* and lead drummer, and then begin the dance. The dancer utilizes specific, improvisational movements to interpret the rhythm being played according to the regional tradition, the song or the *seis* (or metric variation) established. The lead drummer then attempts to interpret the movement of the dancer thereby giving sound to the gestures. This improvisational sound serves as a harmony in addition to the melody (or layer of sound that complements the steady rhythm) of the *buleador*.[49] Combined, these are the elements that necessitate the experience of *bomba* music.

This intricate working of instruments, voices, bodies and improvisational interpretation coalesce to produce the practice of this genre of AfroPuerto Rican music and dance. When the women's costume came into usage more than a half century ago, practitioners sought to supplement the aural with the aesthetic, and thereby enhance the presentational element of *bomba* for professional and commercial purposes. As a result, Puerto Ricans have closely identified the experience (not necessarily the practice) of *bomba* with the women's costume. This has had numerous negative implications including a distorted perspective of the historical context surrounding the exercise of *bomba*, a silencing of the female body, a pacification of Black expression through the dance, and a substitution for the lived experience with the romantic vision the costume produces. As a herald to Victorian era fashion, the confusing (and historically inaccurate)[50] image of the costume may also serve as a signifier for the ambiguous relationship between the United States and Puerto Rico, which officially began at the end of this very fashion epoch.

However, in order to best understand this formal association and its influences on *bomba* (and more specifically the women's costume,) it is important to trace some of the events during the final decades of Spanish occupation (and just before "American" intervention) that lead to Puerto Rico's dubious affiliation with the United States.

Puerto Rico and the United States

Much of Puerto Rico's experience with Spain was characterized by slavery and other forms of colonial oppression. Although the Atlantic slave trade to the Island was effectively shut down by the British in the 1840s,[51] it was not until March 22, 1873 that slavery was finally abolished. Emancipation in Puerto Rico granted the remaining slave population freedom from individual ownership. However, the Island itself remained the property of the Spanish crown – a colonizer of Puerto Rico's land and bodies for four centuries leading up to this historic date three quarters into the nineteenth century. Oral histories provide documentation for the significant number of Puerto Rican arrivals to the U.S. during the mid-1800s.[52] This diasporic community was steadily growing in size and activity by the late nineteenth century. The first transmigrant Puerto Ricans arrived in the United States in self-imposed exile and in display of other demonstrations of dissatisfaction with Spain. These early diasporic subjects were activists and revolutionaries, aggressively involved in the campaign for Cuban and Puerto Rican independence. It was these *Boricuas*[53] who created the Puerto Rican flag (in New York City in 1895) which remains in use to this day.[54] This action was one of the first[55] to assert an individual Puerto Rican identity separate from that of Spain, demonstrating a growing international political hostility against the European country for its colonial holdings. Three years later, the United States intervened on behalf of Cuba and declared war against Spain. After a few months, Spain agreed to negotiations and ceded Puerto Rico and Guam to the United States. The end of this war terminated the colonial relationship between the Island and Spain, which existed for almost half a millennia, and ushered in an undefined period of ambiguous relationship with the United States which continues through the present date.

In 1899, Hurricane *San Ciriaco* devastated the Island.[56] A year later, opportunistic businessmen from the U.S. traveled to Puerto Rico and offered jobs, housing and other amenities for men and women willing to work the sugarcane fields of Hawai'i. After enduring a lengthy trip from the Island via steamer to New Orleans, *Boricua* laborers were given citizenship upon entry to the Gulf Coast city and then shipped across the southern United States to San Francisco and Los Angeles, where they boarded ships taking them to various sites in the Hawaiian Islands. Upon arrival, many workers found there were either no jobs available, less pay than promised or were forced to split from their families and loved ones. Almost six thousand miles from home, many were stranded and forced to remake their lives in the Hawaiian islands. An estimated 5,000 Puerto Ricans were taken to Hawai'i over 1900-1901.[57] While these unwitting and colonized bodies were given citizenship in order to make them legally eligible to work in Hawai'i, those still living in Puerto Rico would wait at least sixteen more years when in 1917, the Jones Act made all Islanders U.S. citizens so that they could enlist to fight in the First World War on behalf of the United States.

In the 1940s and 1950s the United States increased its presence in and affiliation with the Island. In 1941, Vice Admiral Ben Morell began work to make *Vieques* (one of the islands in the Puerto Rican archipelago) the largest U.S. naval base in the Caribbean.[58] For the next sixty plus years, the small populated island off Puerto Rico's east coast would be used for military exercises including aerial bombs and other weapons, depositing harmful radiation in the soil and water supply. In the next decade, Luis Muñoz Marín became the first democratically elected governor of Puerto Rico. Early during his time in office, he obtained the official status of "commonwealth" for the Island, a form of colonial relationship that remains until this day. Muñoz Marín also changed the blue color in the flag from royal blue to navy blue in an effort to demonstrate Puerto Rico's allegiance to the United States.[59] The U.S. presence in Puerto Rico has been marked by economic oppression and a lack of concern for islanders' health (high levels of radiation in *Vieques*) and community life (the abandoned *Boricuas* in Hawai'i.) In spite of this, Islanders have migrated to the U.S. in large numbers since the 1930s in search of better economic and social opportunities for their families. As a result, according to the 2000 census reports, there are approximately as many *Boricuas* in Puerto Rico as there are on the continental United States. The circular trafficking of money, ideas, bodies, and traditions have created fertile opportunities in the Diaspora for displays of Puerto Rican culture. Hence, it is in the continental United States where the *bomba* costume has proliferated in use amongst non-practitioners and practitioners alike.

The *Bomba* Costume for Women

Few sixteenth and seventeenth century chronicler's reports or church records from Puerto Rico survived the various battles (of the eighteenth century and before) waged to secure the militaristically desirable island from the Spanish.[60] For this reason, investigations related to *bomba* and other experiences of slave and free blacks are limited by scant information. The documentation available for a *bomba* study is limited to descriptions from travelers and other references in official documents. As in most slave societies, enslaved and free Blacks wore clothing that was styled after the plantation owners and aristocratic classes. As a result, *bomba* dance is reported[61] to have served as a tool for mimicry. The *paseo* (or promenade) described earlier was similar to the African American cakewalk in that it served as an opportunity to imitate the parading of the elite classes. *Figura* was also used to mime exaggerated poses made by men during social and ballroom (or *salon*) dancing. The women's skirt lifting used to create elaborate *piquetes* (or *bomba* dance gestures) is purported to have been an act of passive aggression that disrupted social standards of modesty. By lifting the top skirt, a woman exposed her undergarments (bloomers or petticoats) to the *primo* drummer, other musicians, and members of the *soberao*[62] (or circle of onlookers and participants) as she mocked aristocratic values of modesty; skirt lifting by *bomberas* recalls "an old accepted means for African women to protest against men's actions" reported by historian Claire Robertson.[63] This ancestrally resistant behavior has become a standard for female *bomba* dance and continues to be used as a favorite means to *pedir golpes* (or request slaps) from the *primo* drummer. This mimicry turned mockery turned *Elegancia* calls us back to a discussion of the contemporary costume.

The costume, used prominently by many commercial practitioners and other performers for approximately fifty years, beckons back to the time of post emancipation (in Puerto Rico and the United States) and the post Reconstruction era at the end of the nineteenth century. It is modeled after a mid-late Victorian era dress and has long sleeves that arrive at the wrist, a high collar that covers most of the neck, and a full skirt that arrives near the ankle. This costume is "traditionally"[64] white with color accents whose elements include jewelry, a head scarf, an apron, and ribbons or ruffles sewn onto the blouse and the petticoat. Rafael Cepeda, widely referred to as the patriarch of *bomba*, details costume specifics in the following excerpt:

> *El traje del bailador de Bomba, puede ser de algodon o de lino ingles, siempre y cuando se habla. El traje de la dama, bailadora de Bomba, debe ser blanco o mezcla con volantes adequado en tela de irlanda. El enagua se le cosen lazitos de cinta y encaje, y nunca se debe tocar a bailar. Ay que bailar con firmeza, nunca perder la figura. El orgullo del bailador de*

Bomba es pintar la figura mas elegante, y el tocador del barril, ritmo constante con certeza.

The costume for male *bomba* dancers, may be cotton or English linen, always and whenever they dance. The costume for female *bomba* dancers should be white or a mixed pattern with an adequate amount of ruffles in Irish cloth. The petticoat has lace and bows made of ribbons sewn onto it; it is never touched during the dance. It is important to dance with firmness, never losing one's figure. The pride of a *bomba* dancer is in painting a very elegant figure and for the drummer, in confidently maintaining a constant rhythm. (Cepeda)

    This costume conjures up a delicate time in U.S. and Puerto Rican history. As already detailed, Puerto Ricans were actively congregating in New York City in support of the Island's independence from Spain. Their relationship with the U.S. was deepening and the awareness of happenings in the United States was permeating the social landscape of the Island through transmigration. This relationship would become more intimate after the Island's cession from Spain to the U.S. in 1898. In the last decade of the nineteenth century, Chicago hosted the World's Columbian Exposition in 1893 in an effort to pay tribute to modernity and the newest technology of the day. Although Black bodies were all but excluded from the fair's main events and attractions, the exposition did serve to popularize an image of Black labor (albeit a racist trope) through the work of Nancy Green hired by a pancake company to play the character of Aunt Jemima.[65] Since that time, this image has haunted Black women in the United States and has contributed to racist and essentialist notions of Black women as domestic workers. Invoking bigoted stereotypes of overweight, middle aged, Black women thought to be passive and appeasing, the Aunt Jemima image is an incarnation of the Mammy.[66] The comment at the beginning of this text by a White southerner to a *Boricua* dressed in the *bomba* costume, reifies the presence of this ideology as an undercurrent of White and Black relations today.

    Other readings of this costume may examine this invented tradition[67] as a reaction to the negative representations of Black culture or as an attempt to capitalize on the commercial image of the U.S. mammy trope. The Aunt Jemima image proliferated for decades and permeated Puerto Rican culture as seen in the brand image of Yaucono, a popular Island based coffee. The 1963 image presented on the company's website boasts a very dark skinned mammy with robust red lips. A 2006 photograph of the brand's iconic character (on display in a public gymnasium in Puerto Rico's capital city) demonstrates a marked lightening of the mammy image. She was no longer *Mama Ines la negra* (or "the Black woman."

This is the name identified by the company for their 1963 incarnation of her.) What is clear from the 2006 representation is that she had been transformed in both name and literal color to *Yauconita la trigueña* ("the brown woman.") T*rigueña* is identified earlier in the this paper as an ambiguous color category most commonly used in Puerto Rico to describe people who may not be identified as white.)[68] The 2006 image is light brown with pink lips, a much more safe and "respectable" or "less offensive" ethnic reference via this company icon; however, the other mammy signifiers remain: the apron, the thick Black woman, the turban/head wrap, and the gesture of this woman in service through her stance of offering a cup of coffee. The first word of the original title of this image, *"Mama Ines,"* is the Spanish translation of "momma," the word with which "mammy" shares etymology, and may explain why the image title changed from *Mama Ines* to *Yauconita*[69] (or "little" *Yaucona/o* or from Yauco where this coffee is grown.) As this image came into Island circulation in the decade following the creation of the costume, one might conclude that the professional *bomba* groups of the mid-twentieth century understood the commercial marketability of the placating image and capitalized on it well before the *Yaucono* coffee company considered appropriating the icon. Perhaps, the mammied *bomba* costume inspired the brand image.

While Puerto Ricans who employ the *bomba* costume may not be aware of the linkages it makes in a U.S. performance context, the performativity of the costume itself engages people in the United States influenced by racist notions of "the mammy." However, should the creators of this costume have carefully considered the iconography they were heralding through the use of this image, it is possible to read the use of the costume as an act of resistance and reappropriation of the mammy image.[70]

La Llamarada,[71] a popular Puerto Rican novel of the 1930s, detailed a *bomba* scene the lead protagonist observed from a distance. The description the narrator provides includes references to *bomba* as savage, ancestral, and primitive. The widespread popularity of the novel paralleled the peak of the Negritude Movement of the same decade and contributed to conflicting representations of blackness. Luis Palés Matos, the most lauded negritude poet of Puerto Rico, was a white man who wrote poetry reinforcing the trope of the hypersexualized *mulata* body. In this context, the costume becomes a savior of the female body[72] in that the fabric leaves little skin uncovered; the stark white cloth serves as an impenetrable shield against the lustful and roving male gaze and discourages the coveting of erogenous zones by androgonizing the body (thereby "effeminizing"[73] the wearer.) The costume becomes a mask that hides the body and serves to erase the presence of the black body in the practice. After decades of this erasure, the black wearer has been joined by brown and white bodies that wear the mask of the costume and signify to the (now historical) blackness of the genre through the costume but no longer physically represent it themselves.

This "browning" or lightening of the genre, I propose, is directly related to the costume use. With increased use of the women's *bomba* costume by mid-twentieth century commercial practitioners, other groups quickly followed suit and appropriated the presentational *bomba* fashion. This standard has been duplicated throughout the Island and the Diaspora and is synonymous with the genre in the collective imaginary. This is clear by the many artistic representations of a costumed female with a male dancer in the absence of *barriles* (*bomba* drums) or other instruments necessary for the practice. The dress of *bomberas* then becomes a prospect for spectacle, and an opportunity for slippage occurs – from respect of the tradition to a chance to "dress up as Black." Below is a comment[74] made by a white performer after having experienced live *bomba* for the first time.

> WAOOOOOOOOOOOO. QUE TREMENDO BOMBAZO, ahora si se lo que es. Que experiencia mas exitante. La pase divino, de ahora en adelante me concentrare a bailar la bomba mas que nada, aunque tenga que pintarme la cara negra y la bemba colora.

> Wow! What a tremendous *bombazo*.[75] Now I know what [*bomba*] is. What an exciting experience. I really enjoyed it. From this time forward I am going to concentrate on dancing *bomba* above anything else, even if I have to paint my face black and my big lips red. (Anonymous)

This comment recalls the mammy images already shown here to parallel the *bomba* costume. This woman, like many other costume bearing performers in the Diaspora, is of a class and social status that supersedes most of the *bomba* practitioners living on the Island. During staged presentations, this and other costumed performers "pass" as practitioners by employing this mask of AfroPuerto Rican culture. Because most Puerto Ricans are uninformed about black history and cultural practices from the Island, the costume itself lends authenticity to the performance. In this way, white bodies can parade the black mask of the costume (ironically often white) and defy racial boundaries of representation. This "white privilege" cannot be inversely practiced by black bodies that are always marked different (or Other) and therefore renders the rampant use by white performers as problematic.

The 2001 *Raices* film produced by *Banco Popular de Puerto Rico* (highlighting the AfroPuerto Rican genres of *plena* and *bomba*) was broadly disseminated and quickly sold out all stock. The widespread viewings of this film in the Diaspora lead Puerto Ricans of all classes to embrace and recognize these African derived elements of *Boricua* culture. As a result, middle class, diasporic dance troupes, committed to promoting folkloric genres of Island dance, adopted *bomba* into their repertoires through the purchase of the video's accompanying CD (or other *bomba* CDs,) development of simple choreographies (which is contrary to the improvisational nature of *bomba* dance,) and the order of costumes from local seamstresses to imitate the ones they saw used in *Raices*. The exclusion of improvisational dance, song, and live drumming in these presentational or homage performances indicates that a new representation of *bomba* has been created that is based on the image of the costume for women. Gone are the interplay and communication between *primo* drummer and dancer and the sung stories of famous dancers, relationships gone awry, and plantation burnings. This essence of *bomba* has been withheld from unknowing masses eager to associate themselves culturally with the beautifully staged *bomba* performances on the beach and on decrepit former plantations[76] prolific in the *Raices* film. After the release of this video in 2001, the costume became a means to become connected to black culture and for many of these groups, has served as a stand-in for the blackness of the genre. In the Diaspora, the centuries old history of poor blacks in Puerto Rico – through use of the costume – has been replaced with the enthusiastic performance of appropriation by primarily white, U.S. based, middle class, Puerto Rican bodies. I claim that this has resulted in a lightening (read "whitening") of that form, which transitions *bomba* from the space of exclusively black expression to one of creolized or pan-Puerto Rican expression. This essentialization of the genre has changed it and created a new experience of the music and dance form in some Puerto Rican communities in the Diaspora.

Conclusion

This analysis has demonstrated the costume to deemphasize blackness. However, the costume has also made accessible (to the average Puerto Rican) an experience, that was until recently, still relegated (thru abhorrence, ignorance, and fear)[77] to the practice of black communities. This has resulted in a shift of representation from *bomba negra* to *bomba trigueña* as it is no longer limited in practice or exhibition to black bodies but may be seen on stages throughout the Island and the Diaspora by people who qualify as performers, perhaps as Puerto Rican, and most unlikely as black.

Female practitioners in the Diaspora and in Puerto Rico have begun to release themselves from use of the costume for varying reasons; some of those reported to this author over the years include: the costume is too archaic; the costume represents colonialism; the costume represents folklore yet the genre has never gone out of practice; the skirt was appropriate when women did not wear pants; and the costume conjures images of the mammy. The last sentiment is one closest to my own experience as a practitioner. I wore the costume for many years but stopped using it when I understood its historical inaccuracy and close relation to the mammy trope. By disavowing the costume (and, in some instances, skirt usage altogether) women are reappropriating their bodies, reclaiming the agency lost or covered by the costume, and ironically, moving toward an aesthetic and dance vocabulary reminiscent of the liberated *bomba* dance of Loiza. While some practitioners invoke the mammy image in their own work, many of the current generation have shunned it and are creating more distinction between their work and that of the costumed performers of the Diaspora.

The racist U.S. trope of the mammy infiltrated *Boricua* culture over the last one hundred years and stimulated a response that may be seen as resistant or compliant. The result is an African diasporic practice that has become whitened in Puerto Rican culture and may now be referred to as *bomba trigueña*.

* The research and analysis represented in this paper is part of the ongoing education, practice, and development of this author. Therefore, the information detailed herein may not succinctly match other researchers or practitioners. This is the sum of my own experience and reflection at the time of this publication and is sure to continue to expand and metamorphose through time.

** I make two grammar related usages that are conscious and political choices. One, I do not hyphenate AfroPuerto Rican; I believe doing so continues to contribute to the elision and marginalization of Black culture and presence in Puerto Rico. Two, I spell Hawai'i the way it is pronounced by the First People of these Pacific islands.

Bibliography

Alvarez, Luis Manuel, and Angel Quintero Rivera. "Bambulaé sea allá: la bomba y la plena." *Raices*. Banco Popular de Puerto Rico, 2001. http://rrpac.upr.clu.edu:909/~lalvarez/Articulos/bambulaeseaalla.htm. (Accessed November 26, 2006.)

Alvarez Nazario, Manuel. *El Elemento Afronegroide en el Español de Puerto Rico: Contribucion al Estudio del Negro en America*. San Juan: Instituto de Cultura Puertorriqueña, 1974.

Aparicio, Frances. "Ethnifying Rhythms, Feminizing Cultures." *Music and the Racial Imagination*. Edited by Ronald Radano and Philip V. Bohlman. Chicago: University of Chicago Press, 2000.

—. "A White Lady Called the Danza" and "A Sensual Mulatta Called the Plena." *Listening to Salsa: Gender, Latin Popular Music, and Puerto Rican Cultures*. Middletown: Wesleyan University Press, 1997.

Arrizón, Alicia. "Race-ing Performativity Through Transculturation, Taste and the Mulata Body." *Theatre Research International* 27 (2002): 136-152.

Baralt, Guillermo A. *"Buena Vista": Life and Work on a Puerto Rican Hacienda, 1833-1904*. Chapel Hill: University of North Carolina Press, 1999.

Barton, Hal. "A Challenge for Puerto Rican Music: How to Build a Soberao for Bomba." *Centro Journal* 16 (2004): 69-89.

—. "The Challenges of Puerto Rican Bomba." *Caribbean Dance: From Abakuá to Zouk*. Edited by Susanna Sloat. Gainesville: University Press of Florida, 2002.

Buckridge, Steeve O. *The Language of Dress: Resistance and Accommodation in Jamaica, 1760-1890*. Kingston: University of West Indies Press, 2004.

Cartagena, Juan. "When Bomba Becomes The National Music of the Puerto Rico Nation . . ." *Centro Journal* 16 (2004): 15-35.

Cepeda, Modesto. "En la Hacienda Caridad." By Rafael Cepeda. Translated by Melanie Maldonado and Priscilla Renta. *Modesto Cepeda y los Patriarcas de la Bomba*. MC, 2005.

De Certeau, Michel. *The Practice of Everyday Life*. Berkeley: University of California Press, 1984.

Emmanuelli Náter, Jorge. "Seven Songs, Seven Seises de Bomba." Workshop for Puerto Rican Organization for the Performing Arts. Chicago, Illinois. September 23 and 30, 2006.

Flores, Juan. "'Bumbun' and the Beginnings of Plena Music." *Divided Borders: Essays on Puerto Rican Identity*. Houston: Arte Publico Press, 1993.

Fraunhar, Alison. "Tropics of Desire: Envisioning the Mulata Cubana." *Emergences* 12 (2002): 219-234.

González Garcia, Lydia Milagros. *Elogio de la Bomba*. Loiza: La Mano Poderosa, 2004.

Gravlee, Clarence C. "Ethnic Classification in Southeastern Puerto Rico: The Cultural Model of 'Color.'" *Social Forces* 83 (2005): 949-970.

Hill Collins, Patricia. "Mammies, Matriarchs, and Other Controlling Images." *Black Feminist Thought: Knowledge, Consciousness, and the Politics of Empowerment*. New York: Routledge, 2000.

Hosbawm, Eric, and Terence Ranger, eds. *The Invention of Tradition*. Cambridge: Cambridge University Press, 1999.

Johnson, E. Patrick. "'Nevah had uh Cross Word': Mammy and the Trope of Black Womanhood." *Appropriating Blackness: Performance and the Politics of Authenticity*. Durham: Duke University Press, 2003.

Klein, Herbert S. *African Slavery in Latin America and the Caribbean*. New York: Oxford University Press, 1986.

Laguerre, Enrique A. *La Llamarada*. 2nd ed. San Juan: Biblioteca de Autores Puertorriqueños, 1939.

Ribes Tovar, Federico. *A Chronological History of Puerto Rico*. New York: Plus Ultra Educational Publishers, 1973.

Rivera, Raquel Z. *New York Ricans From the Hip Hop Zone*. New York: Palgrave Macmillan, 2003.

Roberts, Dorothy. *Killing the Black Body: Race, Reproduction, and the Meaning of Liberty*. New York: Random House, 1997.

Robertson, Claire. "Africa into the Americas?: Slavery and Women, the Family, and the Gender Division of Labor." *More than Chattel: Black Women and Slavery in the Americas*. Edited by David Barry Gaspar & Darlene Clark Hine. Bloomington: Indiana University Press, 1996.

Rosa-Nieves, Cesáreo. *Voz Folklorico de Puerto Rico*. Sharon: Troutman Press, 1967.

Suau, Paloma. *Raices, selections*. VHS. San Juan, PR: Banco Popular de Puerto Rico, 2001.

Sotiropoulos, Karen. *Staging Race: Black Performers in Turn of the Century America*. Cambridge: Harvard University Press, 2006.

Steward, Sue. *¡Musica!: The Rhythm of Latin America: Salsa, Rumba, Merengue and More*. San Francisco: Chronicle Books, 1999.

Totti, Javier. "Puerto Rican Community in Hawai'i." *Centro Journal* 13 (2001): entire issue.

Vega, Bernardo. *Memoirs of Bernardo Vega: a Contribution to the History of the Puerto Rican Community in New York*. Edited by Cesar Andréu Iglesias. Trans. Juan Flores. New York: Monthly Review P, 1984.

Vega Drouet, Hector. "Historical and Ethnological Survey on Probable African Origins of the Puerto Rican Bomba, Including a Description of Santiago Apostol Festivities at Loiza Aldea." PhD diss., Wesleyan University, 1979.

—. "Puerto Rico." *Garland Handbook of Latin American Music*. Edited by Dale A. Olsen and Daniel E. Sheehy. New York: Garland Publishing, Inc., 2000.

Wyatt, Gail Elizabeth. *Stolen Women: Reclaiming our Sexuality, Taking Back Our Lives*. New York: John Wiley & Sons, Inc., 1997.

Notes

[1] Bomba is one of the two genres of AfroPuerto Rican music and is approximately 400 hundred years old. Hector Vega Drouet, "Historical and Ethnological Survey of Probable African Origins of the Puerto Rican Bomba, Including a Description of the Santiago Apostol Activities at Loiza Aldea," (PhD diss., Wesleyan University, 1979), 138.

[2] My own experience as a costumed performer, fall of 2004.

[3] Also referred to in this paper as "the Island."

[4] "Presentational groups" is used here to refer to ensembles, mostly dance companies, using a women's bomba costume but no other elements of bomba practice for performance (identified later in the paper.)

[5] "The Diaspora" is used here to refer to the population of Puerto Ricans in the continental U.S.

[6] Tainos were the first nation people of Boríken, known today as Puerto Rico. Federico Ribes Tovar, *A Chronological History of Puerto Rico*, 9.

[7] Ibid.,12.

[8] Ibid., 29.

[9] Ibid., 323.

[10] For more information, see Manuel Alvarez Nazario's *El Elemento Afronegroide en el Español de Puerto Rico*, (San Juan: Instituto de Cultura Puertorriqueña, 1974).

[11] Danza was an elite dance primarily relegated to the upper classes of Puerto Rico and most popular in the 19th century. Sue Steward, *¡Musica!: The Rhythm of Latin America: Salsa, Rumba, Merengue and More*, (San Francisco: Chronicle Books, 1999), 94.

[12] Frances Aparicio's "A White Lady Called the Danza" and "A Sensual Mulatta Called the Plena," in *Listening to Salsa: Gender, Latin Popular Music and Puerto Rican Popular Cultures* (Middletown: Wesleyan University Press, 1997).

[13] Plena is another of the two genres of AfroPuerto Rican music and is approximately one hundred years old. Juan Flores's "'Bumbun' and the Beginnings of Plena Music," in *Divided Borders: Essays on Puerto Rican Identity* (Houston: Arte Publico Press, 1993).

[14] Sue Steward, *¡Musica!: The Rhythm of Latin America: Salsa, Rumba, Merengue and More*, (San Francisco: Chronicle Books, 1999), 94.

[15] For more information, see Frances Aparicio, "A White Lady Called the Danza" and "A Sensual Mulatta Called the Plena," in *Listening to Salsa: Gender, Latin Popular Music and Puerto Rican Popular Cultures* (Middletown: Wesleyan University Press, 1997); Alicia Arrizón, "Race-ing Performativity Through Transculturation, Taste and the Mulata Body," *Theatre Research International* 27 (2002): 136-152; or Alison Fraunhar, "Tropics of Desire: Envisioning the Mulata Cubana," *Emergences* 12 (2002): 219-234.

[16] "Performers" will be used here to refer to both practitioners of live, improvisational bomba and others who attempt to represent it through costumed, choreographed presentations to recorded music.

[17] Hector Vega Drouet, "Historical and Ethnological Survey of Probable African Origins of the Puerto Rican Bomba, Including a Description of the Santiago Apostol Activities at Loiza Aldea," (PhD diss., Wesleyan University, 1979), 22.

[18] Herbert S. Klein, *African Slavery in Latin America and the Caribbean*, 106.

[19] Hal Barton, "The Challenges of Puerto Rican Bomba," 186-187.

[20] Herbert S. Klein, *African Slavery in Latin America and the Caribbean*, 106.

[21] Luis Manuel Álvarez and Angel Quintero Rivera, "Bambulaé sea allá," in *Raices* (Banco Popular de Puerto Rico, 2001), http://rrpac.upr.clu.edu:909/~lalvarez/Artic ulos/bambulaeseaalla.htm (accessed November 26, 2006).

[22] "People of color" will be used in this discussion to denote people of African heritage who may or may not have been dark skinned.

[23] A Puerto Rican trope of cultural and ethnic whitening through a process of denied and suppressed Black culture and interracial marriage.

[24] As a practitioner, I participate in ongoing discussions about bomba history, aesthetics, and practice with other bomberos.

[25] Practitioners are defined here as those who engage in live and improvisational bomba.

[26] See Alex Lasalle, forthcoming.

[27] There are conflicting views about whether several communities in the northern metropolitan area of San Juan conflate to qualify as a regional style or whether Santurce (the heart of Cangrejos) itself represents a distinct regional style, eclipsing all the other communities often grouped with it.

[28] An area now part of the metropolitan area of the Island's capital city on the northern coast, Cangrejos was once a town populated by freed and former slaves.

[29] Isolated by nature's design, Loiza is a community that has been historically separated from other goings-on of the Island and was therefore a desirable destination cimarrones or runaway slaves. A former maroon community, Loiza continues to be the town in which the highest number of African descendents lives.

For more information, see Lydia Milagros González García, *Elogio de la Bomba*, (Loiza: La Mano Poderosa, 2004).

[30] Seises are the metrics of bomba song compositions. See Jorge Emmanuelli Náter's "Seven Songs, Seven Seises de Bomba," (workshop for Puerto Rican Organization for the Performing Arts, Chicago, Illinois, September 23 and 30, 2006).

[31] For more information see Luis Manuel Álvarez and Angel Quintero Rivera, "Bambulaé sea allá," in Raices (Banco Popular de Puerto Rico, 2001), http://rrpac.upr.clu.edu:909/~lalvarez/Articulos/bambulaeseaalla.htm (accessed November 26, 2006) and Juan Cartagena, "When Bomba Becomes the National Music of the Puerto Rican Nation . . . ," *Centro Journal* 16 (2004): 18.

[32] These are bomba and plena compositions.

[33] With the exception of some minor foot movement.

[34] Luis Manuel Álvarez and Angel Quintero Rivera's "Bambulaé sea allá," in *Raices*, (Banco Popular de Puerto Rico, 2001), http://rrpac.upr.clu.edu:909/~lalvarez/Articulos/bambulaeseaalla.htm (accessed November 26, 2006).

[35] Personal communication with a New Jersey based bomba practitioner 2004.

[36] Movements enacted to elicit a slap from the lead drummer.

[37] Paloma Suau, *Raices, selections*. VHS (San Juan: Banco Popular de Puerto Rico, 2001).

[38] Personal communication with Norka Nadal in 2007.

[39] After the Haitian revolutionary war, many French colonizers abandoned their Haitian estates and moved to the West Coast of Puerto Rico bringing with them their slaves and therefore these influences.

[40] The name of this rhythm may be a reference to Dutch influence; there were many Dutch merchants who conducted business in Puerto Rico.

[41] Personal conversation with a Chicago-based practitioner in 2001.

[42] There are varying beliefs and practices throughout the Bomba community about the existence of two similar rhythms with almost identical names: cüembe and güembe. Personal communication with Jorge Emmanuelli Náter, 2006.

[43] The second drummer creates a heartbeat that is interpreted by the dancer who in turn is interpreted by the lead drummer. The slaps of the lead drummer create a harmony that rests upon the melodic rhythm of the second drum creating a triangular relationship of music, dance and communication.

[44] Barril transliterated means barrel. In the context of bomba, it is a word used to refer to the drums made of barrels.

[45] Luis Manuel Álvarez and Angel Quintero Rivera's "Bambulaé sea allá," in *Raices,* (Banco Popular de Puerto Rico, 2001), http://rrpac.upr.clu.edu:909/~lalvarez/Articulos/bambulaeseaalla.htm (accessed November 26, 2006).

[46] Melanie Maldonado, interview with Isabel Albizu Dávila and Wilfredo Santiago, March 2005.

[47] The word is simultaneously the name of the genre and the name of the drums.

[48] The maraca is a remnant of Taino culture in Puerto Rico and is fashioned from a dried gourd (of the higuera tree) filled with seeds.

[49] For more descriptions of Bomba drumming, singing or dance, see Hal Barton's "The Challenges of Puerto Rican Bomba," (Gainesville: University Press of Florida, 2002), 39.

[50] The bomba costume uses Victorian era aristocratic fashion as its model but employs signifiers of domestic workers – a head wrap and an apron. This does not coincide with the dress of blacks pursuing social mobility (these women often wore hats and not head wraps) or with the domestic workers and other laborers (these women did not have ready access to white, airy clothe and certainly did not engage in work that would allow them to maintain such clean and adorned outfits.) For more information about clothing worn by enslaved people of the Caribbean and free people of color, see Steeve O. Buckridge, *The Language of Dress: Resistance and Accomodation in Jamaica, 1760-1890* (Kingston: University of West Indies Press, 2004).

[51] Herbert S. Klein, *African Slavery in Latin America and the Caribbean*, 106.

[52] For more information, see Bernardo Vega, *Memoirs of Bernardo Vega: a Contribution to the History of the Puerto Rican*, ed. Cesar Andréu Iglesias, trans. Juan Flores (New York: Monthly Review Press, 1984).

[53] The Taino word identifying people from the Island of Boríken and here used interchangeably with Puerto Rican.

[54] There have been three variations of blue color in the flag that will be discussed later in the paper.

[55] A previous flag was created by Island-based revolutionaries and was used in El Grito de Lares of 1868, considered the first revolutionary act towards independence and autonomy for Puerto Rico.

[56] For more information, see Guillermo Baralt's *"Buena Vista": Life and Work on a Puerto Rican Hacienda, 1833-1904*, 118.

[57] For more information, see Javier Totti, "Puerto Rican Community in Hawai'i," Centro Journal 13 (2001): entire issue.

[58] Federico Ribes Tovar, *A Chronological History of Puerto Rico*, 483.

[59] The color of the blue field was changed in the mid-1990s after approximately forty years as navy blue.

[60] Hector Vega Drouet, "Historical and Ethnological Survey of Probable African Origins of the Puerto Rican Bomba, Including a Description of the Santiago Apostol Activities at Loiza Aldea" (PhD diss., Wesleyan University, 1979), 24-25.

[61] Information I have learned during my six and a half years as a practitioner.

[62] For more information, see Hal Barton, "The Challenges of Puerto Rican Bomba," in *Caribbean Dance: From Abakuá to Zouk*, ed. Susanna Sloat (Gainesville: University Press of Florida, 2002).

[63] Claire Robertson, "Africa into the Americas?: Slavery and Women, the Family, and the Gender Division of Labor," 10.

[64] According to the initial established use of this family.

[65] See, Karen Sotiropoulos, S*taging Race: Black Performers in Turn of the Century America* (Cambridge: Harvard University Press, 2006), 19-20.

[66] For more information on the mammy trope, see Patricia Hill Collins, "Mammies, Matriarchs, and Other Controlling Images," *Black Feminist Thought: Knowledge,*

Consciousness, and the Politics of Empowerment (New York: Routledge, 2000); E. Patrick Johnson, "'Nevah had uh Cross Word': Mammy and the Trope of Black Womanhood," *Appropriating Blackness: Performance and the Politics of Authenticity* (Durham: Duke University Press, 2003); Dorothy Roberts, *Killing the Black Body: Race, Reproduction, and the Meaning of Liberty* (New York: Random House, 1997); and Gail Elizabeth Wyatt, *Stolen Women: Reclaiming Our Sexuality, Taking Back Our Lives* (New York: John Wiley & Sons, Inc., 1997).

[67] Eric Hosbawm and Terence Ranger, eds, Invention of Tradition (Cambridge: Cambridge University Press, 1999).

[68] See the table at the beginning of the paper.

[69] The image is referred to as Mama Ines on the company's historical time line (http://www.yaucono.com/History/history3.htm) but is referred to as Yauconita in the image's web address (http://www.yaucono.com/images/yauconita.gif.)

[70] For more information, see E. Patrick Johnson, "'Nevah had uh Cross Word': Mammy and the Trope of Black Womanhood," *Appropriating Blackness: Performance and the Politics of Authenticity* (Durham: Duke University Press, 2003).

[71] Enrique A. Laguerre, *La Llamarada*, 2nd edition (San Juan: Biblioteca de Autores Puertorriqueños, 1939), 341.

[72] In the aforementioned and numerous other texts, the female body became a display in the public realm, which is often gendered as male.

[73] My own signifyin' to the concept "emasculating."

[74] This excerpt was taken from personal communication received directly from the performer via email. Anonymous, e-mail message to the author, November 8, 2004.

[75] Bomba jam session

[76] "Stages" used in the recording of scenes in *Raices*. Paloma Suau, *Raices, selections*. VHS (San Juan: Banco Popular de Puerto Rico, 2001).

[77] For more information, see Cesáreo Rosa-Nieves, *Voz Folklorico de Puerto Rico* (Sharon: Troutman Press, 1967), 64.

BOB MARLEY: POSTCOLONIAL ACTIVIST AND (R)EVOLUTIONARY INTELLECTUAL

ADAM M. LOYD

The success of the European colonial expansion required the complete subjugation of the indigenous populations in the lands they occupied. The physical oppression was accomplished through brute force and military might, yet the long-term suppression of the colonized populations required the enslavement of their minds. In depriving the people of their identity and culture, the colonizers destroyed these populations' sense of humanity, worth, and the right to justice. It is of little surprise then, that much of the art, literature, and music of the postcolonial era take as their subject the rediscovery and reclamation of these lost cultural identities as a first step toward freedom. These artists and intellectuals have chosen to be activists, by giving voice and direction to their communities until such time as each individual has regained his or her own identity and voice.

Among this tradition of activist-artists, Bob Marley stands out as an extraordinary postcolonial figure. An organic intellectual in the Gramscian model, Marley was dissatisfied with the culture of oppression in which he was raised and sought to defeat the structural inequity that he and other Jamaicans routinely faced. Rastafari, a religion based on black-African empowerment, became his new paradigm for understanding the world. Rastafari revealed to Marley his long, lost identity, and with this revelation came a great sense of power and purpose. Marley believed that the same truth which set him free could do so for all in the African Diaspora, and the weapon he chose to spread this message was music. As his lyrics reflect, Marley believed that his music has the power to affect real social change: "Music you're, music you're the key / Talk to who, please talk to me / Bring the voice of the Rastaman / Communicating to everyone / How I, How I know, How I, How I know / And that's how I know / A Reggae Music, chant down, Chant down Babylon."[1] With Rastafari's truth and Reggae music, Marley felt that Babylon, i.e. Western oppression, could be brought down.

Marley's songs trumpet the grass-roots calls for justice, the affirmation of black African culture, the importance of understanding black history, and the need for revolutionary struggle in reclaiming one's cultural identity. Yet, unlike many of his contemporaries, Marley's view of the postcolonial world was neither stagnant, nor rigidly confined by a political ideology. In fact, over time, Marley's understanding of justice and black identity evolved from a Marcus Garvey inspired, unquestioned support of negritude, to a more Mahsweta Devi-like call for universal love that transcends race and nationality. This shift in understanding can be traced to several factors that I will discuss; however, these reasons aside, Marley's unwavering dedication to the cause of justice along with his ability to evolve toward a more perfect understanding of that goal distinguish him as an icon of the postcolonial effort to rebuild a lost people.

In order to analyze Marley's songs as an example of postcolonial activist expression, we must first examine the three major influences on his work: Jamaican history, Rastafari, and Marley's personal history.

Backdrop: The Shaping of a Prophet

Like many Caribbean islands, Jamaica was one of the first lands to be colonized by Europe and one of the last to gain independence. First claimed by Spain in 1509, Jamaica was taken over by the British in 1670, at which time it became one of the world's largest slave markets. Jamaica remained under British control until 1962. Since then, despite having a pluralistic, democratic government, Jamaica still suffers from many of the structural inequalities left over from British rule. Not only is the population divided by race, with a hierarchy that distinguishes whites, browns, and blacks, but the economic chasm between the haves and have-nots is one of the largest in the world.[2] Jamaica's political parties recognized early on that with the majority of Jamaicans living in poverty, the nation's underclass constituted a potentially powerful voting bloc. As such, with no economic relief to offer, they needed to find some means of appealing to poor, black Jamaicans; they needed to represent themselves as understanding the people. Their solution? The token adoption of a Jamaican subculture known as Rastafari.

Rastafari finds its roots in Jamaican born, Pan-African supporter, Marcus Garvey. Born in 1887, Garvey was one of the early supporters of the return to Africa movement. Many point to his call for blacks to look to Africa for a redeemer king as the start of Rastafari. The Rasta religion proclaims that, for centuries, Western society has hidden and rewritten history, including the bible, in order to keep the black race from knowing the truth: that it is the center of human civilization. Developing out of

Ethiopianism, and the reinterpretation of biblical texts (particularly Psalm 68:31), Rastafari posits that Jesus was merely a prophet and that Ethiopian Emperor Haile Selassie was God incarnate. Ethiopia replaces Israel as Zion and the call is made for the African Diaspora to return to the homeland. "For the Rastafari brethren, 'Zion,' the promised land of Ethiopia, was both precolonial utopia and the imminent future of black people who were destined to survive the time span of Babylonian hegemony."[3] While not widely followed as a religion, the Rastafarian message of black empowerment, the lauding of black culture, and the affirmation of the black individual as a superior being that transcends the human condition, reverberated with many blacks who were emerging from colonial oppression. As Anthony Bogues writes, "Rastafari engages the most fundamental question of the black body and African person: *Who am I?* . . . In one fell swoop Rastafari makes God and man the same being . . . The consequence is that this move defines Africans as humans by announcing in Rastafari theology that a black human is God."[4]

With its historic connection to Africa and the continued suffering of a black underclass, Jamaica became a stronghold for Rastafari. However, relatively few Jamaicans actually practiced the religion, and the Rastas' anti-establishment behavior, and impoverished state set them at odds with the police and often made the general population wary. Still, Rastafari's principles of black pride and black power permeated the consciousness of poor Jamaicans. Rastafari linked Jamaica's struggles with the struggles of all black people and gave the people hope that a forgotten glorious past could be theirs again. On the other hand, for the postcolonial Jamaican elite Rastafari became the ideological symbol of Jamaica's poor blacks. Ironically, while the police were persecuting true Rastafarians, the politicians used the trappings and symbols of Rastafari to show their solidarity with the people and gain the common man's political support.

Into this historical, religious, and social environment came a young musician named Robert Nesta Marley, aged 17 years at the time of Jamaica's independence. The son of a black mother and an absent white father, Marley spent the better part of his early life in the urban squalor of Kingston, just adjacent to the even poorer area of Trenchtown. Marley was drawn to the inhabitants of Trenchtown. There he meets fellow band members Peter McIntosh (later Peter Tosh) and Neville "Bunny" Livingston (later Bunny Wailer), and participates in "the Trenchtown youths' defiance of mainstream social norms and their resistance to the colonial structures dominated by white colonials and the light-skinned Jamaican middle class."[5] The immersion in Trenchtown's rebel culture soon led Marley to Rastafari, of which he quickly became a devoted follower. Rastafari provided a context in which Marley could make sense of the inequity he saw around him; he learned of his lost, half-told history, that Africa is Zion, and that a living black man is God. This revelation changed Marley forever. As Anita Waters explains, "Scanty history, when revealed as such, is oppressive in retrospect. The consequences that the revelation triggers often demonstrate how deeply patterns of social interaction, justifications of dominance and submission, religious ideas, the very meaning of social existence, are rooted in historical consciousness."[6] For Marley, Rastafari supplied the vital piece of knowledge that was missing from his life: it told him who he was by giving him his historic identity and, with it, the ability to demand justice.

Rastafari came to define Marley's world view and informed all his musical-lyrical endeavors. Fundamentally, Marley understood that justice for oppressed peoples could only come when they regained their lost identity. This identity was a birthright that colonialism had denied them and that Rastafari's truth could restore.[7] Reggae became Marley's weapon against oppression; he strongly believed that through his Rasta inspired music, enslaved minds could be freed.

Music as Truth: Marley's Message of Emancipation

Looking at his lyrics, Marley's political and cultural philosophy go through a gradual shift, from supporting revolution and negritude to an idealized, one-world love that transcends race and nationality. What remains constant, however, is the guiding force of Rastafari in which Marley's evolving philosophy is framed. Though, chronologically, there is some overlapping in the shifting philosophical message of his songs, Marley's view of the postcolonial world can be divided into three general stages: revolution and black empowerment, disillusionment with African neocolonial politics, and universal love. In order to understand the reasons behind this shift and its effects on Marley's music and message, we shall examine several songs from each of the three periods which are representative of his interpretation of Rastafari and the postcolonial world at those moments in time.

Stage I: Pan-African Unity, Negritude, and Revolution

Marley's early musical expression reflects the enthusiasm and desire for action that is typical of a new convert recently imbued with the power of truth. Having learned that everything he thought he knew was false, Marley was anxious to spread the word and lift the veil of colonial lies from the eyes of all in the African Diaspora. This period of Marley's career, from roughly 1966 to 1975, includes two iconic songs that are representative of the philosophical bent expressed in most of his music at this time. Both songs come from Marley's second album, 1973's *Burnin'*, which "established [him] as a songwriter of radical political thought. He was dangerous. The decision to include the lyrics of the songs on the liner notes . . . gave the listeners a chance to come in full contact with the tough political spirit that permeated his work."[8]

The first of these songs, "Get Up, Stand Up," is a call-to-arms aimed at all those still oppressed by the historical remains of colonial lies. Clearly expressing the Rasta ethos, "Get Up, Stand Up" describes the need for black unity, the fight against false history, and the necessity of struggle as means to achieve justice.

> (Get up, stand up: stand up for your rights!
> Get up, stand up: stand up for your rights!
> Get up, stand up: stand up for your rights!
> Get up, stand up: don't give up the fight!)
>
> Preacherman, don't tell me,
> Heaven is under the earth.
> I know you don't know
> What life is really worth.
> It's not all that glitters is gold;
> 'Alf the story has never been told:
> So now you see the light, eh!
> Stand up for your rights. Come on!
>
> . . .
>
> Most people think,
> Great God will come from the skies,
> Take away everything
> And make everybody feel high.
> But if you know what life is worth,
> You will look for yours on earth:
> And now you see the light,
> You stand up for your rights. Jah!
>
> . . .
>
> We sick an' tired of-a your ism-skism game –
> Dyin' 'n' goin' to heaven in-a Jesus' name, Lord.
> We know when we understand:
> Almighty God is a living man.

> You can fool some people sometimes,
> But you can't fool all the people all the time.
> So now we see the light (What you gonna do?),
> We gonna stand up for our rights! (Yeah, yeah, yeah!)[9]

The message of the chorus is obvious enough: a call for the people to rise up and claim their right to justice. The verses, however, are where Marley's real Rasta philosophy is contained. He begins by challenging the Church and its duplicity in hiding the black peoples' true history. Marley rejects Jesus and the promise of a heavenly afterlife. Instead, in accordance with Rastafari, he explains that our earthly existence is what holds real value. Once this truth is understood, the people will rise up. The second verse remains with this theme, emphasizing that Christianity wrongly justifies people's suffering, holding out heaven as their reward. "[I]nstead of their freedom, [black slaves] were given only a King James Bible with which to make the brutal world of the plantation meaningful."[10] Marley warns that being told that suffering in this life is good or noble is a terrible fraud meant to keep Africans in a state of oppression. In the song, the final verse adds an exclamation point to his argument. There, Marley explicitly calls Christianity a game and a lie. He proclaims Selassie, a living man, as God and announces Western theology that its ruse is up; the people will no longer be deceived and will rise up to take their rightful place.

Marley sets himself apart from many postcolonial activists in directly charging Christianity with the same crime of colonial oppression as the European governments that occupied the "Third World." In Marley's Rastafarian conception, the imposition of a Western religion, a white God, and a false theological history, were as responsible for stripping black people's identities from them as having to accept European economics, education, languages, and philosophy.

The second song of this thematic period, also from *Burnin'*, is entitled "I Shot the Sheriff." One of Marley's most popular (and most covered) songs, "Sheriff" directly addresses the issue of justice for the oppressed.

> (I shot the sheriff
> But I didn't shoot no deputy, oh no! Oh!
> I shot the sheriff
> But I didn't shoot no deputy, ooh, ooh, oo-ooh.)
> Yeah! All around in my home town,
> They're tryin' to track me down;
> They say they want to bring me in guilty
> For the killing of a deputy,
> For the life of a deputy.
> But I say:

Oh, now, now. Oh!
(I shot the sheriff.) - the sheriff.
(But I swear it was in self-defense.)
Oh, no! (Ooh, ooh, oo-oh) Yeah!
I say: I shot the sheriff – Oh, Lord! –
(And they say it is a capital offence.)
Yeah! (Ooh, ooh, oo-oh) Yeah!

Sheriff John Brown always hated me,
For what, I don't know:
Every time I plant a seed,
He said kill it before it grow –
He said kill them before they grow.
And so:

. . .

Freedom came my way one day
And I started out of town, yeah!
All of a sudden I saw sheriff John Brown
Aiming to shoot me down,
So I shot - I shot - I shot him down and I say:
If I am guilty I will pay.

. . .

Reflexes had got the better of me
And what is to be must be:
Every day the bucket a-go a well,
One day the bottom a-go drop out,
One day the bottom a-go drop out.
I say:[11]

The narrative in this song tells of a man who is persecuted by the police for spreading dangerous, presumably Rasta, ideas that must be stamped out before they disseminate. The man, truth having set him free, is about to leave his oppressive confines when he sees the sheriff about to shoot him. In self defense, he kills the sheriff, and is defiantly willing to pay the price if self survival is deemed a crime. However, he is not accused of this crime (perhaps because it was clearly in self defense), but is wanted for a murder he did not commit, the killing of a deputy.

On its surface, "Sheriff" is one man's tale of trouble with the law. However, Marley's message is more complex. He is speaking of a system which repeatedly denies justice to an entire social class. As Dawes notes, "the 'freedom' that meets this figure who is both sharecropper and slave is one that undermines the authority of the sheriff, who is clearly not simply the law but the larger social structure that works against the persona of the piece."[12] The system equates the poor with being guilty; their social status puts them outside the community of respectable, law-abiding citizens. Moreover, fighting back, even for self preservation, is punished. It is a dire picture that Marley paints. That is, until the final verse where he warns the abuse, and continued denial of justice will soon end. A corrupt system that keeps drawing from the well of injustice will eventually find itself falling asunder.

It is not certain whether Marley believed that his songs would cause the masses to rise up, or the elite's eyes to open in sudden recognition of Jamaica's woes, but he did believe that people were listening and that Rastafari's message needed to be told. Nobody else had written the stories of Jamaica's poor, so Marley spoke for them, taking the obscure Trenchtown and putting it on the postcolonial cultural map. Shedding light on the injustices endured by impoverished Jamaicans, and tying their fate to that of all Africans, Marley's call for revolution took on a certain formidability which had the result of both encouraging and altering him.

Stage II: Rethinking the Nature of Zion

The second period of Marley's philosophical song writing evolution runs from 1975-1980. On the whole, Marley's songs in this period lose much of their militancy and take on a more reflective pose. Early on, his attention is on promoting Pan-Africanism, lauding black culture, and proclaiming Africa as the promised land. However, several personal experiences (an assassination attempt, exile, the rise of black neocolonial governments, Selassie's death, and Jamaica's 1980 election violence) eventually create cracks in Marley's unquestioned acceptance of an idealized Africa and the universal righteousness of the black race.[13] While Marley suffered no loss of faith in Rastafari, he came to understand that finding Zion was more complicated than the African Diaspora simply returning home. Songs written after 1976 echo this doubt and sense of personal betrayal.

The most profound of Marley's perception altering experiences was the attempt on his life. While Marley was an activist on behalf of his people, he tried to remain politically neutral, supporting neither Jamaican political party, nor any particular politician. That is until 1976. Jamaica's leftist Prime Minister, Michael Manley, was campaigning for re-election on the platform of improving the economic situation for his nation's poor. Part of Manley's rhetoric included Rastafari inspired messages such as calling

Jamaica a black nation and advocating stronger ties with Africa. Marley, with some reluctance, agreed to play a thinly veiled political event billed as a national cultural concert. Two days before the show, a gunman, presumably funded by the opposition party, attempted to assassinate Marley and his band mates at their home. Luckily, none of the wounds were fatal and Marley defiantly carried on the performance as scheduled. Fearing for his life and feeling betrayed by the very people he was trying to help, Marley soon left Jamaica for 18 months on a self-imposed exile. Over the rest of his life, never again did he spend an extended period of time in his home country.

Numerous songs, in this era of Marley's exploding international fame, bear the markers of his shift from negritude to a critique of its unquestioned adherence. Yet, two songs, in particular, capture Marley's shifting perception of Africa and Zion—they are 1977's "Exodus," from the album of the same name, and the 1979 tune, "Zimbabwe" off *Survival*.

. . .

> Men and people will fight ya down (Tell me why!)
> When ya see Jah light. (Ha-ha-ha-ha-ha-ha-ha!)
> Let me tell you if you're not wrong; (Then, why?)
> Everything is all right.
> So we gonna walk - all right! - through de roads of creation:
> We the generation (Tell me why!)
> (Trod through great tribulation) trod through great tribulation.
>
> Exodus, all right! Movement of Jah people!
> Oh, yeah! O-oo, yeah! All right!
> Exodus: Movement of Jah people! Oh, yeah!
>
> Yeah-yeah-yeah, well!
> Uh! Open your eyes and look within:
> Are you satisfied (with the life you're living)? Uh!
> We know where we're going, uh!
> We know where we're from.
> We're leaving Babylon,
> We're going to our Father land.

. . .

> Jah come to break downpression,
> Rule equality,
> Wipe away transgression,
> Set the captives free.[14]

Like many of Marley's songs, the lyrics' immediate impression usually belies the artist's real intention; only upon closer examination does the intended message become clear. That is the case with "Exodus." At first, the lyrics appear to be a straightforward call for African unity and a return to the fatherland. Yet, while "Exodus" does retain the theme of a return to Zion, the exodus from Babylon that Marley sings about is more exclusive than it appears. It is not the entire African Diaspora he is addressing, but only the believers in Rastafari—"Movement of *Jah* people." Those who recognize their cultural history and identity, whose eyes are open, who like Moses, are part of an enlightened group will leave Babylon. However, those who do not examine their lives and look for truth are left behind. In this re-conception of Rastafari's message, Marley finds that, "To the true Rasta, Ethiopia is more than a territorial entity: it is a moral destination."[15] Marley does not set limits on those who may turn to Rastafari's truth (if not as religious followers, then as philosophical adherents), but his exclusion of those who do not demonstrates a significant departure from his former view of black unity.

Released in 1979, "Zimbabwe" is one of Marley's most overtly political songs. Again, on its surface the song is a cry for freedom, a call to arms for the liberation of the, then, still colonized African nation. The song became an anthem for Zimbabwe's freedom and many credit Marley with helping to affect the nation's actual liberation in 1980.[16] In fact, Marley was invited to perform his song at Zimbabwe's celebration of independence; the theoretical power of activist music was fully realized in practical application at that moment. Yet, for all the positive aspects of a free Africa, Marley could not contain his concerns with the corruption, violence, and neocolonialism he saw perpetrated by blacks on blacks. His idealized Zion proved not to exist in the real world and his music reflects this disappointment.

> Every man gotta right to decide his own destiny,
> And in this judgement there is no partiality.
> So arm in arms, with arms, we'll fight this little struggle,
> 'Cause that's the only way we can overcome our little trouble.
> Brother, you're right, you're right,
> You're right, you're right, you're so right!
> We gon' fight (we gon' fight), we'll have to fight (we gon' fight),
> We gonna fight (we gon' fight), fight for our rights!
>
> Natty Dread it in-a (Zimbabwe);
> Set it up in (Zimbabwe);

> Mash it up-a in-a Zimbabwe (Zimbabwe);
> Africans a-liberate (Zimbabwe), yeah.
> No more internal power struggle;
> We come together to overcome the little trouble.
> Soon we'll find out who is the real revolutionary,
> 'Cause I don't want my people to be contrary.
> . . .
>
> To divide and rule could only tear us apart;
> In everyman chest, mm - there beats a heart.
> So soon we'll find out who is the real revolutionaries;
> And I don't want my people to be tricked by mercenaries.
> . . .
>
> Set it up in-a Zimbabwe (Zimbabwe);
> Africans a-liberate Zimbabwe (Zimbabwe);
> Every man got a right to decide his own destiny.[17]

Marley opens the song with a solidly postcolonial declaration that all men have a right to justice, to form their own futures. United, they will find freedom, but only after armed struggle. He then, in the chorus, links Jamaican Rastafarians (dreads) with Zimbabweans and all Africans who must be as one in their path towards liberation. The very next verse, though, expresses Marley's wariness at what may come with this freedom. He warns against internal fighting and the possibility that some who are now revolutionaries will become the next oppressors. In the chorus, he repeats his call for a united revolution, followed once more by a warning in the next verse. If African rulers divide their people for power's sake, it undermines all Africans. Marley cautions the revolutionaries to watch for such people, mercenaries who would use revolution only to take the place of European oppressors. The final chorus reiterates the call for revolution and freedom in Zimbabwe, and he closes the song reminding his listeners what they are fighting for: the rights and justice for each individual.

The even split between Marley's call for Zimbabwe's freedom and his dire warnings that oppressors come in all races and can be disguised as revolutionaries, demonstrates his disillusionment with postcolonial Africa. As Farred notes,

> [Zimbabwe] reveals the ways in which Marley's critical paradigm has shifted from his earlier, optimistic mode to his mature, critical one . . . [H]is concern about 'spiritual wickedness' is supplanted by his attacks on the disturbing ways in which Zion and Babylon resemble each other. The differences between the two conceptual spaces can no longer be reduced to a racial marker; *Zion* may denote a black African nation, but it does not

inevitably follow that this is a democratic society without 'spiritual wickedness,' corruption, and the oppression and exploitation of blacks by blacks.[18]

Marley's exile from Jamaica exposed him to the practical reality of the African Diaspora. His experiences traveling the world increased his desire for strength through Pan-African unity, but also shook his unquestioned faith that everything black is noble. Both the overtly political and skeptical "Zimbabwe" and the more subtle "Exodus" represent Marley's difficulty at reconciling his belief in an African Zion with the brutal reality of the postcolonial continent. What emerges in his songs is the vision of an imperfect Zion, a potential paradise for the African Diaspora, but as yet, politically and spiritually lacking.

Marley's shift from militant negritude to a more reasoned, critical look at the black world came as the result of both personal and nationalistic disappointments. Much of the exuberance and hope for a heaven-like future following independence were lost as casualties of economic imperialism, neocolonialism, and black on black betrayal. As Vargas Llosa notes, "When he visited Africa he discovered that the continent was far from being the land of salvation for blacks that he had exalted in his credo and his songs, and from then on, he became less concerned with 'negritude' and more ecumenical, and his pacifist preaching and calls for spirituality were more intense."[19] Marley's exile from Jamaica provided him with a more worldly perception of the African Diaspora, but while he recognized and grappled with its failures, he never gave up hope that the Rastafari ideal of black unity could one day be achieved. The message, though challenged by real-world events, still needed spreading and Marley's growing international popularity made him the ideal advocator of Jah's work.

Stage III: Hybridity—Rastafari's One Love

The final phase of Marley's career extends from 1980 until his death from cancer in 1981 and includes several posthumously released songs. With a predominantly white following and fans spanning the globe, Marley became one of music's biggest stars. His 1984 compilation album, *Legend*, has sold over 10 million copies in the U.S. alone,[20] and in 1999 *Time* magazine "pronounced the album *Exodus* to be the most important pop recording of the twentieth-century."[21] For his new fans, Marley's message of love, unity, and freedom often overshadowed his damning of Christianity, condemnation of Western imperialism, and cries of economic inequality. He, too, found an appreciation for his interracial following.

After three decades Marley allowed himself to embrace both of his racial heritages, and he discovered a new interpretation of Rastafari that transcended race. In this last phase of his career, Marley decided that Rastafari and Zion were not the exclusive domain of blacks; "downpression" effected people of all races, and as the birthplace of all humanity Africa could be a paradise on earth for all who were ready to make it so – a true land of hybridity. The tenet of Rastafari which stood out most for Marley at this point was universal love, the brotherhood of humankind relying on righteous people coming together, regardless of their origins. The commonly used Rasta phrase "I 'n I" (derived from the title: Emperor Haile Selassie I, and indicating God's unifying divinity within us all, is the Rastafarian inclusive alternative to the "othering" "me and you") is evidence that love has always been Rastafari's central message.[22] The two songs that most clearly espouse this transcendental view of Rastafari are "One Love / People Get Ready" and "Redemption Song."

Although "One Love" was released on 1977's *Exodus*, technically before Marley's final transition period, it aptly describes the ultimate interpretation of Rastafari's message that Marley would arrive at: global unity achieved through love. The fact that the song is part of an earlier era shows that Marley was at least toying with this view of Rastafari while trying to make sense of the troubling events in Africa and his loss of unquestioned negritude.

> One Love! One Heart!
> Let's get together and feel all right.
> Hear the children cryin' (One Love!);
> Hear the children cryin' (One Heart!),
> Sayin': give thanks and praise to the Lord and I will feel all right;
> Sayin': let's get together and feel all right. Wo wo-wo wo-wo!
> Let them all pass all their dirty remarks (One Love!);
> There is one question I'd really love to ask (One Heart!):
> Is there a place for the hopeless sinner,
> Who has hurt all mankind just to save his own beliefs?
> . . .
>
> As it was in the beginning (One Love!);
> So shall it be in the end (One Heart!),
> . . .
>
> Let's get together to fight this Holy Armagiddyon (One Love!),
> So when the Man comes there will be no, no doom (One Song!).

> Have pity on those whose chances grows t'inner;
> There ain't no hiding place from the Father of Creation.
> Sayin': One Love! What about the One Heart? (One Heart!)
> What about the - ? Let's get together and feel all right.
> I'm pleadin' to mankind! (One Love!);
> Oh, Lord! (One Heart) Wo-oooh!
>
> ...[23]

Marley begins the song with a call for unity among all those who would answer in praise of God. He then redefines his earlier distinction between Zion and Babylon, not based on race or nationality, but on deeds. It is those who speak ill of others and sinfully betray mankind for their own benefit, or in the name of their people, that now represent Babylon. Marley declares that the lost glory of the past, before colonialism destroyed the world, will be again; humanity uniting as one world and one love can create this paradise on earth. Together, the Armageddon of violence and poverty can be defeated and the oppressors of the world deprived of their power to bring doom. Marley is so confident of the power of universal love that he even asks that pity be taken on the enemies of Zion, for their sins will eventually be accounted for by God. His final entreaty is to literally plead with mankind to love one another and pay homage to God for making such a love possible.

"Redemption Song," from the *Uprising* album, is one of the final releases prior to Marley's death. The song incorporates everything Marley had preached about Rastafari and tell of the ability to overcome any obstacle if people are united in God's love. David Moskowitz describes the song this way:

> 'Redemption Song' is the most powerful and personal of the tracks on the 1980 Tuff Gong/Island Records release *Uprising*. Powerful due to its message and personal because it is the only track Marley released singing alone with only his acoustic guitar for accompaniment . . . Ian McCann said of the track, 'as for the message, casting aside fears of man's vain and warlike science for a belief in a greater power, no more eloquent appeal on behalf of any religious belief was ever constructed.'[24]

Marley's central message is that the keys to freedom are within each of us, that we need only change our paradigms of thinking about each other and the world to free ourselves from our divisive, colonial mindsets. Moreover, this freedom can be achieved through something as simple as music, that spreading enlightenment and love through the sharing of song is enough to save the world. Most importantly, Marley's message is a universal one; he does not reserve redemption for any race or nation. As George Stephens explains,

> When Marley released his 'Redemption Songs' in 1980, he sang to hundreds of millions: 'Emancipate yourselves from mental slavery / None but ourselves can free our minds.' This is a vision of emancipation and redemption firmly rooted in slavery, but it relocates the issue of emancipation and redemption in a transracial context: emancipation from mental slavery cannot take place within a merely racial framework.[25]

To Marley, we are all potentially slaves or free men depending on how we view and interact with the world.

> Old pirates, yes, they rob I;
> Sold I to the merchant ships,
> Minutes after they took I
> From the bottomless pit.
> But my hand was made strong
> By the 'and of the Almighty.
> We forward in this generation
> Triumphantly.
> Won't you help to sing
> These songs of freedom? -
> 'Cause all I ever have:
> Redemption songs;
> Redemption songs.
>
> Emancipate yourselves from mental slavery;
> None but ourselves can free our minds.
> Have no fear for atomic energy,
> 'Cause none of them can stop the time.
> How long shall they kill our prophets,
> While we stand aside and look? Ooh!
> Some say it's just a part of it:
> We've got to fulfil de book.
>
> . . . [26]

In the first verse Marley takes us back to the start of the African Diaspora, to the moment where millions of blacks lost their freedom, their identities, and their links to justice. Yet, God carried them through the centuries and led them to today, to a generation that Marley feels can finally triumph over injustice. Moreover, the power to succeed can be found in something as common as music; songs of redemption are the only weapon Marley has at his disposal and they prove, to him, to be enough. It is the second verse where Marley reveals the key to freedom: the emancipation of the mind, a task that each individual must accomplish for him or herself. Once a person finds his or her identity nothing can stop them. Later, he explains that tragedies will still occur, but as freedom spreads, there will be less and less need to fear domination. He even alludes to his own death in referencing atomic energy (Marley blamed his cancer on low level radiation) and notes that not even that will stop time's march toward the day of universal freedom. Marley's final lines invite us all to join in this redemption and carry on his work by singing freedom's songs.

"Redemption Song" and "One Love" essentially summarize Marley's ultimate and final view of life and the true meaning of Rastafari. They chronicle his Rastafarian beliefs and the journey that brought him to his final understanding of Africa, Zion, and the living God within us all. Rastafari provided Marley with his lost identity when that was needed. It gave him the strength and drive to help other downpressed people to learn their history and demand their just and rightful future. It also allowed Marley to question the failings of Africa and black leaders to fulfill the promise of Zion, and, finally, it eventually led to his personal unification and the ability to see beyond race, beyond nationhood, beyond humanity's differences and to call for one love between all mankind. "One Love" represents Marley's hope for the future, and "Redemption Song" is Marley's farewell, and his reassurance that everything will be alright.

Conclusion

The history of Jamaica is similar to the history of many colonized lands, and its emergence from colonial oppression opened doors for the boldest of its disenfranchised population. Like many postcolonial intellectuals, Bob Marley used his freedom to discover who he was, to learn the lost cultural identity that colonialism had denied him, and to use that identity as a way to contextualize and make sense of an unjust world. Rastafari provided the answers Marley was looking for. It taught him that he was from a noble race, that his people were part of divinity, and that Zion was to be found for all black people in their African homeland. The empowering truth of Rastafari and the lies and deceit perpetrated by the West inflamed Marley and set him on a revolutionary, activist mission to fight oppression and spread Rastafari's truth to the entire African Diaspora. Choosing the only weapon he possessed, Marley crafted songs of Pan-African unity, the call for armed struggle, and depicted the injustices suffered every day by his very own community in Trenchtown, all through the lens of Jah's love.

What sets Marley apart from many of the postcolonial artists and theorists who emerged alongside him is his ability to reevaluate and reinterpret the status and history of the postcolonial world and adjust his message accordingly. Always relying on the framework of Rastafari as his philosophical and moral guide, in a relatively short period of time, Marley transformed his position from the blind acceptance of negritude and the need for armed rebellion to a transnational, transracial belief in the unity and brotherhood of all good men and women. From racial division, violence, and anger Marley evolved towards unity, peace, and one love. This transformation should not be interpreted as Marley's belief that injustice and racism were a thing of the past, nor as an abandonment of his people's cause. Instead, Marley's shift in position marks an intellectual maturing and a realization that to defeat racism, nationalism, and the structural remnants of colonial thought, we must look beyond the colonial paradigm of "us and them," look beyond race, and see not "you and me" but "I and I."

Today, Marley's legacy and message threaten to be lost due to their white-washing via commercialization and consumerism. Marley's image has been appropriated by pot-smoking teenagers, t-shirt peddlers, Caribbean travel bureaus, and record companies. This iconic freedom fighter and spiritual leader is having his music stripped of its meaning, left as nothing more than background tunes for good times, as if he were another Jimmy Buffett. Babylon is encroaching upon all that Marley achieved, and it is because of this that I wrote this paper. It is my hope that continued, and expanded, scholarship on Marley will return him (and his philosophy) to his proper status as one of the outstanding postcolonial thinkers of his age.

Bibliography

Bogues, Anthony. *Black Heretics, Black Prophets: Radical Political Intellectuals*. New York: Routledge, 2003.

Chude-Sokei, Louis. "Post-Nationalist Geographies: Rasta, Ragga, and Reinventing Africa." *African Arts* 27 (1994): 80-84, 96.

Dawes, Kwame. *Bob Marley: Lyrical Genius*. London: Sanctuary, 2002.

Farred, Grant. *What's My Name?: Black Vernacular Intellectuals*. Minneapolis: University of Minnesota Press, 2003.

Gilroy, Paul. "Music: Could You Be Loved? Bob Marley, anti-politics and universal sufferation." *Critical Quarterly* 47 (2005): 226-245.

Homiak, John. "Rastafari Voices Reach Ethopia." Review of *The Emperor's Birthday*, by John Dollar. *American Anthropoligist* 96 (1994): 958-963.

Marley, Bob. "Chant Down Babylon." The Words of Bob Marley. http://www.bobmarley.com/songs/songs.cgi?babylon (accessed August 20, 2006).

—. "Exodus." *The Words of Bob Marley*. http://www.bobmarley.com/songs/songs.cgi?exodus (accessed August 20, 2006).

—. "Get Up, Stand Up." *The Words of Bob Marley*. http://www.bobmarley.com/songs/songs.cgi?getup (accessed August 20, 2006).

—. "I Shot the Sheriff." *The Words of Bob Marley*. http://www.bobmarley.com/songs/songs.cgi?sheriff (accessed August 20, 2006).

—. "One Love / People Get Ready." *The Words of Bob Marley*. http://www.bobmarley.com/songs/songs.cgi?onelove (accessed August 20, 2006).

—. "Redemption Song." The Words of Bob Marley. http://www.bobmarley.com/songs/songs.cgi?redemption (accessed August 20, 2006).

—. "Zimbabwe." The Words of Bob Marley. http://www.bobmarley.com/songs/songs.cgi?zimbabwe (accessed August 20, 2006).

Moskowitz, David Vlado. *Robert Nesta "Bob" Marley: Music, Text, and Context*. Ann Arbor, Mi: Bell & Howell Information and Learning Company, 2001.

Mulvaney, Rebekah Michele. *Rastafari and Reggae: A Dictionary and Sourcebook*. New York: Greenwood Press, 1990.

Stephens, George. *On Racial Frontiers: The New Culture of Frederick Douglass, Ralph Ellison, and Bob Marley*. Cambridge: Cambridge UP, 1999.

Vargas Llosa, Mario. "Trench Town Rock." *The American Scholar* 71 (2002): 53-56.

Waters, Anita M. *Race, Class, and Political Symbols: Rastafari and Reggae in Jamaican Politics*. New Brunswick: Transaction Books, 1985.

Walters, Angela. "How I Learned African History from Reggae." *Issue: A Journal of Opinion* 24 (1996): 43-45.

Notes

[1] Bob Marley, "Chant Down Babylon," January 1997.
[2] Anita M. Waters, *Race, Class, and Political Symbols: Rastafari and Reggae in Jamaican Politics*, 9, 29.

[3] Louis Chude-Sokei, "Post-Nationalist Geographies: Rasta, Ragga, and Reinventing Africa," 80.
[4] Anthony Bogues, *Black Heretics, Black Prophets: Radical Political Intellectuals*, 154.
[5] Grant Farred, *What's My Name?: Black Vernacular Intellectuals*, 228.
[6] Waters, *Race, Class, and Political Symbols: Rastafari and Reggae in Jamaican Politics*, 1.
[7] Angela Walters, "How I Learned African History from Reggae," 43.
[8] Kwame Dawes, *Bob Marley: Lyrical Genius*, 41.
[9] Bob Marley, "Get Up, Stand Up," January 1997. Complete lyrics can be found at the web site.
[10] Paul Gilroy, "Music: Could You Be Loved? Bob Marley, anti-politics and universal sufferation," 229.
[11] Bob Marley, "I Shot the Sheriff," January 1997. Complete lyrics can be found at the web site.
[12] Dawes, *Bob Marley: Lyrical Genius*, 80.
[13] Farred, *What's My Name?: Black Vernacular Intellectuals*, 254.
[14] Bob Marley, "Exodus," January 1997. Complete lyrics can be found at the web site.
[15] George Stephens, *On Racial Frontiers: The New Culture of Frederick Douglass, Ralph Ellison, and Bob Marley*, 205.
[16] Ibid.
[17] Bob Marley, "Zimbabwe," January 1997. Complete lyrics can be found at the web site.
[18] Farred, *What's My Name?: Black Vernacular Intellectuals*, 264.
[19] Mario Vargas Llosa, "Trench Town Rock," 56.
[20] Recording Industry Association of America (RIAA), "Diamond Awards," RIAA, http://www.riaa.com/goldandplatinumdata.php?table=tblDiamond.
[21] Gilroy, "Music: Could You Be Loved? Bob Marley, anti-politics and universal sufferation," 227.
[22] Rebekah Michele Mulvaney, *Rastafari and Reggae: A Dictionary and Sourcebook*, 39.
[23] Bob Marley, "One Love / People Get Ready," January 1997. Complete lyrics can be found at the web site.
[24] David Vlado Moskowitz, *Robert Nesta "Bob" Marley: Music, Text, and Context*, 157.
[25] George Stephens, *On Racial Frontiers: The New Culture of Frederick Douglass, Ralph Ellison, and Bob Marley*, 218.
[26] Bob Marley, "Redemption Song," January 1997. The Words of Bob Marley, January 1997, http://www.bobmarley.com/songs/songs.cgi?redemption (accessed August 20, 2006). Complete lyrics can be found at the web site.

Chapter Three

Mapping the Caribbean: Migration, Landscape, and Identity

"Mapping the Caribbean: Migration, Landscape, and Identity" focuses on the subject of Caribbean identity through means as diverse as film, architecture, memory, migration, and the influence of nineteenth-century Russian writers on the works of the Caribbean writer Claude McKay. The collection of essays presented respond to an exploration of the theme of identity that widens the perspective of a single Caribbean identity and shows the myriad possibilities for retrieving and re-conceptualizing that authors have at their disposal. Tatiana Tagirova presents in her essay "Feodor Dostoyevsky and Claude McKay: A Cultural Dialogue with the Dominant Western Ethnocentrism" an engaging study of how "Russian literature of the nineteenth century plays an important role in McKay's formulation of a solution to his dilemma of a dual cultural identity and in his development as a writer." Double consciousness, which in McKay is a struggle to reconcile his Afro-Caribbean identity with Western influence, is in Liamar Durán Almarza's study of Josefina Baez's performance texts a desire to re-configure a "fragmented sense of self" resulting from the uprootedness of migration.

Uprootedness in one's own country is presented by Tania Cepero López's examination of film. Cuban filmmaker Tómas Gutierrez Alea's *Strawberry and Chocolate* serves as a vehicle for a first-hand look at the film's engagement with the theme of 'tolerance' and its repercussions on the Cuban psyche by desconstructing Cuban identity and reconstructing "a definition of identity that moves away from binary opposition." The use of film as a reflector of Cuban society, as "the eye that saw us," is also transferable to Lavina Liburd's problematizing of landscape in the post-independence developments in the built environment of Basseterre, the capital of St. Kitts and Nevis. In Liburd's essay entitled "Disjunctions and Deformations: Memory and Landscape in the West Indies," architecture serves to examine "the symbolic role of the built environment and individual artifacts in the self-definition of the nation moving forward." Liburd's contention is the lack of "memory landscapes" in favor of buildings and spaces that "illustrate the dominance of former colonizers." This discussion of the lack of "historical" reconstruction in the built environment of Basetterre prioritizes the importance of memory as a vehicle for historical reconstruction and sense of identity, a theme that is amply discussed by Aida Luz Rodriguez in her essay "Caribbean Women's Fiction and Strategy of Memory." How aspects such as landscape, location, race, gender, spirituality, class, personal/familial relations correlate to memory and how they are an essential part of self-formation is discussed by Rodriguez in a detailed analysis of the works of Caribbean writers Paule Marshall, Zee Edgell, Michelle Cliff, and Elizabeth Nuñez-Harrell. Raquel Puig in "The Imagined Nation in Cristina García's Monkey Hunting" explores identity and the concept of nation. Coining the concept of Benedict Arnold's 'nation' as an imagined community, Puig problematizes this unified 'imaginary plane' of the nation, "that is formed by the hegemonic nucleus, or the people," and instead proposes, as Michael Hardt and Antonio Negri, that the "unitary experience of a nation subject needs to exclude oppositional differences."

Disjunctions and Deformations: Memory and Landscape in the West Indies

Lavina Liburd

Introduction: Postcolonial Caribbean

This paper looks at the idea of the postcolonial in the Caribbean context. It focuses specifically on post-independence developments in the built environment of Basseterre, the capital city of St. Kitts and Nevis, and attempts to put these developments in context with international discourses of identity and heritage. As with other societies, what has come to be classified as postcolonial thought/discourse emerged in St. Kitts-Nevis well before official Independence. As elsewhere it became a driving force in the process of moving towards Independence. In describing the process I reference regional thinkers and writers, situating St. Kitts-Nevis within this larger arena. This is partially because these ideas emerged somewhat simultaneously across the region as a result of political and intellectual interaction, and partially because of the paucity of documentation within the country itself. Within this chapter, I also briefly outline the road from Crown Colony to Independence for St. Kitts-Nevis, linking it with significant developments in the built environment and outlining the development of the social structure of the state.

> We will manage only by recognizing what our situation is, by identifying the tools and resources available to us, by truly uniting ourselves and by working as a nation, albeit an embryonic one, to ameliorate, if not overcome our present difficulties.[1]

Articulations of nationalism in the Caribbean tend to locate the moment of origin of the nation in the present postcolonial era, and in the soil of the 'new world'. This invokes consideration of the primordial versus modern character of the nation, and the motifs of national mythology as discussed by Anthony Smith. Here the myths of origins in time and space are clearly articulated. The myths of ancestry, migration and liberation, can be highly afro-centric in popular discourse, but also include the relocation of European, Asian and Middle-Eastern populations who came or were brought to the region.

> There can be no Mother India for those whose ancestors came from India . . . There can be no Mother Africa for those of African origin, and the Trinidad and Tobago Society is living a lie and heading for trouble if it seeks to create the impression or allow others to act under the delusion that Trinidad and Tobago is an African society. There can be no Mother England and no dual loyalties; . . . There can be no Mother China, even if one could agree as to which China is the mother; and there can be no Mother Syria or Mother Lebanon. A nation, like an individual can have only one mother. The only Mother we recognize is Trinidad and Tobago and mother cannot discriminate between her children. [2]

Shalini Puri examines the above quote from Eric Williams quite closely in the light of the actual practice of politics in Trinidad and Tobago. Here Williams attempts to invoke intra-ethnic unity and mitigate the rhetoric of Afro-Caribbean nationalism. He invokes the language of hybridity and the locus of a particular landscape to produce an identity different from ancestral identities, yet one that acknowledges multiple heritages. However as Puri notes, highly racialized political practice also resorts to "tearing *apart* the fabric of "the people" along racial lines" in order to consolidate racialized voting blocs. (17)

Derek Walcott begins to give us a framework for an aesthetic expression of Caribbean/ West Indian identity that invokes a particular approach of freedom. As analyzed by Olaniyan,

> . . . the most productive stance is to envision the region as a liminal space not beholden or accountable to either side [the formerly dominant or the formerly dominated]. The aesthetics proper to this space Walcott calls . . . "mulatto"(9), neither purely black nor purely white; a hybrid aesthetics free to speak in Creole, English, or both, or appropriate forms from the diverse cultural traditions that make up the Caribbean—European, African or Asian.[3]

Yet even here there is hierarchy and division. The term "mulatto" traditionally implies a mix of black and white, effectively excluding Asian and Native American influences, in spite of the permission to appropriate the Asian. Creole also implies naturalized white or mulatto in its variable usage. Additionally, in invoking the freedom to borrow from 'the diverse cultural traditions that make up the Caribbean', Walcott expresses a nationalist's limitation as to what may be considered authentic. That is, we are not beholden to either, but to all of the above. Walcott's vagueness also allows us the freedom to translate forms from one medium to the other—music to architecture, building to art, landscape to music—however his own ambivalence between mimicry and innovation and mimicry as innovation does not allow us to embrace this formulation uncontested.

Disjunctions

I argue that there are important disjunctions between the conceptions of local identity embodied in the current Heritage discourses operating in Basseterre, and other expressions of postcolonial local and regional identity. I suggest that these disjunctions stem from the historical alienation of the majority of the population from the urban built environment which they are now asked to valorize as heritage, and that differences in perception between class and ethnic groups are at the root of contestations over space which play out in the built environment of Basseterre. I will use two 'novels of formation' Zee Edgell's Beka Lamb, and Merle Hodge's Crick, Crack, Monkey set in Belize and Trinidad respectively to illustrate the conception of the connection between 'people' and 'landscape' in postcolonial Caribbean thought. I then contrast this conception of identity with that used in the heritage discourse in downtown Basseterre through two examples.

ILLUSTRATION 3.1 AERIAL VIEW OF BASSETERRE

ILLUSTRATION 3.2 BASSETERRE, INDEPENDENCE SQUARE

There are multiple directions in current development in Basseterre. Basseterre is the oldest city in the Federation with an eighteenth and nineteenth century core of colonial Georgian buildings, but it is also a working city. Its function as the governmental and commercial center of the Federation, with two working ports and an airport nearby, has posed a considerable challenge to conservation efforts. The St. Christopher Heritage Society endorses the approach of decentralizing development, and accommodating the growth of commercial, institutional and governmental functions on planned sites outside of Basseterre in order to preserve as many of the colonial buildings in Basseterre as possible. The relocation of the Eastern Caribbean Central Bank headquarters to a new campus in the suburbs of Basseterre is one example of this trend. The construction of the new Caribbean Development Bank headquarters in downtown Basseterre is symptomatic of a parallel tendency, which continues the development of the city as the center of the political, social, and economic life of the federation. There is a strong preference and tendency for Governmental and quasi-Governmental offices to remain in and expand in Basseterre, keeping ministries centralized in the Capital city. This has led to the location of Government ministries in locations as diverse as the Pelican Mall, originally intended to be an entirely commercial development, and in new buildings on Port Zante, an area of reclaimed land primarily intended for commercial development to serve cruise ship passengers disembarking at the deep-water port. The continuing development of Basseterre also often threatens structures the Heritage Society would like to see listed as 'historical' although the provenance/significance of such structures is not always clear.

Concomitant to this is the loss of older "vernacular" structures as well as the decrease of "green-space" in the city and the increased use of temporarily vacant lots for parking. The city typically contained small gardens associated with buildings that initially served both commercial functions below and residential above. Such townhomes are in the process of becoming entirely commercial space.

ILLUSTRATION 3.3 TOWNHOMES IN BASSETERRE

The eighteenth century core of "Georgian" buildings have generally been successfully adapted to retail and commercial use. This adaptation is a compromise between preservation and a process of "commodification" represented by the activities of the "Beautiful Basseterre" committee of the Chamber of Industry and Commerce. The "Beautiful Basseterre Committee", which was most active between 1985 and 2002 was concerned primarily with the aesthetic image of the city, based on a traditionalist motif not necessarily historically 'authentic'. During this period, new construction in Basseterre became almost exclusively in a traditionalist vein. The approach also spread to new construction in the suburbs of Basseterre and to some extent throughout St. Kitts. This approach is very much geared to creating a pleasant cohesive experience for the foreign tourist. Consequently, the recent explosion of informal vending—always an element of the city historically—after the opening of the new deep-water port, is of great concern to this group. Although somewhat stimulated by the tourist industry, this activity does not fit the desired image of "the gentleman's city," a terminology I borrow from Ananya Roy's article *The Gentleman's City* in the collection *Urban*

Informality: Transnational Perspectives, which investigates contestations over the removal of informal activity from the streets of Delhi, India.

ILLUSTRATION 3.4 THE 1792 COURTHOUSE

ILLUSTRATION 3.5 THE 1893 TREASURY BUILDING

The built environment of Basseterre reflects the colony's continued imbrication in globalized discourses over centuries. The British and French both held portions of St. Kitts for almost 100 years. The port town of Basseterre initially developed around a French fort. After the French ceded their holdings to the British in 1713, the town was taken over by the British and became the Capital of the colony. Consequently, the oldest buildings in Basseterre reflect both French and British influences. Most have been classified as a variation of the Georgian style common to the British colonies of the Caribbean. These buildings, typically two stories, have also been referred to as "blouse and skirt" buildings with their characteristic whitewashed wooden tops and cut-stone bases. Distinctive 'quoining' is often though not always seen around openings and at corners of the stone base. The French influence is seen in the use of verandas typically on the upper level overhanging the sidewalk. Decorative wooden fretwork at railings and eaves is also typical. However, the few institutional buildings from the early colonial period reflect strong Palladian influences. The Courthouse was initially built as a commercial structure but was then bought and converted by the local Assembly in 1792. The Treasury, probably the first colonial building constructed specifically for governmental purposes, was built in 1893.

ILLUSTRATION 3.6 NATIONAL HOUSING CORPORATION

ILLUSTRATION 3.7 1965 GOVERNMENT HEADQUARTERS AT LEITH

Later colonial buildings also reflect globalized discourses. Many were built in the 1960s to accommodate the expanding bureaucracy necessary for internal self-government and associated with the 'welfare state.' The Central Housing Authority, now the National Housing Corporation, from which an extensive low-income housing program is still administered, the main post-office, electricity department, and Social Security Administration buildings all date from this era. The entry of the SSA has been modified from the original open breezeway connecting to a central courtyard. It now forms an air-conditioned lobby and reception area. The original Government Headquarters building (GHQ) was completed in 1965.[4] Built to accommodate the local House of Assembly, it marked the granting of internal autonomy to elected local representatives in 1967. It is clearly modernist in its construction as are many of the institutional and commercial buildings of this era. However, with its central courtyard, as well as louvers and brise-soleil at the façade, it is also a fine example of Tropical Modernism. Continuing into the late 1980s, commercial building also tended towards a stripped down modernism, or a vernacular that continued the 'blouse and skirt' tradition. The original materials of the traditional style were often replaced with plastered concrete block, and color or veranda placement designated top and bottom.

ILLUSTRATION 3.8 WEST SQUARE STREET, CIRCA 1990

ILLUSTRATION 3.9 CENTRAL STREET, 2004

I have attempted to describe the end of the colonial era and emergence of postcolonial ideas in the Caribbean and St. Kitts-Nevis in particular. I have followed this with a discussion of developments in and contentions over the built environment of Basseterre in order to set the stage for an exploration of how issues of identity and identifications inform these conflicting priorities. The following section addresses questions of identity and its relationship to landscape and the built environment.

Identity, Culture, Landscape

Crick, Crack, Monkey by Merle Hodge is a cogent critique of many aspects of post-Independence Trinidadian Creole society. Creole in Trinidad refers to the mixed descendents of African and European inhabitants as opposed to the considerable Asian Indian community. The usage in Belize is similar. The main character is Cynthia/Tee whom we follow from early childhood through adolescence. Between the boisterous rural world of her Tantie who raised her and the color-class strivings of her Aunt Beatrice who takes her to live in 'town' for high school, Hodge shows the studious and intellectual Tee as genuinely conflicted. She locates hope for stepping outside these social tensions in Tee's grandmother Ma-Josephine, a market woman who lives in the bush, and in the values embodied in the landscape she inhabits.

The bush (emphasis mine) is characterized as fearful, originary, powerful, and backward; the perspective clearly varying with generation, class, and socialization as discussed by Abrahams in the chapter "Symbolic Landscapes and Expressive Events" and by Edgell in *Beka Lamb*. In both novels it becomes the location of hope, a source of liberatory power and is reinforced as a connection to ancestry. The bush was the place to which slaves escaped in many of the Caribbean territories. Here they built communities isolated from the plantation system of the lowlands, and outside the direct control of colonial and local authorities. Ma, the matriarch of the family in *Crick, Crack Monkey* resides in the forested hills and valleys of Pointe D'Espoir, the symbolically named 'Peak of Hope'. In this initial moment we are presented with the bush as "an enchanted country"[5] richly fertile, ancient and closely linked to the mythologies of the people which were retentions from Africa.

> . . . hills thickly covered with every conceivable kind of foliage, cool green darknesses, sudden little streams that must surely have been squabbling past in the days when Brar Anancy and Brar Leopard and all the others roamed the earth outsmarting each other. . . . We returned with our baskets full of oranges, mangoes, chennettes, Ma bent under a bunch of plantains that was more than half her size.[6]

This is also the only site in the novel where we see the transmission of oral culture. To confirm the sense of origin and ancestry associated with the montane forest landscape, Hodge creates an association between Tee and a specific ancestor, Ma-Josephine's "tall proud straight grandmother." (21) Ma asserts that Tee is her grandmother come back again. In keeping with her nationalist allegorical and cautionary project, Hodge at this point introduces a perilous moment in the development of Tee's consciousness, and by allegory that of the society as a whole: Ma cannot remember her grandmother's "true-true name." (21)

The representation of *the bush* (emphasis mine) as the site of the true soul and power of the people or nation is more subtly presented in Edgell's *Beka Lamb*. Edgell shows us the perceptions of this landscape as the location of inscrutable power through the legend of "Tataduhende," a story used to frighten children (138), and as the place to which one retreats in time of trouble (135). But, she also shows us the social devaluation of these wild areas as the place where the superstitious Black Caribs lived (66), and a signifier of traditions which must be left behind to gain social advantage (70). In both novels, the beach, which is also symbolically the edge before departure, is presented as the socially mobile place to vacation. In fact, choosing to vacation in "Sibun Bush" (70) is one of the markers she uses to show the nationalistic transformation of Beka and her mother Lilla away from bourgeois, Eurocentric aspirations.

Vacationing at *the shore* (emphasis mine) is clearly presented in both *Beka Lamb*, and *Crick, Crack Monkey* as a place of opportunity for social mobility. It is also presented as a place of pain and disillusionment. In *Beka Lamb*, the Lamb family vacations yearly at the caye, an island off the shore of Belize. Beka's family inhabited the space under the house of her father's boss, Mr. Blanco, demonstrating the multiple layers of social relations. The significance of "the house bottom" is noted a number of times in the novel as the place where washerwomen worked.[7] It is invoked by Beka's grandmother for negative reinforcement to encourage her to study. Edgell also points out that although they vacationed in such close proximity, the Blanco and Lamb children never met. It is also at the shore that Beka's best friend Toycie engages in a relationship that eventually costs her sanity and her life. Edgell juxtaposes her return from a secret mignight tryst with the appearance of deadly man-o-war jellyfish along the beach. Paradoxically it is Beka, in her role as allegory for the nation that we see threatened by the jellyfish.

> . . . Toycie yelled, 'Watch you foot, Beka! Man-o-war!' Beka leaped to sandy ground, her flesh prickling as she saw the transparent, purple coloured sac, bloated with poison, half-covered by seaweed only a short distance from where her foot had been. . . . 'They're all along the beach today,' she said.[8]

Both novelists create strong identifications with aspects of the natural and cultivated landscape but not with the city or town. In *Crick, Crack Monkey*, the town is presented as a site of alienation and oppression. Tee's experiences are of constant rejection because of her village upbringing and the dark color of her skin. Her Aunt Beatrice's insistence on her association with the 'right people' (emphasis mine) leads her to internalize and resent her apparent "niggery-ness" (85). Edgell, in contrast, engages the cultivated landscape in her allegorical project but presents no internal or formative experiences relating to the urban landscape as she does with the bush and the shore. She takes us rather dispassionately on a Sunday walk through the typical elements of a city—the museum, Government house, the cathedral, the barracks, the 'crazy-house', the segregated clubs.

The idea of identification with the natural and/ or cultivated landscape as an essential element of identity particularly *national* identity is central to many discourses of nationalism.[9] In discussions regarding design, it is often presented as a counterpoint to architectural 'styles' or methods of working which come to be seen as alien even if they were previously established as hegemonic and 'national' or 'universal'. The Picturesque movement in nineteenth century England is an excellent example of this process. The 'Picturesque' developed from an assertion of naturalized irregularity in the landscape as an exemplification of national identity. This was from identity and indigenized culture. Much of the experience positioned in opposition to the neoclassical styles in Architecture and baroque landscape planning which a growing segment of the design, intellectual, and political circles felt were alien impositions inappropriate to the culture and environment of England. In this case the discourse on landscape was also related to anti-monarchical and parliamentary movements.[10]

Edgell and Hodge create the forest or 'bush' as a place internal to a liberated postcolonial identity while the shore is framed as an exterior, threatening space. The town or 'road' is presented as an alien and dangerous space, separate of the shore and the town is shown as shaped by interactions with the elite of society, typically white or 'light-skinned' families. Thus indirectly, the formal built environment is seen as part and parcel of elite, expatriate culture. These multiple formations of identity and aspiration reveal a distinct lack of connection, even an antipathy to the historical urban environment. This formulation is not unique. Any number of utopian movements have decried 'the city' as diseased and corrupted, and have elevated the countryside as closer to the 'spirit' of the nation. This was true of the Heimatschutz discourse (Otto 1983) in early twentieth-century Germany which opposed 'Zivilisation' in favor of 'Kultur' (Herf 1984). It was also true of the social movements in the early nineteenth century in the United States which advocated slum clearing and re-planning of the city. What we have in the work of these Caribbean writers is somewhat different. It is a profound disconnect from colonial society and the urban environment created for the planters, craftsmen and merchants. They seek to provide a grounding for emerging nations in the soil of the land *to which they are now native* – as we referenced at the beginning of this paper in discussing the transplanted, and modern versus primordial character of Caribbean nations. They also seek to advocate a direction for development, which does not reify either the hierarchies of class and color or their associated landscapes, which pervade Caribbean society.

Typology and Fantasy

In contrast to these assertions, there is a completely different aspect of identity production in operation in downtown Basseterre. In the early 1990s, the Beautiful Basseterre Committee of the Chamber of Industry and Commerce (CIC) spearheaded an initiative to promote "traditional style on a scale unequalled regionally". A historic zone was proposed for downtown Basseterre and owners of "existing incompatible buildings within the zone" were encouraged to "consider changes that will make them more harmonious with their traditional surroundings" (Anonymous 1985). At this time, design guidelines intended to cover renovation and new construction were also commissioned for the area.

Heritage tourism seems to have been an important consideration in undertaking the project. Protecting a commodifiable expression of identity in the built environment has been seen to motivate influential business groups who stand to benefit directly from the attraction of foreign tourists to the city. The nomenclature "Beautiful Basseterre" instead of "Historic Basseterre" is telling of the motivations, goals, and intended results of the committee's activities. This type of heritage discourse is less concerned with the preservation of historical artifacts than with creation of a sense of place *imagined* to have been historically authentic. To quote the committee's manifesto:

> It is a satisfying pleasure to slowly meander from one area of the city to another. One is continuously reminded of a bygone era . . . perhaps less frantic, perhaps more caring and certainly more beautiful than most comparable cities of today. (Anonymous 1985)

This discourse is particularly curious in a context where 95% of the population gained the franchise only 50 years ago, and lacked significant economic opportunity as little as 80 years ago. This narrative of a 'bygone era', however, is common to postmodern discourses, which seek to negate the theoretical 'alienation' of modernity. As is typical in the discourse of 'tradition', the nostalgia invoked does not refer to a particular historical moment or era, but to a sort of generalized vision of an idealized past.

In the case of downtown Basseterre, the 'sense of place' produced by the new construction is one that is more formal and ornate than the adjacent historical buildings would suggest the city has ever been. As photographed by a member of London's Georgian Group on behalf of the colonial office in 1951 (Acworth 1951), the typical building type consisted of a stone ground floor and a simple wooden upper floor with a hip roof. Quoining around the windows and doors was common, but only at the ground floor. Wooden shutters were employed at both doors and windows often without glazing behind.

ILLUSTRATION 3.10 PHOTOGRAPH BY ACWORTH CIRCA 1951

The renovations of the Kassab building into the home of Court's, a regional household goods chain, and the renovation of several buildings owned by the Ram's corporation are key examples of what the Beautiful Basseterre Committee terms 'traditional style recoveries.' The historical typologies of Basseterre are often absent or warped in these 'recoveries.' The appeal is to a generic idea of 'tradition' and not the specific historical realities of Basseterre.

Disjunctions and Deformations 153

ILLUSTRATION 3.11 KASSAB AND RAM'S BEFORE RECOVERY

ILLUSTRATION 3.12 KASSAB AND RAM'S AFTER RECOVERY

Interestingly, Government support for the "Beautiful Basseterre" project has been slow to materialize. A historic zone has not been officially declared, and design review for new construction and remodels has not been instituted. However, with the buy-in of local merchants the 'traditionalizing' of Basseterre proceeds apace. Additionally, the first public sector projects in the post-Independence era have taken on a neo-traditional, postmodern style. This can be attributed to heavy pressure from the Chamber of Industry and Commerce and the St. Christopher

Heritage Society. The first such project was the renovation and expansion of Government Headquarters.

As noted earlier the original Government Headquarters building (GHQ) completed in 1965 was built to accommodate the local House of Assembly, and marked the granting of internal autonomy to elected local representatives in 1967. Originally a cogent example of Tropical Modernism, the design featured a central courtyard with a water feature to encourage passive cooling. The use of louvered windows and a shallow cross-section promoted cross-ventilation, and the brise-soleil at the façade provided sun shading to limit solar heat gain in the absence of air-conditioning. The new design of the building partakes in the narrative of tradition, but introduces elements and proportions—such as the medallion at the parapet, and discrete rather than continuous balconies—which are alien to the historical architecture of the island.

ILLUSTRATION 3.13 GOVERNMENT HEADQUARTERS: BEFORE RECOVERY

ILLUSTRATION 3.14 GOVERNMENT HEADQUARTERS: AFTER RECOVERY

Such nostalgia fantasies of a 'better time' reflect an anxiety about the post-colonial future which manifests in the desire to re-validate colonial icons. These imperial returns at the very moment of formal independence have functioned to allow the designation of early-colonial buildings and un-interrogated signifiers of imperial style as 'heritage', while late colonial often modernist buildings, even those that marked significant developments in the nation's path to state-hood are devalued.

Post-colonial Anxieties and Imperial Nostalgias

In *Edge of Empire: Postcolonialism and the City*, Jane M. Jacobs discusses the imperial nostalgias which guided development in the City of London in the late 1980s. She states that these sprouted from anxieties over the loss of empire, and potential loss of pre-eminence in the global financial sector. The resulting need to reaffirm an identity of London as the heart of empire was the generator of townscape conservation interests. I suggest that a similar imperial nostalgia is at work in Basseterre. Key figures in the current development trend in Basseterre are expatriates from other parts of the empire. The end of Empire also has the potential to produce anxiety in the merchant class of St. Kitts-Nevis who, are largely of European, Middle-Eastern and Asian extraction, as the nation begins to attempt to define its identity, often in primarily ethnic and afrocentric terms. Jacobs notes that

Imperialism lingers in the present . . . as a trace . . . a potent memory which can shape trajectories of progress, drive nostalgic returns and establish the structures of difference through which racialized struggles over territory operate.[11]

(De)formations

Heritage includes not just physical artifacts, but also the experiences and events that surround the artifacts, and experiences that may not be clearly connected to artifacts at all. Pierre Nora discusses these in terms of 'lieu de memoire' and 'milieu de memoire' that is to say realms and environments of memory. These concepts encompass both physically represented collective memories and those that form intangible cultural environments. He asserts that representation often replaces lived experiences which are in danger of fading into the past. From my viewpoint the 'recovery' of the Government Headquarters building represents a lack of recognition of an important national lieu de memoire. My second example is that of an unbuilt milieu de memoire seeking representation.

The Middle Passage Memorial project was a Caribbean-wide project initiated in the late 1990s. The goal was to place an identical memorial to the experience of slavery in each nation and territory of the Caribbean region. Specifically the memorial seeks to commemorate the harrowing "Middle Passage", leg in the 'triangle trade' between Europe, Africa, and the Americas on which slaves were transported from Africa to the Americas. It has been estimated that one-third of captives taken from West Africa did not survive the Atlantic crossing. These fledgling attempts to memorialize the painful history of the trans-Atlantic slave trade within the precincts of the Capital City have come into direct conflict with conservation interests. The discussions around the placement of the Middle Passage memorial reveal a tendency towards the strategy of erasure and re-inscription of meaning. The site most strongly proposed and most discussed for the placement of the memorial has been Independence Square. However, the proposal was not to place the new intervention within the boundaries of the square, creating its own precinct, but to place it within the central formal garden, *taking the place of* the existing fountain. This was an attempt to *claim the symbolic center* for a foundational national experience. The contentious public debate has to date resulted only in the vandalism of the fountain by 'persons unknown', and a stalemate which precludes the realization of the commemorative precinct.

ILLUSTRATION 3.15 FOUNTAIN AT INDEPENDENCE SQUARE

ILLUSTRATION 3.16 FOUNTAIN AFTER BEING VANDALIZED

The committee formed to realize the project included government representatives, representatives from the St. Christopher Heritage Society as well as prominent private citizens. However, opposition to this proposal has come from both the Heritage Society and the Beautiful Basseterre Committee on the grounds that the fountain was installed to commemorate the initial provision of plumbing to Basseterre in the mid-twentieth-century. The apparent clash of 'heritage' and 'national' interests has repeated itself in multiple episodes. In the current situation, national space, whether for bureaucratic or commemorative purposes, must be constantly fought for and negotiated within Basseterre. This would seem to be a no-win situation in which the disposition of a site hinges on the relative significance of particular histories as perceived by different interest groups.

In this context, how do we achieve recognition for sites connected to significant national histories and ensure that the thrust for conservation and traditional style replication also allows room for expressions of emerging national identities and commemorative functions? How do we ensure that this neo-traditional thrust does not sacrifice the distinctive history of Basseterre for the image of a traditional colonial city? In Basseterre we are witnessing what happens when international preservation and heritage discourses impact a society where memory landscapes are not a primary form of memorial, and when these are post-colonies asked to valorize as "national heritage" the buildings and spaces which illustrate the dominance of former colonizers. The result is that what is seen in the built landscape and read as local identity becomes contentious. But the contestation here is between the seen artifact and the unseen but remembered history, between the built and *unbuilt* environments.

Conclusion

Postcolonial liberatory strands pervade Caribbean literary and artistic production. However, Architecture is not yet clearly a part of this expressive regime. In fact neo-colonial influences often seem to operate in the realm of the built environment. We have seen that these are driven by Post-colonial anxieties of the merchant classes, as well as the nostalgia aspects of Heritage tourism. In Basseterre, as elsewhere, this has resulted in commodification of the built environment for external consumption. In Architectural History public buildings and monuments are often deemed to reflect the experiences, identity, and aspiration of nations. The current collection of revamped and new structures in Basseterre seem to primarily reflect the hegemony of the globalized discourses, largely uninflected to reveal local particularity of experience and history. However, recent contestations over space make clear an underlying instinct in the public sector to resist the hegemony of postmodern 'heritage' discourse. Conversely, the dubious results also betray a current lack of direction and clarity in post-colonial thinking about the symbolic role of the built environment and individual artifacts in the self-definition of the nation moving forward.

Bibliography

Abrahams, Roger D. *The Man-of-Words in the West Indies: Performance and the Emergence of Creole Culture.* Baltimore: Johns Hopkins University Press, 1983.

Acworth, A. W. *Buildings of Architectural or Historic Interest in the British West Indies; a Report with Proposals as to the Best Means of Protecting Them from Damage or Destruction (Otherwise Than by Acts of God).* London: H.M. Stationery Off, 1951.

Anonymous. *Robert Llewellyn Bradshaw 1916 – 1978.* (Funeral Program). 1978.

Anonymous. *Chamber of Industry and Commerce, Beautiful Basseterre Committee Manifesto.* (Unpublished Manuscript), circa 1985.

Edgell, Zee. *Beka Lamb.* London: Heinemann, 1982.

Herf, Jeffrey. *Reactionary Modernism: Technology, Culture and Politics in Weimar and the Third Reich.* Cambridge, UK: Cambridge University Press, 1984.

Hodge, Merle. *Crick Crack, Monkey.* London: Heinemann, 1981.

Holston, James. *The Modernist City: An Anthropological Critique of Brasília.* Chicago: University of Chicago Press, 1989.

Inniss, Probyn. *Historic Basseterre: The Story of Its Growth.* Basseterre: P. Inniss, 1979.

—. *Whither Bound, St. Kitts-Nevis?* S.l.: s.n., 1983.

—. *Historic Basseterre: The Story of a West Indian Town.* Basseterre: P. Inniss, 1985.

Jacobs, Jane M. *Edge of Empire: Postcolonialism and the City.* London; New York: Routledge, 1996.

Nora, Pierre, and Lawrence D. Kritzman. *Realms of Memory: Rethinking the French Past.* European Perspectives. English-language ed. 3 vols. New York: Columbia University Press, 1996.

Olaniyan, Tejumola. "Derek Walcott: Liminal Spaces/ Substantive Histories." In *Caribbean Romances: the Politics of Regional Representation,* edited by Belinda Edmondson. Charlottesville and London, University Press of Virginia, 1999.

Otto, Christian F. "Modern Environment and Historical Continuity: The Heimatschutz Discourse in Germany." In *Art Journal* 43 (1983): 148-157.

Puri, Shalini. "Canonized Hybridities, Resistant Hybridities: Chutney Soca, Carnival, and the Politics of Nationalism." In *Caribbean Romances: the Politics of Regional Representation,* edited by Belinda

Edmondson. Charlottesville and London, University Press of Virginia, 1999.

Roy, Ananya. "The Gentleman's City". In *Urban Informality: Transnational Perspectives*, edited by Nezar AlSayyad and Ananya Roy. New York: Lexington, 2003.

Smith, Anthony D. *The Ethnic Origins of Nations.* Oxford, UK and New York, NY: B. Blackwell, 1987.

Tzonis, Alexander, and Liane Lefaivre. "Critical Regionalism." In *Critical Regionalism: the Pomona Meeting: Proceedings,* edited by Spyros Amourgis. Pomona, Calif: College of Environmental Design California State Polytechnic University. xii, 336. 1991.

Notes

[1] Robert Llewellyn Bradshaw, Premier of the Associated State of St. Christopher-Nevis-Anguilla, Statehood Day Address 1974, quoted in Anonymous 1976, 3.

[2] Dr Eric Williams, First Prime Minister of Trinidad and Tobago, quoted in Puri 1992, 16.

[3] Olaniyan, "Derek Walcott: Liminal Spaces/ Substantive Histories," 199.

[4] Innis, 58.

[5] Hodge, *Crick Crack, Monkey* 16.

[6] Ibid.

[7] Edgell, *Beka Lamb,* 2.

[8] Ibid., 49-50.

[9] Smith, *The Ethnic Origins of Nations*, 183-90.

[10] Alexander Tzonis and and Liane Lefaivre, "Critical Regionalism," 6-7.

[11] Jacobs, *Edge of Empire: Postcolonialism and the City,* 158.

STAGING TRANSCULTURATION: BORDER CROSSINGS IN JOSEFINA BÁEZ'S PERFORMANCE TEXTS

LIAMAR DURÁN ALMARZA

In his article, "Y con ustedes, Josefina Báez, de La Romana al infinito," Miguel D. Mena states that, in order to get to know the Dominican Republic "in its most intense borders" one must travel to New York.[1] This idea is also present in Yolanda Martínez-San Miguel's *Caribe Two Ways: Cultura de la migración en el Caribe insular hispánico,* where she defends that, given the intensity and continuity of migrations between the Caribbean and New York, it is not surprising that Manuel Ramos Otero, the nuyorican poet, identifies the city as part of the Caribbean archipelago.[2] For her, New York represents a "symbolic, economic and geographic extension of the Hispanic Caribbean reconfiguring traditional notions of classical insular experience"[3] thus revealing itself as one part of the Caribbean where transnational and multiethnic communities emerge only to begin a problematic dialogue with celebratory discourses on both US multiculturalism and narrow conceptions of Caribbeanness. In her view, despite the fact that diasporic communities make clear the limitations of national boundaries, these borderlines also offer the possibility of new conceptualizations of official discourses on nationality, ethnicity and culture.[4] In this way, "the limit stops being . . . a site of resistance and entrenchment to become that space where the constitutive heterogeneity of a community or a nation is recognized" (My translation).[5]

Similarly, Homi K. Bhabha states in his celebrated collection *The Location of Culture* that in the process of translation between cultural systems there emerge "interstitial spaces" where those practices that resist acculturation exist.[6] It is in those "contact zones," borrowing Mary Louise Pratt's terminology,[7] that hybrid patterns of cultural identity and signification occur, and where cultural difference is constructed and negotiated. In Bhabha's words, it is in these in-between spaces that "the intersubjective and collective experience of *nationess*, community interest, or cultural value are negotiated."[8]

Beatriz J. Rizk, who in her article "El tercer espacio: el arte del performance en tres dramaturgas latinas de Estados Unidos" explores the artistic production of various Latina performers in the US, points out that these "Third Spaces," as Bhabha calls them, have been explored by many Latino and Latina researchers, who have identified them as the "geopolitical spaces" emerging in those places where borders, whether geographical, cultural or identitarian, are being negotiated.[9] In her view, these metaphorical borders come into being in the space between hegemonic culture and marginality, and, like Bhabha and Martínez-San Miguel, she defends that they usually develop into alternative sites for the appropriation and reformulation of elements from the dominant culture that go "beyond the assimilationist's dream, or the racist's nightmare, of a 'full transmissal of subject-matter,' and towards an encounter with the ambivalent process of splitting and hybridity that marks the identification with culture's difference."[10]

The hybridity that characterizes those interstices is presented as a powerful alternative to monolithic conceptions of cultures and societies, and its capacity to resist homogenizing discourses has been pointed out by many, from various disciplines and perspectives. One of the most recognized approaches is that of Chicana author Gloria Anzaldúa, who in her *Borderlands/La Frontera* explores the means through which what she calls "the new mestiza"[11] (and by extension, all Latinas/os) negotiate and shift among different cultural systems in order to come to terms with their personal and collective identity. For Anzaldúa,

> cradled in one culture, sandwiched between two cultures, straddling all three cultures and their value systems, la *mestiza* undergoes a struggle of flesh, a struggle of borders, an inner war. Like all people, we perceive the version of reality that our culture communicates. Like others having or living in more than one culture, we get multiple, often opposing messages. The coming together of two self-consistent but habitually incompatible frames of reference causes *un choque*, a cultural collision.[12]

These *choques* or cultural collisions are explicitly explored in the works of Dominican-American performer Josefina Báez, who locates her artistic production in the interstitial spaces that these borderlands represent.

In *Dominicanish*, Josefina Báez, born in La Romana but who has lived in New York for decades, brings together diverse cultural forms to illustrate the complexity of Dominican experiences in the diaspora. Both the text and performance challenge traditional binary conceptions of linguistic, gender and ethnic practices creating a unique "Third Space" in which a multiplicity of borders are crossed and transgressed once and again in order to contest narrow cultural and identitarian definitions.

At this multi-dimensional third space Báez explores some of the issues that migrant communities visit and revisit in the process of redefining personal and collective identity. In this sense, the concepts of space and place themselves are of particular importance given the fact that migrants must always reconfigure their sense of geographic space and belonging, something that in many cases implies getting used to inhabiting those metaphoric borders that are situated "neither here nor there." As Angela Bammer states, for these communities, "home" becomes a hybrid location at the "imaginary point where here and there . . . are momentarily grounded" then situated "*both* here *and* there."[13]

In order to recreate this feeling, Claudio Mir, the theatrical director of the performance explains that the actions in *Dominicanish* "take place in no particular place, not a street, not a house, not a courtroom. It is as if Josefina is suspended in an undefined place, a place that lets you travel instantly between distant points."[14] However, this place that for Mir is "undefined" has found its location in Báez's creative universe: for her and her protagonist, "Home is where theater is."[15] In this sense, the stage becomes "a site of resistance inscribed in the body of the performer and the performative space where the theater also functions as a border, a space not here or there, but rather a neither nor location."[16]

At this interstice "La Romana, New York, India, the suspended space between here and there, now and then" (My translation)[17] collide and clash to explore "the changing geographies of the city and the transcultural experience of globality, in order to emerge renewed and to perform Dominican identity in movement."[18]

Those physical and geographical borders are not the only limits consciously trespassed and deconstructed, and, in order to fully understand the different dimensions that the text explores, we consider, as Sophie Mariñez does,[19] that *Dominicanish* must be analyzed from different perspectives to account for its complexity.

A first approach from a literary point of view will reveal one more interstice where the piece is situated: defined as a "performance text," this work transcends traditional literary genres blending together poetry, popular culture slogans, references to Indian philosophy and song lyrics, among others. Furthermore, in an attempt to incorporate some of the visual magic of the stage into the printed edition of *Dominicanish*, a photographic animation presenting the artist performing kachipudi movements that is set in motion each time the pages of the book are turned has been included. The disruption of the stillness of the written text creates a textual and visual "pastiche,"[20] a hybrid that illustrates more accurately the fragmented lives of migrant communities.

This fragmentation and hybridization of forms and genres is also to be found in the underlying cultural aspects that the text/performance brings to the fore. In that sense, the play is full of references to the various layers that contribute to the formation of the narrator's personal identity. In regards to ethnicity, for instance, by defining herself as a "Dominican York," she positions herself in opposition to the official discourse on Dominicanness in the Dominican Republic where, as Silvio Torres-Saillant explains,

> dominican-yorkers exist . . . as subalterns who occupy the lowest position in the moral order. . . . Thus, one cannot proudly assume a dominican-york identity. . . . without positioning as adversary with regards to that nemesis of ours that Creole middle-class represents. To speak as a dominican-york involves the acknowledgment of an intrinsic marginality. It implies recognizing oneself as the voice of alterity (My translation).[21]

Paradoxically, that intrinsic marginality that Torres-Saillant refers to situates the narrator in the margins not only of Dominicaness but also in those of Americaness, since, as Yolanda Martínez-San Miguel points out, --"Dominicanyorkers become "the other," in the context of both the US and the island."[22] Despite the adverse circumstances, Báez chooses to look at the bright side and so she states in her preface to *Dominicanish*:

> I am a Dominican York. And as such I am exposed to endless constant and varying stimuli. They enrich my personal culture in unexpected ways. The text, as well as the stage performance of Dominicanish illustrates the creation and state of my personal universe (translated by Lantigua).[23]

Taking as a starting point this personal universe, Báez develops a piece in which traditional notions of Dominicanness are transformed into what she calls *dominicanish,* a term she coins to denote both her personal version of being a Dominican in New York ("not quite Dominican") and her particular idiolect of Spanglish.

When asked about her work, she insists that her art is an excuse for the exercise of her spirituality, which relies on the teachings of Advaita Vedanta philosophy, positioning herself explicitly against the prevalent Catholicism on the island. Advaita Vedanta's non-dualistic understanding of reality seems to be very much in line with Báez's experiences as a migrant who deals with multiple cultural traditions, and who, as a transcultural subject has to reconfigure her sense of personal identity moving beyond the logic of binary oppositions, and generating "a multiplicity of trinities that create unexpected bonds."[24]

In *Dominicanish*, we witness the process of growth of a little migrant girl into an adult woman as she comes to terms with her ethnic and linguistic identity as a New Yorker of Dominican origin, a path in which symbols and languages are constantly reformulated and appropriated to account for the painful metamorphosis that migrants suffer when facing a new reality.

The English language is one of the first sources of conflict for the little girl upon her arrival in New York City, as she expresses at the very beginning of the play, when she says:

> I thought I would never learn English.
> No way I will not put my mouth like that
> No way jamás ni never no way
> **Gosh** to pronounce one little phrase one must
> Become another person with the mouth all
> twisted Yo no voy a poner la boca así como
> un guante.[25]

However, as time goes by and she becomes more fluent in the language and more knowledgeable of the society in which she lives, she finds in the music and lyrics of The Isley Brothers the tools she needs to reconstruct her alienated identity:

> In a cloud of smoke I found my teachers.
> In an LP jacket I found my teachers
> . . .
>
> Los hermanos Isley
> The Isley Brothers
> . . .
>
> Repeat after them.[26]

This move allows her to renegotiate at the same time her ethnic, linguistic and racial identity, navigating away from the official Dominican discourse that denies the African roots of Quisqueyan population. As Aida Heredia puts it,

> the Dominican Republic suffers from a politics of social and cultural identity informed by a concept of nationalism that is rooted in the supposed ideal of a Spanish origin. With this self-conception of the Dominican

people as a repository of the ideal of the Spanish past, the classes which exercise economic, intellectual and political power on this Caribbean island have persuaded the Dominican majority that Dominicans do not have links, in any profound sense, with the peoples of Africa brought to the island as exploited or unpaid labour.[27]

In contrast, in *Dominicanish*, the narrator celebrates her Africanness listening to the songs of soul and jazz music and vindicating her black roots by asserting, "Con afro black is beautiful. Black is a color. Black is my color"[28] while at the same time signaling her bonds with other African-American communities in the US. By doing so, she is not only moving away from the dominant Dominican discourse on race but also from one of the main racial ideologies in the construction of "latinidad" that, as Laó-Montés explains, "defines Latinos as a third race, as it were, in between black and white."[29] This assumption, based on the notion of 'mestizaje' and racial hybridism, was developed in nineteenth century Latin American nationalist thought in an attempt to distance themselves from the black/white hierarchy that dominates Western racial ideology. However, since "Latinos/as" as "mestizos/as" are located in a subordinate position in relation to 'whites' but above the category of 'blacks,' the colonial hierarchy is in fact being reproduced. Moreover, this discursive framework, that has become dominant in Latin American and Latino/a identitarian discourses, contributes to the creation of an imagined community based on a fictitious ethnicity that homogenizes Latinas/os in racial terms and, as a result, brings about the invisibilization of the Afro-Latino community.

Conversely, the narrative voice in *Dominicanish* finds her agency as a black Dominican-American woman by reading and listening to the songs of Billie Holliday and The Isley Brothers:

> Repeat after them
> my teachers the Isley Brothers
> Repeated a whisper
> whispered a little louder
> Sing a song sang a song
> sang a whisper
> . . .
>
> Growing smooth soft hard Growing
> hard Sweet memory growing soft
> . . .
>
> Last Saturday my teachers sang in Soul Train

Now I don't care how my mouth look I like
what I'm saying.[30]

The references to popular culture as the source of her knowledge also function as an indication of her working-class consciousness, as it is in the lyrics of the jazz and blues songs that she learns English and not in the education she receives in school:

> SAT scores doubled but in no university catalog
> I found my teachers: The Isley Brothers.
> I did no see a class, department,
> major, minor, sororities, fraternities
> *groovin' with soul.*[31]

Later in the text, she affirms, in the same light:

> Higher education took me to places of pain and
> pleasure History in black and white
> Distinguished teachers: Pearl Bailey, Earth
> Fantasy, Wind September, Reasons and Fire,
> Ella Fitzgerald, Louis Armstrong and the dearest
> of all, my favorite Ms. Billie Holiday.[32]

Her class consciousness is also revealed in the extracts from the Panchatantra[33] that she includes in the performance-text. This awareness can be seen in the following passage where she reflects not only on the existence of different social classes in society—and the often overlooked interdependency among them—but also on the fate of lower class communities and individuals in a globalized world:

> But then again,
> Kings and servants depend on
> each other
> There can be no king without a servant
> And no servant without a king
>   . . .
>
> But then again, how can servants be well?
> It is said that the poor, the sick, the dreamers
> and the fools always go into exile.
> *Poor, sick, dreamers and fools exile.*[34]

And it is in exile in the urban, working-class New York neighborhood of Washington Heights, the Dominican enclave par excellence in the city, where she retrieves those components of her Dominican self that were obliterated when she started her formal education. It is important to note that, as Alberto Sandoval-Sánchez and Nancy Saporta-Sternbach point out, elementary education plays a very important role in the formation of transcultural identities in the U.S. since, in most cases, schooling "involves the imposition of English and the subsequent erasure of ethnic, ancestral values. For some Latina students, their first contact with English is when they enter the public school system, which operates, in most cases, as an instrument of the dominant culture."[35]

The community and *el barrio* function in this context as a powerful device to counteract the pressure of compulsory assimilation into mainstream culture. As Jorge Duany notes in his *Quisqueya on the Hudson: The Transnational Identity of Dominicans in Washington Heights*,

> Washington Heights serves as an intermediary point of settlement, a place where Dominicans can speak Spanish, meet fellow Dominicans, attend mass in Spanish, shop in *bodegas*, listen to *merengue*, and remain encapsulated within Hispanic culture.[36]

It is when she walks through the streets of the *barrio* that our narrator feels confident again to express herself in Spanish and to incorporate references to the Latino subculture into her discourse:

> Suerte que la 107 se arrulla con Pacheco[37]
> Pacheco tumbao[38] añejo
> Pacheco flauta   Pacheco su nuevo tumbao el
> maestro el artista Tremendo Cache
> compartido en cruz[39]
> Juntos de nuevo   como al detalle   Tres de Café y
> dos de azúcar[40] Con el swing del tumbao y
> reculando como Ciguapa[41]. [42]

However, despite celebrating her Dominican heritage and culture, she does not embrace these traditions without questioning them. In her "Letanía de la decencia," one of the poems that serves as source for the performance text, she challenges some of the assumptions and beliefs that shape women's roles and acceptable behavior in the Dominican and Latino/a society, thus incorporating gender in her poetic analysis of the formation of transcultural identities:

> *Me chulié en el hall*
> Metí mano en el rufo
> Craqueo chicle como Shameka Brown

Hablo como Boricua
Y me peino como Morena
...

Me junto con la muchacha que salió preñá
Salgo con mi ex
Hablo con el muchacho que estaba preso.[43]

Exile and migration have positively impacted the protagonist since she is now able to recognize that racism and sexism underlie some of the popular beliefs in the Dominican Republic. As many other migrants, she experiences what Michel Pêcheux calls "disidentification"[44] with their culture of origin allowing her to reconstruct her alienated identity free of learned prejudices. As Sandoval-Sánchez and Saporta-Sternbarch write,

> For those who inhabit the margin or border—spiritually, physically, or metaphysically—disidentification signifies flexibility, straddling, oscillation, and liminality in a constant juggling of identities as a "survival strategy" [Muñoz 1999: 5] within the dislocations and contradictions of the subjects' cultural presence.[45]

Towards the end of the text the narrator is ready to acknowledge her transformation and it is then when she affirms:

Now I am another person
Mouth twisted
Guiri[46] guiri on dreams
Guiri guiri business
Even laughing
Laughing in Dominicanish
There is no guarantee
Ni aquí ni allá
Not even with your guiri guiri papers.[47]

One of the most interesting aspects of the play is perhaps that, as Silvio Torres-Saillant states, Báez's *Dominicanish* is an important intervention in the consideration of the cultural experiences of Dominican diasporic communities. For him, the most relevant feature of *Dominicanish* is that "it offers an open ontological frame" where everything that is present in the life of migrant communities can be considered to take part in the formation of Dominican nationhood in and outside the island.[48] In his "Frontispiece" to the *Dominicanish* he affirms that the play "resists and combats rigid definitions of culture"[49] evoking this resistance "lyrically in a language stemming hybridity from the clash and the fusion of English and Spanish."[50]

Interestingly, Sandoval-Sánchez and Saporta-Sternbach in their analysis of Latina solo performances in the US also consider hybridity as one of the characteristics of the genre. From this perspective, Báez's plays can be inscribed in two different but related traditions: that of Latina Theater in the US and that of Dominican artists in the diaspora. One of the aspects in which both traditions conflate, is in the presence of transcultural subjects[51] who, as the protagonist in Dominicanish "claim their own agency in all its hybridity."[52] This hybridity, as the authors of *Stages of Life* observe, should not be taken as a given, but rather as something that "is constructed as a process whereby protagonists (and audiences) problematize the multiple strands of their identity simultaneously."[53]

As it has been argued throughout this paper, Báez vindicates in her *Dominicanish* those interstitial spaces—borders—where diasporic communities dwell and reconfigure their fragmented sense of self as spaces for aesthetic creation and alternative identitarian definitions. Despite the fact that, as Báez points out, "'there is not guarantee' neither here nor there,"[54] (My translation) implying that the construction of one's subjectivity is never a complete process but "always on the way to the home of constancy,"[55] (My translation) the energy she transmits in her performance represents a song of hope for all those who, as the protagonist in the text, must negotiate their lives "chewing English and spitting Spanish."[56]

Bibliography

Anzaldúa, Gloria. *Borderlands/La Frontera*. San Francisco: Aunt Lute Books, 1999.
Báez, Josefina. *Dominicanish*. New York: Ombe, 2000.
—. Personal Interview. 22 February 2007.
Bhabha, Homi K. *The Location of Culture*. London: Routledge, 1994.
Duany, Jorge. *Quisqueya on the Hudson: the Transnational Identity of Dominicans in Washington Heights*. New York: The CUNY Dominican Studies Institute, 1994.
Heredia, Aida. "The Journey Inward: Sherezada Vicioso's 'Un extraño ulular de voces traía el viento'". In *Daughters of the Diaspora. Afra-Hispanic Writers*, edited by Miriam de Costa-Williams. Kingston and Miami: Ian Randle Publishers, 2003
Lantigua, Juleyka. "Review of *Dominicanish*. A Performance Text, by Josefina Báez". *Caribbean Studies Newsletter* 28:2 (2002):6.

Laó Montes, Agustín. "Introduction. Mambo Montage: The Latinization of New York City". In *Mambo Montage. The Latinization of New York*, edited by Agustín Laó-Montes and Arlene Dávila. New York: Columbia University Press, 2001.

Mariñez, Sophie. "*Dominicanish*, de Josefina Báez: la translocalización de los símbolos". *Agulha. Revista de Cultura.* http://www.revista.agulha.nom.br/ag21baez.htm (accessed February 13, 2007).

Martínez-San Miguel, Yolanda. *Caribe Two Ways: Cultura de la migración en el Caribe insular hispánico*. San Juan: Ediciones Callejón, 2003.

Mena, Miguel D. "Y con ustedes, Josefina Báez, de La Romana al infinito". Ediciones del Cielonaranja, http://www.cielonaranja.com/menajosefinabaez.htm (accessed March 8, 2007).

Muamba Tujibikile, Pedro. *Quinientos años: hacia un desencubrimiento de la identidad caribeña*. Santo Domingo: CEDEE, 1991.

Pêcheux, Michel. *Language, Semantics, and Ideology*. Translated by Harbans Nagpal. New York: St. Martin's Press, 1982.

Pratt, Marie Louise. "Arts of the Contact Zone". *Ways of Reading.* http://www.nwe.ufl.edu/~stripp/2504/pratt.html (accessed April 3, 2007)

Rivera-Servera, Ramón. "A Dominican York in Andhra." In *Caribbean Dance From Abakuá to Zouk. How Movement Shapes Identity*, edited by Susanna Sloat, 152-164. Gainsville, Fl.: University Press of Florida, 2002.

Rizk, Beatriz J. "El tercer espacio: el arte del performance en tres dramaturgas latinas de Estados Unidos." Citru.doc: cuadernos de investigación teatral. México: CONACULTA, INBA, Centro Nacional de Investigación Teatral Rodolfo Usigli-CITRU, Vol. 1 (2005): 84-93.

Rodríguez, Néstor E. *Escrituras de desencuentro en la República Dominicana*. México DF: Siglo XXI Editores, 2005.

Sandoval-Sánchez, Alberto and Nancy Saporta-Sternbach. *Stages of Life. Transcultural Performance and Identity in U.S. Latina Theater.* Tucson: University of Arizona Press, 2001.

Torres-Saillant, Silvio. *El retorno de las yolas. Ensayos sobre diáspora, democracia y dominicanidad*. Santo Domingo: Ediciones Librería Trinitaria, 1999

——. Frontispiece to *Dominicanish,* by Josefina Báez, 13-14. New York: Ombe, 2000.

——. "No es lo mismo ni se escribe igual: la diversidad en lo dominicano."

Desde la Orilla: hacia una nacionalidad sin desalojos. Ed. Torres-Sailllant et al. Santo Domingo: Ediciones Librería Trinitaria, 2004: 17-46.

Notes

[1] Miguel D. Mena, "Y con ustedes, Josefina Báez, de La Romana al infinito". Ediciones del Cielonaranja, http://www.cielonaranja.com/menajosefinabaez.htm.
[2] Yolanda Martínez-San Miguel, *Caribe Two Ways: Cultura de la migración en el Caribe insular hispánico*, 322.
[3] Ibid., 325.
[4] Ibid., 270.
[5] Ibid., 271.
[6] Homi K. Bhabha, *The Location of Culture*, 2.
[7] Mary Louise Pratt, "Arts of the Contact Zone. Ways of Reading". http://www.nwe.ufl.edu/~stripp/2504/pratt.html.
[8] Bhabha, *The Location*, 2.
[9] Beatriz J. Risk, "El tercer espacio: el arte del performance en tres dramaturgas latinas de Estados Unidos", 87.
[10] Bhabha, *The Location*, 224.
[11] Gloria Anzaldúa, *Borderlands/La Frontera*. (1999)
[12] Ibid., 100.
[13] Quoted in Sandoval-Sánchez, Alberto y Saporta-Sternbach, Nancy. *Stages of Life.Transcultural Performance and Identity in U.S. Latina Theater*, 155.
[14] Josefina Báez. *Dominicanish*, 9-10.
[15] Ibid., 37.
[16] Alberto Sandoval-Sánchez and Nancy Saporta-Sternbach, *Stages of Life. Transcultural Performance and Identity in U.S. Latina Theater*, 97.
[17] Sophie Mariñez, "Dominicanish, de Josefina Báez: la translocalización de los símbolos". Agulha. Revista de Cultura. http://www.revista.agulha.nom.br/ag21baez.htm
[18] Ramón Rivera-Servera, "A Dominican York in Andhra" in *Caribbean Dance From Abakuá to Zouk. How Movement Shapes Identity*, ed. Susanna Sloat, 152.
[19] Mariñez, "Dominicanish."
[20] Mena, "Y con ustedes."
[21] Silvio Torres-Saillant, *El retorno de las yolas*, 20.
[22] Martínez-San Miguel, *Caribe*, 274-75.
[23] Báez, *Dominicanish*, 7; Translation in Juleyka Lantigua, Review of *Dominicanish. A Performance Text*, by Josefina Báez, 6.
[24] Báez, Dominicanish, 6.
[25] Ibid., 22.
[26] Ibid., 26-27.

[27] Aida Heredia, "The Journey Inward: Sherezada Vicioso's 'Un extraño ulular de voces traía el viento,'" in *Daughters of the Diaspora*. *Afra-Hispanic Writers*, 326.
[28] Báez, *Dominicanish*, 26.
[29] Agustín Laó-Montes, "Introduction. Mambo Montage: The Latinization of New York City", in *Mambo Montage. The Latinization of New York*, 9.
[30] Báez, *Dominicanish*, 27-28.
[31] Ibid., 34.
[32] Ibid., 48.
[33] Indian collection of fables and tales, originally written in Sanskrit between the Third and Fifth Century AD.
[34] Ibid., 40-41.
[35] Sandoval-Sánchez and Saporta-Sternbach, *Stages*, 49.
[36] Jorge Duany, *Quisqueya on the Hudson: the Transnational Identity of Dominicans in Washington Heights*, 46.
[37] Johnny Pacheco is one of the most influential figures in salsa music. Born in the Dominican Republic, his family moved to New York when he was a kid and it was there that he would later become an internationally renowned star.
[38] One of the styles of salsa music..
[39] It refers to Celia Cruz, one of the most well-known salsa singers, with whom Pacheco collaborated in various occasions throughout their careers.
[40] "Tres de café y dos de azúcar" is one of the most famous songs by Pacheco.
[41] Mythical women who are believed to inhabit the mountains in the Dominican Republic and whose feet are turned backward to avoid being followed.
[42] Báez, *Dominicanish*, 42. "Luckily 107th Street lulls with Pacheco/ Pacheco tumbao añejo/ Pacheco flute /Pacheco his new tumbao / the master the artist/ Tremendous Cache / shared in Cruz/Together again/ perfect ensemble/ Tres de Café y dos de azúcar/ With tumbao's swing and / walking backwards like a Ciguapa" (My translation).
[43] Ibid., 43. "I made out in the hallway/ I messed around in the rooftop/ I crack gum like Shameka Brown/ I speak like a Puerto Rican/ and I do my hair like a Black woman/…/I hang out with the girl who ended up pregnant/ I date my ex/ I talk to the guy who was in jail" (My translation).
[44] Michel Pêcheux, *Language, Semantics, and Ideology*, trans. Harbans Nagpal, 157-59.
[45] Sandoval-Sánchez and Saporta-Sternbach, *Stages*, 6.
[46] "Guiri" is an informal word for foreigner or tourist.
[47] Báez, *Dominicanish*, 47.
[48] Silvio Torres-Saillant, "No es lo mismo ni se escribe igual: la diversidad en lo dominicano" in *Desde la Orilla: hacia una nacionalidad sin desalojos*, 17.
[49] Silvio Torres-Saillant, Frontispiece to *Dominicanish*, by Josefina Báez, 13.
[50] Ibid., 14.
[51] I am using the notion of "transcultural subject" as proposed by Sandoval-Sánchez and Saporta-Sternbach who in Stages of Life. *Transcultural Performance and Identity in U.S. Latina Theater* offers a model for analyzing Latina plays and

performances based on the theories of transculturation developed in the Latin American tradition.
[52] Sandoval-Sánchez and Saporta-Sternbach, *Stages*, 6.
[53] Ibid.
[54] Báez, *Dominicanish*, 47.
[55] Ibid., 7.
[56] Ibid., 49.

Deconstructing Cuban Identity: Senel Paz's *The Wolf, the Woods and the New Man*: and its Film Adaptation *Strawberry and Chocolate* by Tomás Gutiérrez Alea

Tania Cepero López

An Introduction of Sorts

As my mom drove us to the Karl Marx Theater,[1] I silently negotiated with our loyal but not always reliable Lada: "Please don't die on us." We were headed for the opening night of the XV International Festival of New Latin American Film which would open with the release of Tomás Gutiérrez Alea's latest movie, *Fresa y chocolate* (*Strawberry and Chocolate*), the film adaptation of Senel Paz's short story *El lobo, el bosque y el hombre nuevo* (*The Wolf, the Woods and the New Man*).[2] We wondered how much of the story's irreverent political criticism would have been passed on to the movie, but mostly we were hoping to see a lot of it, tons of it; we were silently praying for a deluge of criticism of the Revolution, of Fidel Castro, of everything and everyone.

We, praise the Lada, made it to the theater in time to feel the room becoming quieter by degrees. And there it was, the initial scene, which was grotesque, sexual and darkly funny, and which made us laugh uncontrollably. Was it really that funny? Looking back I realize we laughed to release the tension. And it seems to have worked, for as the laughter rose within us, we felt our backs relax ever so slowly. By the time the final scene arrived, and the credits started rolling, we all became part of a warm standing ovation that lasted for what seemed to be an eternity. The cast members stepped onto the stage, and we all clapped, as if this was the last time we would ever clap, as if our lives depended on it. They looked back at us, as if saying "you are welcome."

As we drove back home that night to Cojímar, my mother, my sister and I, who usually refused to acknowledge, or rather hope that anything "good" could ever happen in Cuba, realized that we had witnessed a historic event and, dared we say it, a "good thing." As I laid myself down to sleep a few hours later, I wondered if we would have an unannounced blackout later that night. Those were the worst, the unannounced ones. I thought then about having to get up at five the next morning to catch a bus and go to college, an almost impossible feat, yet not as painful to anticipate this particular night. Tonight, I thought, "it feels good to be Cuban."

Today, as I look back, I realize that in 1993, the year *Strawberry and Chocolate* was released, I hated being Cuban. I hated that I could not walk into a hotel lobby without fear – of being told to leave, or worst, the fear of being mistaken for a prostitute. I hated blackouts. I hated "come candelas," literally "fire eaters," an euphemism for radical communists. In short, I hated being Cuban because this place where I had been born, by mistake I was sure, was the source of all my problems, or should I say of all my hatred? But the night I saw *Strawberry and Chocolate*, for the first time in a long time, I did not hate anyone or anything, and for the first time in a really long time it felt good to be Cuban.

As it often happens, memory and academic research have served me well as I try to make some sense of that night almost fourteen years ago, when I first saw *Strawberry and Chocolate*,[3] a film that will always remain in my memory as the movie that brought Cuba back into my identity. Like Senel Paz's award winning story *The Wolf, the Woods and the New Man*, *Strawberry and Chocolate* followed the tumultuous friendship of David and Diego who are developed, on the surface, as dialectic opposites. David is a heterosexual, homophobic, and naive college student from the countryside who is also a faithful member of the Communist Youth League while Diego is a gay, older, educated urbanite who has been rejected by the Revolution that David so proudly embraces.

While it is practically impossible to determine the box office numbers - in a country where information is manipulated on a daily basis - we do know that the movie broke several box office records. When asked about the movie's success during an interview in 1995, Tomás Gutiérrez Alea recalls "the long lines to see it" during the three months that the movie was shown in Havana.[4] When asked if he had any idea of the number of Cuban viewers who had seen the film, Alea replied: "*Strawberry and Chocolate* may hold the record for the greatest number of Cuban viewers, I don't know. But at any rate, it is the film which has attracted the greatest number of viewers in the shortest period of time." The film directors, Tomás

Gutiérrez Alea and Juan Carlos Tabío, as Dennis West points out, again and again attributed the success of the film to its universal theme of tolerance. Alea calls the film during the same interview "a well told story with a theme that many people wanted to discuss in public. A theme that up until this time had remained rather marginalized," and he quickly adds: "I'm not referring just to the theme of homosexuality, but rather to the theme of tolerance in general."[5]

I think we can all agree that one of the major themes of the film and the story is indeed the need for mutual tolerance or acceptance of the other, in this case the homosexual. I believe, however, that both the film and the story's main contribution is to Cuban, not to Universal culture because the short story and the film did for Cuban identity what Derrida did for literary theory, specifically, and Western thought in general when he published *Of Grammatology* in 1967. Derrida showed us how Western culture depends on binary oppositions that are always placed in hierarchical order. In this hierarchy, one term is highly valued while the other one is found to be almost worthless.[6]

Derrida analyzed, for example, how Linguistics gives primacy to speech and tends to see writing as secondary.[7] These terms, however, can never sustain the antithesis upon which they depend, as "the meaning of each term depends on the trace of the other that inhabits its definition."[8] In similar fashion, Alea, in *Strawberry and Chocolate,* deconstructed the binary oppositions upon which Cuban National identity depends to define itself within the ideological culture of post-revolutionary Cuba, where heterosexual has been privileged over homosexual, national has been privileged over foreign, and revolutionary has been privileged over counterrevolutionary through political and everyday discourse.

As Alea deconstructed Cuban identity, perhaps unknowingly,[9] he also reconstructed a definition of identity that moves away from binary opposition and is connected to Fernando Ortiz's notion of *cubanía* as "a complete Cubanness" that is also "felt, conscious and desired" (My translation).[10] Identity then (that which is identical to the self but also dependant on the other) although constructed by Cuban culture and society, belongs to the individual and not to those in power. Alea's definition of Cuban identity is then closely related to Gustavo Perez Firmat's definition of *cubanía* which he describes as a "mystery and a fact" that does not "depend on place of residence or country of citizenship" and which "has little to do with language or demeanor, and – perhaps most importantly – which cannot be granted or taken away." For Perez Firmat, in short, *cubanía* is a "willingness of the heart."[11]

So perhaps I should say that while Alea deconstructs Cuban national identity, *Strawberry and Chocolate* reconstructs an alternative definition of national identity that, as a cultural and social construct, oscillates between private and public, and individual and collective realms. But to be Cuban, the film argues, is also to accept each individual's right to an identity that is both collectively and individually constructed. In addition, what joins individual and collective identities is the condition of *cubanía* which is not imposed by an ideology, but grows out of a mutual respect between the selfsame and the other, and from the self's and the other's desire to belong to a common cultural tradition: a communal and individual "willingness of the heart."

In post-revolutionary Cuba, Paz and Alea argue, heterosexual is privileged over homosexual, revolutionary over counter-revolutionary, socialist over capitalist or imperialist, male over female; national is privileged over foreign. In addition, both the short story and the film set the audience up to realize that "these terms can never sustain the antithesis on which they depend as the meaning of each element in the binary pair depends on the "trace" of the other that inhabits and constructs its definition.[12]

Between Reality and Imagination: the Historical Context of *Strawberry and Chocolate* and *The Wolf, the Woods and the New Man*

Emilio Bejel, in his book *Gay Cuban Nation,* provides an insightful analysis of how the rejection of homosexuality has contributed to the formation of the Cuban identity since the late 1800s. During Cuba's wars of independence against Spain (1868-98), for example, the image of the military hero was at its height.[13] José Martí, the hero of Cuba's independence movement and to this date Cuba's National Poet, created through his fiction a "sort of manly poet" as the ideal model of behavior for all Cuban men.[14] There is and has been for a long time, Bejel argues, "a seemingly obvious relationship between notions of Cuban nationalism and homosexuality."[15] As the title of his book indicates, Bejel ultimately argues that "Cuban nationhood has been defined, in part, by its rejection of gayness and queerness."[16] It was not, however, Bejel explains, until after Fidel Castro's rise to power in 1959 that homophobia was institutionalized in Cuba. The dark years that followed the triumph of the Revolution came to be known as *el quinquenio gris*, "the gray quinquenium (My translation)." This is also the time period that precedes *The Wolf, the*

Woods and the New Man, which is set during the late 1970's and before the Mariel boatlift.

In 1965, Castro had told an American journalist that a homosexual would never "embody the conditions and requirements of conduct that would enable us to consider him a true revolutionary, a true communist."[17] Sadly, for the next fifteen years or so, and to this day, these homophobic feelings have been put into actions, and while at times blatantly, and at times more subtly, the persecution of homosexuals has never stopped. From the mid to late 1960s, the UMAP (Military Units to Aid Production) were instituted. The UMAP were conceived as part of a "rehabilitation" program for people (mostly men in military age) who were thought to be "antisocial."[18] This category included anyone who refused to study or work, Jehovah's Witnesses who refused to serve in the military for religious reasons, young delinquents, and, of course, the "immoral," among whom homosexuals were included.[19] In 1984, Nestor Almendros and Orlando Jiménez Real produced and released *Improper Conduct*, a documentary that records dozens of testimonies from people who were sent to the UMAP. Among them were writers, gay men, and other people who fell under what the revolutionary laws defined as people who exhibited "dangerous or extravagant attitudes" and thus eligible for the UMAP.[20]

In this documentary, José Mario, one of the first to write in exile about the UMAP, jokingly recalls a big sign that welcomed him and his fellow "rehabilitation candidates" to the camp: "*El trabajo os hará hombres. Lenin*" ("Work shall make you men. Lenin"). An ironic play on words, José Mario notes, on the sign the allied forces found at Auschwitz: "Work shall set you free."[21]

Luckily for José Mario and many others, the UMAP were short lived thanks to the outrage and protests at the international level. Renowned European intellectuals such as Graham Greene, Gian Giacomo Getrinelli, and Jean Paul Sartre voiced their objections. In 1965, while the UMAP camps were in full swing, Allan Ginsberg visited Cuba. He, too, openly voiced his objections to this new type of "authoritarianism that was dominating Cuban politics at the cultural level."[22] He was finally expelled from Cuba, which ironically made his point all the more valid.

The UMAP were finally closed in 1968, approximately two years after they were instituted, but the persecution of homosexuals continued in new, improved ways. To eradicate homosexuality as a social evil was one of the main goals of the Cuban revolution. It was part of its campaign against all social evils engendered by capitalist society. The Revolution considered homosexual behavior as dangerous as gambling or prostitution and "aspired to cleanse the country of everything that its leaders and many of its people had seen as national ills."[23]

In 1971, the First Congress of Revolution and Culture was held in Havana. In the Congress declaration, the participants defined "homosexual deviations" as a "social pathology" that must be "rejected" as a matter of "militant principle." Moreover, the delegates agreed not to allow in any way "these [homosexual] manifestations or their propagation."[24] In practice, gays were banned from government jobs or any other jobs that dealt with young people. After this Congress, new laws were also passed which allowed for sentences of thirty years in prison, and even death for any "crimes against the normal development of the family."[25] Later on, in 1979, laws were passed which authorized the arrest of people who had not done anything wrong, but exhibited "an eccentric appearance" or "showed symptoms of being dangerous." These "precautionary laws" were supposedly therapeutic and rehabilitative in nature, and allowed for the internment in "special labor facilities" or "mental institutions" for at least 1 and up to 4 years.[26] Some of Cuba's most accomplished intellectuals were driven into obscurity because they were openly gay or because their works treated homosexuality as something other than a social ill to be eradicated by this new and better Socialist regime. In 1961, Cuba's best-known playwright at the time, Virgilio Piñera, was arrested for twenty-four hours. His detention, although brief, was a cause of concern for Cuban intellectuals. His work was never published in Cuba again until after his death, when the Revolution decided to reclaim him as one of the greats of Cuban letters.[27]

In 2002, Tracey Eaton from the Dallas Morning News traveled to Cuba and met with a group of gay men, who testified to the continued institutionalized persecution of homosexuals. One of the gay men interviewed, José Miguel, did say, however, that although institutionalized homophobia is alive and well, cultural homophobia is not as strong.[28] In part, I believe, because of films like *Strawberry and Chocolate*.

This fierce persecution of homosexuals, however, must be also analyzed as the persecution of an entity that was seen as the antithesis of the New Man, the man of the Revolution. The government's persecution, arrest and attempts to "rehabilitate" was also geared towards the redefinition of Cuban identity as the rejection of anything – including but not limited to sexual orientation – that was perceived as an obstacle to the revolutionary process. In other words, if you were against the revolution, you were not Cuban. If you were against the Revolution, you only had one choice, to "enter" it or to "leave" the country. And to enter the Revolution, you had to conform to the ideal of the "new man." As Bejel points out,

Piñera was "victimized by the 'virilization' of the 'new man' of the Cuban Revolution."[29] The "new man" was the ideal new subject in this new ideal society. The "new man," therefore, was to be "free of the impurities of the bourgeois past, willing to sacrifice for his country, ready to renounce utilitarian values, and eager to posses a great disposition and aptitude for struggle (a physical struggle, if need be) for nationalist and socialist ideals" In short, the "new man" was to be "virile and highly macho."[30]

The homosexual then was seen as representative of everything that the "new man" was not. He was the impurity from the past that must be removed in this new society that was to be inhabited by the "new man." Even if the Revolution was not exactly sure of what the "new man" would turn out to be, it was dead sure of what the "new man" was never to become: a homosexual or what was even worse, an effeminate. The Cuban Revolution's sentiments towards homosexuals were clearly expressed in one of the state's newspapers which was called, not surprisingly, *Revolution:* "No homosexual represents the Revolution, which is a matter for men, of fists and not feathers, of courage and not trembling, of certainty and not intrigue, of creative valor and not of sweet surprises."[31] In part, the Revolution's homophobic policies stemmed from the Soviet Union, where homosexuality had been illegal since 1934. But even more so, it was related to the idea of the "new man" for as homosexuality was considered a social ill the only way to achieve the ideal of the "new man" was to free him of such evils.[32]

During this period of heightened and active homophobia, intellectuals could have just given up homosexual discourse to stay out of sight and out of trouble. Instead, and perhaps because artistic creativity tends to defy institutions of power and ideological generalizations, gay-themed works appeared, and gay and lesbian people rebelled against the system as much as they could.[33] The homosexual is and has been for centuries a dissident within a Cuban culture that drags its hatred of homosexuality from its colonial past, and its patriarchal culture of "machismo," but after the Revolution the homosexual became a political dissident *ipso facto*, but as the persecution increased some gays became twofold dissidents because of their sexual orientation (although perhaps even more for effeminate behavior) but also because of their criticism of the Revolution, something the powers at be would definitely not tolerate.

The most talked-about case was José Lezama Lima's masterpiece *Paradiso,* which was published in 1966. Since then, Lezama Lima has been considered one of the most accomplished Latin American writers of the twentieth century.[34] The government's initial reaction was to remove the book from circulation. But again, several revolutionary intellectuals exerted their influence and the book was put back on the shelves.[35] *Paradiso* was a breakthrough for homosexuals because it presented homosexuality as a supranatural substitute for heterosexual relations. Because of *Paradiso*, Bejel argues, homosexuality becomes an "emblem of poetry: it is a search for the similar that transcends time and reproduction. It aspires to a creativity that goes beyond the 'natural,' toward a state Lezama Lima defines as 'beyond the limits'."[36] *Paradiso* proposed homosexuality as something comparable to artistic creation, an alternate way to look at the world and express one's individuality and, I would add, one's identity.

As Bejel explains in *Gay Cuban Nation,* Lezama Lima's Neo-Baroque style, made the book somewhat less accessible to the general public and therefore less dangerous to the State.[37] But it was precisely this intricate style that made *Paradiso* widely popular and appreciated within the intellectual elite in Cuba, especially among those who had suffered persecution for their sexual orientation. Lezama Lima's work is still considered worthy of only the most knowledgeable and liberal minded readers perhaps because it made homosexuality an expression of art. And for this, homosexuals were eternally grateful. Ironically, *Paradiso* and the controversy around it increased Lezama Lima's reputation as a writer both inside and outside of Cuba. From 1968 to 1971, however, he was involved in a scandal that finally severed his ties with the revolutionary process, and one which also damaged the image of the Revolution once and for all among foreign intellectuals: the Heberto-Padilla scandal. In 1971, Heberto Padilla published a book of poems titled *Fuera del juego (Out of the Game)*, his poems openly expressed his views against the revolutionary process, which Padilla viewed as authoritarian and retrograde. A moral purge ensued, and as Reinaldo Arenas recalls in his memoir *Antes que anochezca (Before Night Falls)*, Padilla was forced to confess to being a "counter-revolutionary" and he listed among many other writers, Lezama Lima as one of his fellow counterrevolutionaries.[38] Although Lezama Lima and his friends denied the accusation, the damage was already done. He was thrust into obscurity as he was denied access to state-run journals and travel permits to participate in international events.

Like Virgilio Piñera, he was eventually erased from the Cuban cultural stage. But this fact made him a martyr among intellectuals, especially among those who had been, like Lezama Lima, made to suffer for their otherness or for voicing a dissenting opinion. I would also argue, that this made him a martyr for Cuban gay intellectuals, who thought he had sacrificed himself not only to remain true to his art, but also to remain true to his identity, one that he divorced from the Revolution's heterosexual, virile, and New-Man soaked identity, and one that was more Cuban because of this.

Cuban National Identity is Deconstructed and Reconstructed in the Imagination

Perhaps because of this sad history of homophobia and persecution, many critics have analyzed *Strawberry and Chocolate* mainly as Alea's attempt to rectify or apologize for the systematized persecution of homosexuals in Cuba after 1959. The historical persecution of homosexuals, however, must be also analyzed as the persecution of anyone or anything that was perceived to be the antithesis of the "new man," the man of the Revolution. The government's persecution, arrest and attempts to "rehabilitate" the other were also geared towards the redefinition of Cuban identity as the rejection of anything – including but not limited to sexual orientation – that was perceived as an obstacle to the revolutionary process.

In other words, if you were against the revolution, you were not Cuban. If you were against the Revolution, you only had one choice, to "enter" it or to "leave" the country, and once you left the country, you ceased to be Cuban. And to enter the Revolution, if you were a homosexual or worse an effeminate, you had to conform to the ideal of the "new man." You had to be, or at least appear to be, strong and manly. You had to walk straight, dress like a man, and talk like a man. If you were a political dissident, you had to keep your mouth shut and follow the beat of the Revolution's drums.

The homosexual, no doubt, was the most visible example of everything that the "new man" was not. He was, in the eyes of the Revolution, the antithesis of the "new man."[39] Even if the Revolution was not exactly sure of what the "new man" would turn out to be, it was dead sure of what the "new man" was never to become: a homosexual or what was even worse, an effeminate. Queerness was exiled from the official definition of Cuban identity, that is to say, the "new man's" identity, in the same way that dissenting attitudes were labeled un-Cuban, unpatriotic and counterrevolutionary. Fidel summed it up best in one of his speeches "dentro de la Revolución, todo; contra la Revolución, nada," "inside the Revolution everything; against the Revolution, nothing."

It is precisely this form of narrow, binary thought process that *Strawberry and Chocolate* questions, as it demonstrates how the Cuban (national) identity has been constructed through the negation or exclusion of the other. Therefore, Diego, in *Strawberry and Chocolate* is representative of the gay man but also of the other in the broadest sense of the word. Diego is the symbol of the "dissenting voice" who according to the Revolution is not meant to be part of the revolutionary process, and is to be rejected or exiled from the "new man's" nation, and the "new man's" identity.

Although there are many differences between the short story and the film,[40] in both texts, the first encounter is marked by the direct opposition of David, a heterosexual, cookie cutter revolutionary, and Diego, an effeminate homosexual, and a "counterrevolutionary." "He came to my table,"[41] David, remembers, and saying, "excuse me," he sat down across the table with his bags, purses, umbrellas, rolls of paper and his cup of ice cream."[42]

In Proustian fashion, Senel Paz constructed his short story as a remembrance of things past, as remembered by David who is also the narrator. Late at night, he heads down to Coppelia. This familiar place triggers a memory of his friend Diego who baptized this ice cream parlor with the more operatic name of "the Cathedral of Ice Cream."[43] And it was in this precise place that Diego and David had met.

It was clear from his appearance, David recalls in the story, that Diego was gay or as David puts it, "it was easy to see the kind of ailment he suffered from", but the ultimate condemning fact, David thought, was that despite the fact that there was chocolate ice cream Diego ordered strawberry.[44] Here, Paz reveals the binary nature of David's system of thought. He identifies chocolate ice cream with heterosexuality, virility, manhood and culturally ascribed gender roles while he connects pink strawberry ice cream with homosexuality, femininity, and effeminate behavior.

When Diego pulls out some "foreign books," David, despite his secret longing to read them, switches his Communist Youth League identification from one of the front pockets of his shirt and places it inside the other pocket. This symbolic gesture is meant to show Diego that David is, unlike Diego, a revolutionary which is to say, a straight man, which is to say a man who is only interested in books that are deemed "good: in ideological terms. As flawed as the logic may seem in this argument, many of us took it be an absolute truth in our daily lives until we encountered *Strawberry and Chocolate*. Diego blackmails David into coming to Diego's house. But before they leave Coppelia, Diego feels the need to make some things clear:

> Before [you come to my home], I want to make some things clear because I don't want you to say later that I wasn't straightforward with you. You are one of those persons whose ingenuity comes off as dangerous. One, I

am a faggot. Two: I am religious. Three: I have had problems with the system; they think there is no place for me in this country, but I won't take none of that, I was born here; I am, first and foremost, a patriot and a Lezamian, and I am not leaving this place, not even if they light my ass on fire. Four: I was in jail during the times of the UMAP. And five: my neighbors watch me; they keep an eye on everyone that visits me. You still wanna go? (My translation)[45]

This meeting marks a turning point in David's life–he, to his own surprise, agrees to go to Diego's house–and most importantly, in the reader's understanding of the world. In a short statement Diego has collapsed almost all the binary structures of meaning that are familiar to David and to his audience, as he deconstructs the official definition of Cuban identity. Diego sees himself as a "patriot" yet he has had "problems with the system." According to the revolutionary binary discourse if you are not with the system, you are against it. And if you are against it, you are a traitor and nothing could be further from the meaning of the word "patriot." Yet Diego, who has been labeled a homosexual by the Revolution, who is defined as an "antisocial," a social evil to be eradicated, pledges his love for the place where he was born, and pledges not to leave Cuba no matter how much they try to push him out.

Diego, both in the short story and the film, sees his identity as the construct of the Cuban nation but also as the result of his deep connection to an invented "Lezamian" nation. He questions the existence of a fixed Cuban nation and Cuban identity. The Cuban nation is for him a place where cultural and literary traditions converge, and also one where sexuality is recognized as part of one's identity.

That Diego sees himself as a citizen of the Lezamian nation is significant because this declaration questions the definition of Cuban identity as dependant on an imposed ideology, or placed within geographical boundaries. This deconstruction of identity in the political realm and its reconstruction in the cultural realm becomes the basis for *Strawberry and Chocolate* which, even more so than the short story, deconstructs the binary oppositions upon which Cuban revolutionary discourse has depended to define Cuban identity through the rejection of the other.

Strawberry and Chocolate: Deconstruction MTV Style

In one of many interviews, the late Alea said, "you make a film because you want to express something to the largest audience possible. So you have to use a language that can reach that audience."[46] Many years before he made *Strawberry and Chocolate,* in his book *Dialectic of the Spectator"* Alea had also envisioned the "cinematic experiment" as "a process of discovering or uncovering *(descubrir),* of rendering visible what was formerly obscured by the ideological anesthesia of everyday life.[47] He felt the need to awaken his spectator to the possibilities of alternative meanings and truths, and the language of contrasts and oppositions served him well to do this in the film *Strawberry and Chocolate.*

Alea emphasized the dependence of Cuban identity on the binary pair of heterosexual /homosexual by discarding Senel Paz's *The Wolf, the Woods and The New Man* and by adopting instead the title *Strawberry and Chocolate.* Here chocolate ice cream is associated with virility, strength and Revolution while the pink strawberry ice cream is associated with homosexual, effeminate behavior, weakness and counterrevolution. *Strawberry and Chocolate* brought to millions of Cuban citizens what the short story had engraved in a few of us: the realization that in defining Cuban identity, especially after the Revolution, we had been so busy with binary thinking that we had forgotten to question the ethical and logical validity of authoritarian affirmations of truths.

The first encounter between Diego and David in *Strawberry and Chocolate* is reminiscent of their first meeting in the short story. David is sitting at a table, eating his chocolate ice cream and reading the official newspaper of the Communist Youth, when Diego's "excuse me" startles him.[48] The polarity of their identities is emphasized by the camera angle, which gives us quick close ups of each character as they speak. It is only towards the end of the conversation, when David has already agreed to follow Diego to his house, that the camera looks over Diego's shoulder as David speaks, or vice versa. But the now famous perfectly symmetrical shots of David's and Diego's profiles talking to each other are nowhere to be seen here, although they do become more and more frequent later in the film, as they start really listening to each other.

Diego is irreverently effeminate in this public space; his hands seem to fly every time he talks. He is loud and self-confident. David, in contrast, is silent and reserved. He speaks with a firm voice in short, angry sentences. The result of the encounter, however, is the same as in Paz's short story, as David, with the hope of getting the photos of his performance in *A Doll's House*, agrees to accompany Diego to his house, or as Diego calls it *la guarida, the hideway*.[49] In this scene, Diego, the homosexual and David, the heterosexual, begin the defy the ideological definition of the "new man." David, the heterosexual is manly but unsure of himself. Diego, however, who is supposed to be the weak link in our journey towards the society of the "new man", is effeminate, yet confident and in control of the situation. The binary pair heterosexual/homosexual has begun to crumble. One depends on the other for its definition, yet David has presumed, until this day, to be superior. This encounter, however, presents the homosexual, Diego, as the one in control of his life and his socially and privately constructed Cuban identity.

Another binary pair is deconstructed as we enter *la guarida*, Diego's nation within the Cuban nation, where images become representative of the fragmented and unstable nature of Cuban National identity. There is especially one wall that visually represents Diego's private yet socially and culturally constructed Cuban identity. For Diego, Cuban identity is a desire to belong to a cultural and literary tradition that is both national and international. Cuban identity is also the recognition of the other in the selfsame. So much is Diego's wall a reflection of an identity imbedded by the other, that almost every object on the wall seems foreign to David. As Diego literally leaves this physical place of identity (he's making tea and then coffee in the kitchen), David unsuccessfully tries to decipher the meanings of all these objects, which will become the starting points of most of their conversations in *la guarida*.

The main wall, which the camera pans out from bottom to top, following David's perception, reveals an abstract painting, as well as portraits of Fernando Ortiz, a renowned Cuban anthropologist, perhaps Lydia Cabrera, a writer, and Rita Montaner, a famous entertainer during the 1940s and 1950s; a Degas' sketch of a ballerina, and a poster of Bola de Nieve, another famous black performer from the 1950s. At the center of the wall, the camera reveals a portrait of Lezama Lima smoking a cigar, and a frontal portrait of José Martí. To the right and left of these, we see a portrait of Gertrudis Gómez de Avellaneda, an early nineteenth century poet, and José María Heredia, another nineteenth century poet who was sent into exile by the Spanish colonial authorities. There is also an oil lamp (commonly used during the National Campaign for Literacy of 1961), a fragment of a colonial iron fence, a pair of ballet slippers in an old frame, and Chango's[50] axe. Two "Cuban Indians" complete this collage that is Diego's identity.[51] His sexuality is not explicitly displayed on the wall, but it is nevertheless present in the form of *El Maestro*, Lezama Lima, who Diego later calls "a universal Cuban" during one of his many conversations with David.[52]

It is only after a long friendship and many, many conversations in Diego's private nation of *la guarida* that David begins to accept Diego and his individual sense of identity. It is also significant that David begins to see in the wall a representation of his own Cuban identity to the point that he feels the need to add iconic revolutionary images to it. One day, David shows up with a copy of the famous frontal photograph of Che Guevara taken by Korda in the early days of the Revolution, a photo of Fidel at La Sierra Maestra and a small flag of the 26th of July Movement with a Santeria necklace like the ones the rebels wore when they came down from the mountains. "Aren't they a part of Cuba too?" David asks Diego, who half amused and half proud of David, nods in agreement, and promptly adds all these symbols of *cubanía* to his wall.[53]

This joint construction of Cuban identity is paramount to the final acceptance of Diego by David, but most importantly it collapses the opposition of the binary pairs upon which the Revolution has based its rejection of the other. David and Diego do not have to choose between Lezama Lima and Che. They recognize that Che, a staunch proponent of the virile "new man", and a foreigner, has the right to be a part of the culturally and ideologically constructed Cuban identity. But Lezama Lima is there too, at the center of it all, exuding a Cuban identity that is homosexual and patriotic. It is precisely this newly constructed Cuban identity through difference that unites Diego and David, a union that does NOT require either of them to give up their own definitions of Cuban identity. In fact, each of their definitions is enriched by their differences.

But in the end, Diego does leave (or is forced out of) Cuba when the Revolution rejects him one last time. This last straw comes, however, when he is persecuted because of his "thinking head" not because of his sexual orientation. Otherness, it seems, is conveniently redefined by the ruling ideology to include all dissenters. Not surprisingly, when Diego pronounces the fatal words "I'm leaving the country", David's first reaction, the one he's been conditioned with by so many years of binary thinking, is to take down the representations of the Revolution from the wall. Before Diego has had a chance to explain that he is leaving because he has no other choice (he has been fired from his job and has been banned from any jobs related to the development of Cuban culture), David has already taken down *his* symbols of identity from the wall.[54] He quickly puts them inside his bag as Diego, visibly shaken by David's reaction, begins to explain the reasons behind his decision to leave. But we would be wrong to interpret David's initial reaction as a political statement, or an act or rejection. Instead, it is a way for David to show that he cares. He feels betrayed, but later seems to understand and accept that Diego has not chosen to leave, but has been forced into exile.[55] And, even if he never puts his symbols of *Cubanía* back on the wall, he does come to terms with Diego's decision. The action of putting the Revolution back on perhaps would have appeared too obviously symbolic. There was, in addition, no practical reason to do so because when David leaves everything that remains in *la guarida* would be confiscated.

After the disclosure of Diego's future exile condition, almost every scene takes place outside of *la guarida*. The friends move from private to public places. And one of those public places is, of course, Coppelia. They return to the place where it all began. In this, the scene that precedes the now famous embrace, there are no shots of Diego and David facing each other as opposites. The camera again switches from one face to the other, and the rest of the shots give us each character's view of the other. David and Diego sit down at the table at the same time and David with laughter in his face, switches ice cream plates with Diego, who simply smiles and looks at David's face. He jokingly takes on Diego's personality, effeminate behavior included. The old David would have never done this, especially not in a public place. But this new David, this "new man", is confident enough as a sexual and a human being to make fun of his self, and laugh with, not at Diego, who visibly moved by Diego's public display of affection exclaims, "You are so beautiful David. Your only defect is that you are not a faggot," and David still jokingly replies, "Nobody is perfect."[56] This is the linguistic equivalent of their embrace in the next and final scene. David, the heterosexual and revolutionary privileged element of the binary pair, has finally accepted that his identity, his meaning, can only be complete with his acceptance of the other, Diego, into his self. While the movie begins and ends in the same physical place, there is no doubt that both elements of the binary pair heterosexual/homosexual have learned to rely on each other for their definition of their individual Cuban identities. The authoritarian spell has been broken.

In 1993, I hated to be Cuban not only because of the blackouts and the self-imposed silence, but also because I felt that I could do nothing to change the status quo, because like most Cubans living on the island I had become a cynic. I chuckled when I read slogans like "100% Cuban," "Fidel we are with you," or "Towards a better future." But as I dived into the muddled memories of my past, as I looked behind me through the lens of *Strawberry and Chocolate*, I have realized that like many other Cubans, in 1993, I underwent an identity crisis. We thought that because we were dissenters, we were not Cuban. We thought that because we were "out of the game," we had ceased to exist as Cubans. But *Strawberry and Chocolate* encouraged us to redefine Cuban identity as a social and individual construct that depends, quite literally, on the other for its existence. Identity, Alea suggested, cannot be imposed upon us any more than sexual orientation.

As he deconstructed the binary pairs we had relied upon for so long, (heterosexual/homosexual,revolutionary/counterrevolutionary, Cuban/foreign) he opened our eyes to a new definition of Cuban identity that is dependant on and respectful of the other. Cuban identity, Alea suggested, is not a status that can or should be given by the State in exchange for our voice, but rather an awareness of our similarities and differences, a willingness to see the invisible thread that connects us to a literary and cultural tradition that is our own because it is different from all the others. And that, Alea suggests, is what makes Cuban identity complex, which is different from complicated. We will only make it complicated if we refuse to acknowledge the other in our Cuban own self.

Bibliography

Bejel, Emilio. *Gay Cuban Nation*. Chicago: The University of Chicago Press, 2001.
Belsey, Catherine. *Poststructuralism: A Very Short Introduction*. Oxford: Oxford University Press, 2002.
Conducta impropria, edited by Nestor Almendros and Orlando Jiménez-Leal. Madrid: Playor, 1984.
Conducta impropria, directed by Néstor Almendros and Orlando Jiménez-Leal. VHS. Cinevista Video, 1984.
Chua, Lawrence. "I Scream You Scream (Tomás Gutiérrez Alea's film 'Strawberry and Chocolate')."*Artforum International* 4:62 (Dec. 1994), htpp://web.7.infotrac.galegroup.com.ezproxy.edu/itw/infomark/ (Accessed March 28, 2005).
Eaton, Tracey. "Gays in Cuba Still Struggling to Find a Place of Their Own." *The Dallas Morning News* (via Knight Ridder/Tribune News Service), August 25, 2002, htpp://web.7.infotrac.galegroup.com.ez proxy.edu/itw/infomark/ (accessed March 28, 2005.)
Strawberry and Chocolate [Fresa y chocolate], directed by Tomás Gutiérrez Alea and Juan Carlos Tabío. DVD. ICAIC: Miramax, 1993.
Howard, Phillip. A. "Strawberry and Chocolate." *The American Historical Review* 102: 4 (October 1997): 1275-1276.
Ortiz, Fernando. "Los factores humanos de la cubanidad" [The human factors of Cubanness]. In *Fernando Ortiz,* edited by Julio Le Riverand. La Habana: UNEAC:1973. 149-157.
Paz, Senel. *El Lobo, el bosque y el hombre nuevo* [The Woolf, the Woods and the New Man]. Mexico, D.F.: Ediciones Era, S.A. de C.V., 2003.
Pérez Firmat, Gustavo. *A Willingness of the Heart: Cubanidad, Cubaneo y Cubanía*. Miami: Cuban Studies Association, 1997.

Smith, Paul Julian. *Vision Machines: Cinema, Literature and Sexuality in Spain and Cuba, 1983-1993.* London: Verso, 1996.

West, Dennis. "'Strawberry and Chocolate,' Ice Cream and Tolerance: Interview with Tomás Gutiérrez Alea and Juan Carlos Tabío." *Cineaste* 1 and 2 (1995), 16-20.

Notes

[1] I don't know what this theater was called before the Revolution, but to us it was the Karl Marx Theater, and it could hold more people than any other theater in the city. Every single seat was taken. After I had finished writing this paper, I compared notes with my mother, and she remembers the theatre being full, but she swears it was the Yara movie theatre, not the Karl Marx theatre. Because memory has become the lens of much of my readings, I chose to leave it as I originally remembered it.

[2] This was in 1993. Paz's short story had been circulated, mostly as a Xerox of a foreign publication, among Cuban readers since 1990. David, a good friend of our family, had lent one of those photocopies to us, but only after we swore to return it to him safe and sound, and soon, as there was a list of close friends who were anxiously waiting for their turn to read it.

[3] Senel Paz still lives in Cuba. His last book was published in Barcelona only a few months ago.

[4] West, "Strawberry and Chocolate, Ice Cream and Tolerance: Interview with Tomás Gutiérrez Alea and Juan Carlos Tabio," 20.

[5] Ibid.

[6] Belsey, *Poststructuralism: A Very Short Introduction*, 75.

[7] Ibid., 77.

[8] Ibid., 75.

[9] Here I am indebted to Dr. Richard Schwartz, my friend and mentor, who in his analysis of Woody Allen's film *Deconstructing Harry* points out that "deconstructionists sometimes succeed in affirming new truths unseen even by the author."

[10] Ortiz, "Los factores humanos de la cubanidad," 157.

[11] Perez Firmat, Gustavo. *A Willingness of the Heart: Cubanidad, Cubaneo y Cubanía*, 8-

[12] Belsey, *Poststructuralism*, 75.

[13] Bejel, *Gay Cuban Nation*, XVII.

[14] Ibid., XVIII.

[15] Ibid., XVI.

[16] Ibid., XIV.

[17] Eaton, "Gays in Cuba Still Struggling to Find a Place of Their Own."

[18] Bejel, *Gay Cuban Nation*, 100.

[19] Ibid.

[20] See *Improper Conduct,* the film, and *Improper Conduct,* the book, a collection that includes the film transcripts and many other interviews that did not make it to the final cut.
[21] Ibid.
[22] Bejel, *Gay Cuban Nation,* 101. See note 15 above.
[23] Ibid., 95.
[24] *Improper Conduct,* 176. See note 16 above.
[25] Eaton, "Gays in Cuba Still Struggling to Find a Place of Their Own; and *Improper Conduct.*
[26] *Improper Conduct,* the film, and *Improper Conduct,* the book.
[27] Piñera's only fault appeared to be his open homosexuality, and his homosexual appearance. Spanish writer Juan Goytisolo was one of many foreign intellectuals who often traveled to Cuba, and who supported the Revolution. In the documentary *Improper Conduct,* he recalls his last meeting with Virgilio Piñera during one of his last trips to Cuba: (. . .) But it was in 1967, while I was in Havana for the third time, that I discovered what was really happening. I received a visit from a great Cuban writer, I'm talking about Virgilio Piñera, a writer of great importance, as important as Alejo Carpentier or Lezama Lima; author of short stories, novels, plays, etc. Virgilio told me then what was going on. He told me about the UMAP, he told me that there were over six thousand homosexuals locked up in these camps, that he himself lived in fear of denunciation and arrest by the Defense Committees of the Revolution. I realized that he was terrified because he did not want to talk in my hotel room or in the hotel lobby. He wanted us to walk in the garden, where we would be safer. Virgilio struck me as a lonely, cornered man…I must say that when I saw him leave, so frail, aged, so marked by his experience…this truly changed me, and it made me reconsider the evolution of the Revolution and doubt it . . . (My translation).
[28] Eaton, "Gays in Cuba Still Struggling to Find a Place of Their Own."
[29] Bejel, 99.
[30] Ibid.
[31] Howard, "Strawberry and Chocolate," 1275.
[32] Bejel, 100.
[33] Ibid., 104.
[34] I first heard of Lezama Lima as a college student in 1996. One of my classmates was a big fan of his work, and she once brought me to a "tertulia," a literary discussion, at Lezama Lima's home, which has been turned into a museum. A year later, this classmate revealed to me, as if she was telling me the greatest secret ever, that she was in fact gay. We laughed it out, and I scolded her for her secrecy, which I saw as an affront to our friendship. Looking back, I understand why she kept it a secret. Being openly gay would have probably gotten her expelled from college. But I also understand now why she was such a devotee of Lezama Lima's work, one of the very few authors in Cuban letters who openly wrote about a homosexual relationship, and who was also ostracized for it.
[35] Ibid., 104 and *Improper Conduct.*
[36] Ibid., 122.

[37] Ibid., 104.
[38] Arenas, *Before Night Falls*. This is perhaps one of the most widely known cases – outside of Cuba – of intellectual repression. For more on the Heberto Padilla affair, see Bejel's *Gay Cuban Nation* and Orlando Jimenez's *Improper Conduct*.
[39] In addition, he became an easy target because of the cultural homophobia and machismo that already existed in Cuba by 1959.
[40] Jesús Barquet discusses three problems he sees in the short story which are dealt with effectively in the film. See Barquet, Jesús. *Paz, Guitierrez Alea y Tabio, Felices discrepancias entre un cuento, un guión y un film* (*Fe de Erratas*, no. 10 (May 1995), 83-86). For more discrepancies between the film and short story see Caballero, Rufo, *Fresa y chocolate: Las ondulaciones del deseo* (*Cuba Literaria*: Publicaciones Cubanas en la red). http://www.cubaliteraria.cu/disidencias/fresa_chocolate.asp (Accessed March 29, 2005))
[41] Because there are no available English translations of *The Wolf, the Woods and the New Man*, I have translated all direct quotes from the story.
[42] Paz, *The Wolf, the Woods and the New Man*, 10.
[43] Ibid., 9.
[44] Ibid.
[45] Ibid., 19.
[46] Chua, "I Scream You Sream."
[47] Alea, *Dialectic of the Spectator*, quoted in Smith, *Vision Machines*, 82.
[48] *Strawberry and Chocolate*, "Chapter 2: Unwanted Company," Dir. Tomás Gutiérrez Alea.
[49] Ibid., "Chapter 3: Looking for Photos."
[50] Chango is the king of the *Orishas* or deities in Cuban Santeria. He is the God of fire and lighting and, most importantly, the epitome of masculinity.
[51] Ibid.
[52] Ibid., "Chapter 6: Firm Principles?"
[53] Ibid., "Chapter 11: Teacher and Student."
[54] Ibid., "Chapter 15: Torn from Home."
[55] Ibid.
[56] Ibid., "Chapter 16: Diego's Farewell."

CARIBBEAN WOMEN WRITERS AND THE STRATEGY OF MEMORY

AIDA LUZ RODRÍGUEZ

The tradition of Caribbean narrative[1] has been one of contestation (a subversion of colonialism and neocolonialism)[2] and complemented by representations of Caribbean identity. In one way or another, Caribbean novelists, to contest ideological conventions while giving emphasis to modes of self-identification, resort to strategic schemes such as memory (the mental process of recalling and remembering facts). Through their narrative frameworks, then, authors such as Paule Marshall, Zee Edgell, Michelle Cliff, and Elizabeth Nunez-Harrell draw from elements clearly linked to neo/colonialism and to Caribbean identity and resort to the narrative strategy of memory. In this essay, thus, I will examine how Caribbean women writers (Marshall, Edgell, Cliff, and Nunez-Harrell) use memory; contest modes of oppression; and resort to historical details to construct narrative worlds as part of a subject-formation process. Primarily, the analysis will highlight characters' recollections and the salient elements in the novels—background (personal/historical past), personal/familial relations, landscape (nation and/or land), location (border/margin, island/metropolis), race, gender, spirituality, class—as they correlate to memory as an essential part within the process of characters' formation. I seek to demonstrate that these characters use memory to recall experiences in order to understand their selves, as for example, Ursa in Marshall's *Daughters*, Pavana in Edgell's *In Times Like These*, Clare in Cliff's *No Telephone to Heaven*, and Marina in Nunez-Harrell's *When Rocks Dance*. Female novelists, while employing the strategy of memory as the capacity to recall and store experiences, create narrative worlds that contest ideology and structures of authority. Especially, as Evelyn O'Callaghan writes in *Woman Version: Theoretical Approaches to West Indian Fiction by Women*, female novelists mold what they express in their works, "interact with 'power structures,'" contest finality and fixation, and adjust ideological influences. Following a similar trend, in the essay, "Introduction: Women and Literature in the Caribbean:

an Overview," Carole Boyce Davies and Elaine Savory Fido assert, "Caribbean women are engaged in women's issues . . . in the region or outside, they bring a special perspective . . . born of the special character of Caribbean life, its unity-in-diversity, its engagement with human rights . . . and . . . survival" (15).Thus, Caribbean women novelists, while depicting "women's issues" within a Caribbean context, contest ideological conventions, emphasize modes of self-identification, and resort to strategy of memory.

Engaging themselves in "women's issues" and through the scheme of memory, Caribbean female novelists develop modes of historical reconstruction and revision in their narratives[3] and dramatize an enactment of recalling and remembering. As such, if action depends on the concepts that the characters remember, and if, as Frantz Fanon affirms in *Black Skin, White Masks*, "to speak is to exist," therefore, to exist the subject must have memory since "to speak" the subject must store and remember language. In *Memory and Dreams: The Creative Human Mind*, George Christos, explains that "memory is enhanced by language" (37). As well, J. Edward Chamberlin in *Come Back To Me My Language: Poetry and the West Indies*, establishes the relevance of language, and how the act of remembering the language will aid the West Indians to recall their past since, as Chamberlin affirms, "for West Indians, language also connects their past and their present" (271). Somehow, the subjects initiate a process of remembering and learning, actions, which, as Christos indicates, "take place simultaneously . . . What a network learns depends on its synaptic structure (or previously stored memory), as this determines which attractors are attained and learned" (51-52). He adds that, normally, "there is a little person inside us, or a 'self,' . . . with 'free will'" (1, 73). Overall, according to Christos "memory is the process (and the information stored by that process) that enables us to carry our experiences into the future, and to look back into our past and use those experiences" (37). The recollections from the past will mold the present that will forge the future. In all probability, then, to subsist, the self needs those memories. In *Searching for Safe Spaces: Afro-Caribbean Women Writers in Exile*, Myriam J. A. Chancy sustains that the subjects in adoptive countries feel alienated and "are left with the solace of memory; it is in this way that the exile may . . . belong wherever s/he is—through memory" (217). Essentially, as Elaine Savory, in "Ex/Isle: Separation, Memory, and Desire in Caribbean Women's Writing" (1998), claims "[t]here is . . . no sustained human relationship without memory" (172-73). Since human beings interact with one another to subsist and use language to communicate (two processes that engage the interaction of memory), therefore, memory constitutes an integral part of a subject's existence. For instance, in Marshall's *Daughter*, Estelle, Ursa's mother, "remembered the letter . . . she had committed to memory" (143). In Edgell's *In Times Like These*, Pavana recalls a "memory of ancient malarial symptoms" (3). In Cliff's *No Telephone to Heaven*, "Memory crosses memory crosses memory" (92). Likewise, in Nunez-Harrell *When Rocks Dance*, memory, "like a sore tooth" (199) induces Marina to accept her African traditions. In sum, to reach self-assertion, the subjects must draw from memory the stored experiences, carry those experiences into the future, and look back into the past to use their accumulated experiences, which will grant the subjects self-clarification.

In *Daughters*,[4] Marshall depicts Ursa Mackenzie as a migrant character in the Caribbean and the United States dealing with social circumstances as she recalls from memory experiences as student, daughter, lover, and worker and as she clarifies her stance in life. As Ursa begins her quest, she validates Christos' concept of the "little person inside us, or a 'self,'" for she speaks to "the monitoring voice inside her" (9).[5] Ursa, too, evokes past experiences and brings forth her cultural background and historical past, a scheme that she begins when she receives "The Mt. H. Alumni Newsletter," which, "before she throws it out," made her feel "as if she's right back on the Mt. H. campus again" (10-11). Through the "Newsletter," Ursa recalls a scene of college memories by remembering an incident that took place twelve years ago, a scene that produces a two-level remembrance, that of her college experience and that associated with Africa and its people. The scene causes the narrative to move from the present temporal instant to the immediate and archaic past while bringing forward a historical recollection of Ursa's cultural background and placing her culture in opposition to that of the other, to be exact, the colonizer evoked through the "Newsletter." Symbolically, Ursa has enacted Edward K. Brathwaite's words, which Simon Gikandi quotes in "Modernism and the Masks of History: the Novels of Paule Marshall." According to Gikandi, Brathwaite explains how "'we find a West Indies facing the metropolitan west . . . and clinging to a memorial past on the other. Within this matrix, she formulates her enquiry into identity'" (169-70).[4] Here, Ursa represents the "West Indies facing the metropolitan" holding on to her "memorial past" and undergoing a self-identity quest.

In her memory, Ursa recallls the rejected proposal "of a paper on Congo Jane and Will Cudjoe" (377) and the thesis statement: "*A neglected area in the study of the social life of New World slave communities has been the general nature of gender roles and relationships [. . .] in the United States and the Caribbean*" (11). In that instant, the figures of

Congo Jane and Will Cudjoe stand as metonymic figures that evoke the slaves and their world, historical information relevant for Ursa's cultural background, for her "Caribbeanness." Her life in New York and her contact with "The Mt. H. Alumni Newsletter" represent her recent memory, while Jane and Cudjoe represent her latent-archaic memory linked to traces of African tradition. Ursa, actually, comes close to Chancy's description of the subjects, who, once they are out of their home country, "are left with the solace of memory" (217). Her recollection, in addition, evinces an act of struggle and resistance against the metropolis, symbolically embodied in the professor who rejects her proposal. Mainly, a mixture of elements interacts in this segment: the historical fact, the struggle and resistance, and the contrast of the Caribbean and American cultures.

Marshall stresses the Caribbean-American contrast even more through Ursa's parents, her Caribbean father, the PM (Primus Mackenzie), a member of Parliament on the island of Triunion, and her mother, Estelle, an African-American woman from the United States. Ursa faces the two worlds (Caribbean-American) when her mother sends her a letter pleading Ursa to come to the island. Concurrently, the letter identifies Ursa as a migrant individual, a feature applicable to Caribbean identity,[6] while Celestine, a household maid, ratifies Ursa's metropolitan influence for "[l]iving up there all these years has changed her" (305). In the letter, Estelle emphasizes that she needs Ursa to help her save the "Government Land" because the PM is going to sell them to an American developer, "I'm afraid of the P and D Board and your father . . . something has to be done to stop those people on the board and to bring your father to his senses' (363). Her mother's letter, likewise, introduces the socio-political theme as part of the neo/colonial atmosphere, which provokes Ursa's dilemma about choosing New York or the Caribbean and induces her to think about her being and her existence. While Ursa vacillates between staying in the metropolis and going back to defend her land and her history, she becomes aware of her position in life.

Important, too, is the fact that the reader gets the information from the letter near the end of the book, which suggests that the whole recounting in the novel has taken place in a non-linear manner. Accurately, "The Mt. H. Alumni Newsletter," along with the flashback (memory recall) about the professor, and the letter from the mother constitute separate blocks of narration that alter the conventional introduction-climax-conclusion narrative sequence. A flashback introduces the race/class issue when Ursa goes to "The Monument of Heroes" which was hidden "where scarcely anybody can get to see them, so as not to offend the white people" (375).

There, her memory recall produces a reverie of her past, as if in a dream, about Estelle, Viney, herself as a child, Lowell Carruthers, Congo Jane and Will Cudjoe. Later, she walks along the beach, "trying to rid herself of the dream" (384). Her memory brings her back to the situation that has brought her to the island, the destruction of "Government Lands beach [which] will be the exclusive property of the NCRC types flown in on the private planes" (385). From a feminine perspective, as Ursa's progression continues, the "external object"[7] necessary for her identification functions in a manner distinct from Bhabha's assumptions because the characters, "The Mt. H. Alumni Newsletter," and Estelle's letter, instead of connecting Ursa to the metropolis, links or connects her to her center of identification, the island.

She cares for her island rather than for her stay in New York, which is, symbolically, the place of the colonizer insinuated through the word "other," for "Jane *and* Will Cudjoe . . . *You* can't call her name or his without calling or at least thinking of the other, they were so close" (377). That way, instead of looking in the eyes of the colonizer[8], Ursa looks back to her island and her historical past, which become an obsession in her imagination, a fantasy, "Triunion! Triunion all over again! . . . Where am I? Which place? What country? Is there no escaping that island? (292). If her cultural background and island stand in the midst of her imagination, at that moment, her memory, by recalling her culture, her island, and her nation, becomes a constitutive part of her transformational process. The island, as a result, functions in the same manner as the nation that Madhava Prasad mentions in "On the Question of a Theory of (Third World) Literature." In the essay, Prasad proposes, "the nation as a frame of reference is a constant presence in cultural production" (78). In that case, within Ursa's memory recall, the nation or nationalistic thoughts participate whenever she refers to the island and its culture. In this regard, in "Gender and Hemispheric Shifts in the Caribbean Narrative in English At the Close of the 20th Century: A Study of Paule Marshall's *Daughters* and Erna Brodber's *Louisiana*," Cynthia James asserts that Marshall's "female protagonists . . . re-establish connections with their West Indian roots . . . to reawaken ancient spiritual connections lying dormant" (2). As Ursa remembers Congo Jane, Will Cudjoe, and the island, her "dormant" connections reawaken.

Her obsession with the island becomes apparent through her fight with Lowell Carruthers. While they argue, he declares "'First comes him, then the little island. . . . Your head's there . . . your body is around. . . . We have the body, but that place . . . ha[s] your head'" (265). His words confirm Ursa's transfer of the remembered "little island" and the shreds of

African culture (Jane and Cudjoe) latent in her memory to her metropolitan world and accentuate her neo/colonial condition which according to Hume is a "longing for something lacking" (20). Definitely, her thoughts have been with the island, she "Misses . . . the PM, Estelle, Celestine, even Astral Forde. Misses the stone faces of Congo Jane and Will Cudjoe . . . Longs suddenly for the little miserable two-by-four island she's been hiding from . . . for the past four years (257). Her longing becomes apparent while she tries to convince Viney, her "'sister/friend,'" (382) to go with her to the island. Viney recaps, "All that stuff about them and that island that stays on your mind . . . The cans and bones keep up such a racket you can't hear your own self, your own voice trying to tell you which way to go, what to do with your life" (112). At the end, her father becomes the object through which she acknowledges herself as she becomes aware that her forehead is a "version of the PM's . . . [that] overshadowed those parts of her face that took after no one but herself. That were simply Ursa. She'd catch her reflection in a mirror and all she would see . . . was his forehead" (408). In this mirror stage,[9] when Ursa looks at her reflection, she sees her father, the PM, who represents her Caribbean side and, hence, her identification with her island.

Similar to Ursa, Pavana Leslie in Edgell's *In Times Like These*, happens to be the subject of a range of social conditions and undergoes a process of self clarification. Per chance, Marshall and Edgell delineate comparable incidents, which demonstrate how writers work on analogous themes, characters, and circumstances. Each writer, Marshall and Edgell, has designed a distinct storyline for the narrative worlds they convey in their novels, even though each narrative sets up some commonality between the two novels and, consequently, the writers' craft. It is as H. Porter Abbott explains in the essay "'What Do We Mean When We Say 'Narrative Literature?' Looking for Answers Across Disciplinary Borders." Abbott believes that sometimes "a genre can activate a particular narrative, and then this narrative can act as a platform on which all kinds of other non-narrative (and narrative) modes can be piled, and yet remain operative" (4). On such basis, it seems evident that, both writers, (Marshall and Edgell) "activate a particular narrative" to deal with women issues and their family/personal relationships. Similarly, in a parallel manner to Marshall, Edgell elaborates a narrative scheme juxtaposing the time sequence and the localities in a looking-back-retrospective manner while controlling the narrative perspective through Pavana, an approach that resembles Ursa's recounting and that Richard F. Patteson takes into consideration in "Zee Edgell: The Belize Chronicles." In the essay, Patteson sustains that "the novel's formal complexity lies less in its wealth of character and incident than in its narrative technique," which is marked by "a bewildering array of time shifts" (68). For Patteson, "the novel's flashbacks are all rendered through Pavana's recollections after she has returned to Belize" (70). Thoroughly, the narrative scheme facilitates the recounting and Edgell's potential to give details of Pavana's life story as Pavana departs from Belize, goes to London, moves to Africa, and returns to Belize. Like Ursa, Clare, and Marina, Pavana has to come to terms with whom she is and has to handle strenuous situations and personal relationships.

Ursa deals with Carruthers, while Pavana has to cope with Alex Abrams, the father of her twins, Lisa and Eric. Upon Pavana's arrival in London, Alex went out of his way to assist her and "protect her, to bring her along . . . to develop abilities she had not known she possessed" (34). By remembering how Alex treats her and the phrase "to develop abilities," implies that Pavana becomes whom she is, that she has developed her personality because of Alex protection and guidance after she undergoes a "long, slow process of growth and discovery" (Patteson 71). Alex guides her "smoothing out what he saw as rough edges, correcting her pronunciation of certain words" (35). To an extent, Alex's protection means her submission and acceptance of his rules, including his political party. Pavana frees herself from the political group and Alex when she begins to understand their actions and "ideologies" (108) and when Alex asks her to have an abortion. By doing so, Pavana becomes Edgell's way to represent one of those women who, as O'Callaghan says, "interact with 'power structures'," (98) contest finality and fixation, and adjust ideological influences. Disappointed, Pavana remembers her days in London, "how much could she have known, as she'd joyfully enlisted as a foot soldier, labouring on the fringes of the set Alex and Moria attracted" (35). Involving herself in politics, with Alex in the midst, Pavana believes that "they were a new breed in the Caribbean" (35). What she means is that this group of people, in their impetus to change the economy and society, might have developed into a new type of Caribbean individual, into a hybrid.[10] Now, in her remembering, and aware of her real self, she sees the London group from another perspective, "implementing a policy of rewarding their friends and punishing their enemies . . . holding on to political power for its own sake, at any cost" (35). Along with Pavana's relationships and political parties and as her memory brings forth Pavana's remembrances of Alex and the London group, Edgell, just as Marshall does, uses other characters to introduce the class/race issue.

Edgell has Moria transmit information that expands the Caribbean context within the narrative. Moria, Alex's sister and an active member in the London group, indirectly furnishes the facts applicable to the concepts of class and race when Pavana remembers a conversation she has with Moria. At that moment, Moria acquaints the London group with her memories and her impressions of the time when Pavana attended mass during her first Sunday in London. In her recounting, describing Pavana's white outfit, Moria affirms, "'[w]ith your black skin and skinny frame, you looked quite the little monkey, so cute'" (36). Following Moria's little vignette, Alex recriminates and reprimands Moira for identifying Pavana with a monkey. Moria, however, justifies her behavior and remarks that "[a]t home people call each other black monkey all the time'" (36). Essentially, Moria has used Pavana's skin color as the signifier[11] of her people in Belize where "the two light-skinned Creole children . . . Alex and Moria grew" (37). The highlighting of skin colors throughout their discussion, points towards a "racially diverse Belize" (143). In Pavana's introspective review of her participation and dealings with political parties, the class/race issue constitutes a persistent factor.

Edgell advances the ideas about class and race through another character, Stoner Bennett, a friend who is a political activist from London and who jeopardizes the lives of Pavana's children by kidnapping them in Belize. Upon his return to Belize, Pavana bumps into Stoner who has come home and who she positions as one of "that class . . . the kind of person who could be depended upon to do the dirty work which everybody else was too respectable to do" (84). With apprehension, Pavana thinks of "her last memory of actually seeing Stoner Bennett [it] was about the time he had become one of the drifters on the fringes of West Indian student life in London" (83). Clearly, Pavana's words imply that Stoner belongs to that class of West Indians who move aimlessly from place to place without a permanent job or position. Pavana also situates Stoner as one of those who represents the "new breed in the Caribbean," that will defend their political ideas "at any cost." Effectively, Edgell creates Stoner as a provocative agent, for Stoner's response to Pavana's exchange induces her to describe herself within the class of the "'brainwashed colonial lackeys'" (85). Identifying herself as "colonial," Pavana evokes Africa, colonialism, slavery, and racism.

Pavana even remembers the time when Stoner went to Africa, an expression highly evocative of colonialism and slavery. As Pavana recollects from reading the newspapers, Stoner had gone to Africa to reclaim his cultural heritage, an action that Pavana considers frivolous or lighthearted for "perhaps all that was simply rhetoric, guaranteed to make newspaper headlines" (85). In her exchange, she identifies with the slaves when she asks Stoner, "'were you pitched out of Africa, the homeland of us slaves?'" (85). Pavana's words place her in the role and position of the slave transferring the remembered shreds of African culture and ancestors latent in her memory to the actual spatial-temporal moment or immediate memory on which the narration develops and on which she makes the recollection. The statement, in synthesis, produces two impressions, the implication that the authorities have him leave Africa and the identification with and, possibly, the recognition of some kind of inheritance from the slaves, the African citizens who were transported to the Caribbean against their will during colonial times through the middle passage, the route travelled by the slave-carrying boats. Further on, Stoner challenges Pavana invoking the color of her skin when he calls her "'Quite the little Brownie, aren't you? Was it the famous Belizean false pride or was it revenge?'" (87). His words give Pavana the attributes and qualities belonging to her people and her country.

Additionally, Pavana's relation with the Minister and his political counterparts, when she accepts to direct the Women's Unit, places Pavana in a position which resembles Ursa's towards the PM and the P and D Board. As well, Ursa's work with the NCRC correlates with Pavana's work, establishing another point of comparison between the two protagonists, that of struggle and resistance against the established political ideologies. To do the work, Pavana has the help of Mrs Cora Elrington while Ursa looks for Mae Ryland. Most important is the fact that through this position, Pavana becomes aware of the matters developing in her country, namely, the socio-political struggles and the "policy of rewarding their friends." It is a period of transition when the community is permeated by confusion, anxiety, intrigue, and political hardships. Appropriately, while recalling the moment when she decides to return to Belize, Pavana concludes, "I feel some resurgence of . . . patriotism in these nationalistic times at home" (20). Her memory has helped Pavana to gradually attain an understanding of herself to become a woman able to handle successfully her family and personal relationships so as not to "lose possession of the self [she] was trying to become" (155). Recalling from memory, she affirms: "'All my life . . . I wanted . . . to stand on my own feet . . . I wanted some control over what happened in my life'" (149). As such, Pavana reaches self-assertion and Edgell shows how writers use the memory-recall strategy along with women's issues within a political, historical, and social context to present a literary dynamic, which provides the necessary interaction in order to enable the use of memory as part of a subject's identification process. Edgell thus has highlighted similar concerns as Marshall while developing Pavana's process of definition. Comparably, Marshall and Edgell use memory as part of an identification process, to deconstruct the linearity of narrative and to control characterization making Ursa and Pavana, respectively, the narrative center in a variety of social settings within a female framework just as Michelle Cliff does for Clare in *No Telephone to Heaven*.[12]

Pursuing strategic features comparable to Marshall's and Edgell's, Cliff emphasizes strategies of memory to delineate a creole[13] consciousness undergoing a self-defining quest within notions of class, race, and gender. Cliff uses a fragmented narrative, a variation of Jamaican English, neo/colonial historical fact, and the intersecting stories of other characters such as Christopher, Harry/Harriet, Paul, and Kitty and Boy Savage (Clare's parents), as part of the scheme to develop Clare's interior quest. Examining these representations, in "With the Logic of a Creole Michelle Cliff," Judith L. Raiskin points out that "Michelle Cliff explores . . . how racial identity is constructed, how race 'means,' and the differences and connections . . . [of] the three countries she has called home" (183). Cliff places her characters in Jamaica, the United States, and England; makes the characters heirs of racially mixed ancestors; and develops a connection with their native land.[14] In "Grounding Self and Action: Land, Community, and Survival in *I, Rigoberta Menchú, No Telephone to Heaven,* and *So Far From God,*" Mayumi Toyosato concludes that in *No Telephone to Heaven* the text "blurs the boundary of personal fulfillment and social responsibility, depicting Clare's identity as tied to the land, community, and action" (303). By tying Clare to the land, Cliff highlights history and uses Clare's scrutiny of "certain places" as the enactment of a memory search for the signs or archives of history and as the resource to signify the limited written records of Caribbean history.[15] Since collective memory has been "wiped out," Edouard Glissant indicates in *Caribbean Discourse: Selected Essays*, "the Caribbean writer must 'dig deep' into this memory, following the latent signs that he has picked up in the everyday world" (64). Inclusively, Glissant recognizes individuals' recollections as "the memories of cultural contact" (134). One way or another, through Clare's depiction, Cliff tags along Glissant's tenets since Clare searches for the "signs" in her "everyday world," which constitute her "memories of cultural contact." In the novel, Cliff put together the fragments of Clare's memory (her remembrances of her culture, of her people, of her life abroad, and of her grandmother and mother), turning the text into a tapestry of her ruminations, which constitute her historical background.

To do so, Cliff manages the narrative movement[16] through a third person narrator, moving back and forward through time interposing Clare's mental recollection of her life with that of her journey on the truck, which is the actual temporal action in the novel. To enhance the fragmented effect, the events "strike her in flashes" (90). It means that the narrative imitates her thinking process imbuing the text with "flashes" of her life while she travels on the truck. To disclose her progression, the narrator says a "question passes through her mind . . . A fragment of memory" (91). Although, "[s]he may interrupt her memory to concentrate on the instant, on the immediate and terrible need" (87). As if looking through a file or at snap shots, or, as if explaining Cliff's strategic scheme, the narrator says, "memory crosses memory crosses memory . . . on the reconstruction of past" (92). Next, the narration focuses on Clare's observation of a painting, which turns into one of the "certain places" of historical records. Again, the narrator inserts a comment which emphasizes that the facts she recalls fade away once she moves from the source which provokes the recalling, thus, validating the expression "*out of sight, out of mind*" (97). For Clare, as the truck jumps, "[t]he painting dims and memory switches" (92). Simultaneously, through the painting, Cliff incorporates themes of motherhood; elements depicted in Marshall's, Edgell's, and Nunez-Harrell's texts. Clare's memory recall of the painting, also, reminds the reader of her mother's desertion and the loss of Clare's childbearing capacity. At that instant, the narrator questions, "Had she a child would she be on this truck? On her way to restoration?" (93). That way, the narrator hints toward Clare's psychological need[17] to restore her own self.

    As she ponders through her mind and once in her grandmother's land, Clare's memory brings reminiscences of yesterdays and Clare recalls "her young self differently now" (173). Again, she wondered about her mother, "it was where she was alive, came alive . . . I was blessed to have her here . . . Here is her" (173-74). Deep in herself, she brings to mind her mother's letters (like Ursa), which convey her commitment to her people, "A reminder, daughter—never forget who your people are. Your responsibilities lie beyond me, beyond yourself. There is a space between who you are and who you will become. Fill it." Openly, her words pass her African tradition to Clare and turn into an obsession in Clare's imagination, that is, the words have become the spur that has provoked Clare's journey through her memory banks. Bearing in mind her duty, Clare enters the river to perform a baptismal ritual (Marina follows a similar ritual). As she enters the water, "[t]he importance of this water came back to her . . . She shut her eyes and let the cool of it wash over her naked body, reaching up into her. . . . Rebaptism" (172). Perhaps, since "Here is her," the "Rebaptism" suggests her way of becoming her individual self for she asserts, "I am in it" (194). Now, in her looking back around the place after her baptism, everything results "familiar" (183). Even, at an interview, Clare emphasizes her identification with the land and her people, "I am a Jamaican . . . I have African, English, Carib in me . . . I owe my allegiance to the place my grandmother made" (189). In her mental quest, Clare places herself in history, "I am in it. It involves me . . . I'm not outside this history—it's a matter of recognition . . . memory . . . emotion" (194). Aware of her new self, Clare admits the need that brought her back, "I returned to this island to mend . . . to bury . . . my mother. . . . I could live no longer in borrowed countries" (191-193). On the truck (the indicator of the actual temporality), and ready to fight the American invasion of her land, Jamaica, the group arrives at her grandmother's land to stop an American company from filming a wrong version of Nanny, the maroon warrior. Having assumed her responsibility, accepted her history, and defended her people against neocolonial powers, Clare dies in the encounter and, finally, she is restored to her land. Her quest corroborates the assumption in Odile Jansen's essay "Women as Storekeepers of Memory: Christa Wolf's Cassandra Project." Jansen emphasizes, "[b]eing able to represent one's history fully and consciously has a curative effect" (38). In effect, although the group is betrayed and annihilated, Clare's restoration to the land implies a healing of Clare's plight. All along, Clare's traced path through her memory banks indicates Cliff's control of the data in an attempt to put together a process of fragmentation and personal identification.

Consistent with Cliff, through a different approach, Elizabeth Nunez-Harrell elaborates Marina's process of self-definition in *When Rocks Dance*. Distinct to Marshall, Edgell, and Cliff, through a third-person omniscient narrator in a straightforward manner, Nunez-Harrell develops a narrative packed with symbols, metaphors, memory recalls, and flashbacks to depict the consciousness of Marina. Nunez-Harrell pulls together familiar and traditional themes associated to neo/colonialism and descendants from Africa, Europe, and the Caribbean. Challenging stereotyped roles of women, Nunez-Harrell situates sex and the body as a means to obtain food and shelter and shows women's power to achieve economic stability. By developing the theme of land ownership and prestige as a life goal (an obsession depicted in Marshall's *Brown Girl, Brown Stones* as well), Nunez-Harrell incorporates memories of Africa, the struggle for survival, and the integration of obeah, spirits, and spirituality.[18] In "Theorizing Spirit: The Critical Challenge of Elizabeth Nunez's *When Rocks Dance* and *Beyond the Limbo Silence,*" Melvin B. Rahming defines "spirit as the infinite source and force that originates and perpetuates the organic interrelatedness of all things in the cosmos" (2).

He adds that spirituality refers to "the degree (or index) of one's consciousness of his or her participation . . . in this cosmic interrelatedness" (2). Both aspects, spirits and spirituality, function as a central sphere linking all the characters and themes in the novel, especially, Marina who, according to Antonio (her husband), her "very existence was determined by the black magic of obeah" (142). To structure the mythical and religious effects, Nunez-Harrell resorts to memory as a means for Marina to attain self-assertion.

Marina, whose body houses nine spirits, has been born for the land.[19] She learns about the value of the land and the oil from the Warao, while Emilia, her mother, transmits her the obsession for the land. The Warao's words promote the insertion of the neocolonial/capitalist aspect through the Americans who want to buy the land to exploit the oil. Adequately, capitalist elements underline women/men relationships,[20] an exchange of stock and shares as women marry or live with a man to obtain land or as men give land to obtain a woman. Equally, the transactions seem to turn women into sexual objects, even though women overpower men. Being an object and knowing the value of her share, Marina uses her body as a tool to obtain power. At such, Marina becomes a representation that allows Nunez-Harrell to challenge the depiction of stereotyped roles of women as sexual objects. Knowing men's desires, Marina preserves her virginity because "[i]t gave her power. Men breathing . . . down her neck, begging . . . .And . . . when they thought they had conquered her, she remained . . . in control, brushing them off" (86). In her reverie, while she waits for Antonio on her wedding night and having married him for the land, she prepares herself for the act that will grant her the land: sex. Once he arrives, "[s]he opened her legs to him. Land. Land. She was born on the land. Land was her birthright. She would not lose it as her mother had" (87). Her body gets her the land and Marina overpowers Antonio who represents colonial hegemony. Using her body and pursuing her dream and fantasy, she challenges fixity and finality and contest power structures.

Assertively, through another episode, Nunez-Harrell italicizes the text to highlight Marina's thinking process so as to broaden the function of memory recollection through an interior monologue. In a mental divagation while in a trance, Marina recalls how she prepares a potion to induce Antonio to give her the land. Meanwhile, she acknowledges her strength and identifies herself as "The almighty Marina using manumust on her husband" (257). Her potion works and Antonio gives her five acres and has the deed made on her name, Marina E. Heathrow. Even during her pregnancy, she will not give up. As Clare does in her grandmother's land, Marina goes to the Tabaquite to reclaim her five acres, to feel the land.

There, as if in a baptismal ritual, she introduces her hands in the earth full of oil, as "[s]he dreamed then of the time when the land would be greaseless" (267). Her obsession for the land has "blinded her" (266). All in all, Marina's representation allows Nunez-Harrel to depict the various functions of memory, that is, as a means to set goals, as an empowering tool, as a mode to journey the past, and as a way to foresee the future.

In Marina's mind, thoughts about obeah begin to settle down, for "[i]n a flash, her mind took her to Alma's backyard" (152). At another instant, just like Ursa, Pavana, and Clare, Marina hears a voice, the voice of a little girl or, perhaps, a self inside her, telling her, "'If I was you, Miss, I'd ask Alma" (198). In her conversation with Antonio, "[a]s if she were in a trance. . . . She felt an incredible force . . . dragging her consciousness up to the surface, pulling it to a reality her conscious mind always shunned" (152-3). Each day Marina resists the force of her memory reminding her of her decision not to accede to obeah. To avoid going to Alma, she has "kept telling herself that she was a modern woman. . . . Obeah might be the answer for some people, but not for her. She would not resort to it . . . she would retain control of herself" (218). Her memory, however, keeps harassing her, and although she resists the force, the voice inside her, "the girl's words stuck in her memory like a sore tooth" (199). Once in Tabaquite, holding on to her land, she admits "obeah had served her. The manumust had worked its magic" (267). After Marina gives birth to twins, a boy and a girl, Marina comes to terms with herself and the African religion, a process that Lea H. Creque-Harris explains in "When Rocks Dance: an Evaluation." In the essay, Creque-Harris indicates that the women attain stability once they accept "the religion and spiritual powers of the African ancestor as syncretized in the new world in the form of obeah" (160-61). Once Marina accepts the traditions of her ancestor, she reaches self-stability. Finally, Marina has her land, and Nunez-Harrell has developed a narrative which incorporates memories of Africa and the struggle for survival through obeah, spirits, and spirituality. Although Nunez-Harrell's approach is different from Marshall, Edgell, and Cliff, in synthesis, in or out of their home country, Caribbean women writers portray women who have to struggle, resist, and surmount overpowering structures.

Apparently, Caribbean women writers, appropriating ideological conventions, represent Caribbean identity and incorporate in the texts multiple narrative strategies to emphasize modes of self-identification. Indeed, Caribbean women authors bring into their narrative worlds the approach of memory as a strategic feature to enhance the working of the mind. From the combination of such feature, Caribbean women writers create texts such as Marshall's *Daughters*, Edgell's *In Times Like These*, Cliff's *No Telephone to Heaven*, and Nunez-Harrell's *When Rocks Dance* although the women writers' background and circumstances differ. Caribbean women writers, certainly, examine modes of oppression, resort to historical details to construct narrative worlds in order to challenge ideology and fixed methods of self-assertion. Therefore, Caribbean texts account for strategic features and themes relevant to Caribbean experience, which include hierarchies of race and class permeated by influences of the history of colonialism, the inheritance of slavery, and the traces of African traditions. One way or another, Caribbean female writers integrate strategic attributes and elements, which corroborate the tradition of Caribbean narrative.

Bibliography

Abbott, H. Porter. "What Do We Mean When We Say 'Narrative Literature?' Looking for Answers Across Disciplinary Borders." *Academic Search Elite.* http://www.EBSCOhost (accessed October 11, 2001).

Bhabha, Homi K. *Location of Culture.* London: Routledge, 1994.

Chamberlin, J. Edward. *Come Back To Me My Language: Poetry and the West Indies.* Urbana: University of Illinois Press, 1993.

Chancy, Myriam J. A. *Searching for Safe Spaces: Afro-Caribbean Women Writers in Exile.* Philadelphia: Temple University Press, 1997.

Christos, George. *Memory and Dreams: The Creative Human Mind.* New Brunswick: Rutgers University Press, 2003.

Cliff, Michelle. *No Telephone to Heaven.* New York: Vintage International, 1989.

Creque-Harris, Lea H. "When Rocks Dance: an Evaluation." In *Caribbean Women Writers: Essays from the First International Conference*, edited by Selwyn Reginald Cudjoe, 159-163. Massachusetts: Massachusetts University Press, 1990.

Davies, Carole Boyce and Elaine Savory Fido. "Introduction: Women and Literature in the Caribbean: an Overview." In Davies and Fido, *Out of the Kumbla: Caribbean Women and Literature*, 1-22.

—. "Talking it Over: Women, Writing, and Feminism." In Davies and Fido, *Out of the Kumbla: Caribbean Women and Literature*, IX-XX.

Davies, Carole Boyce and Elaine Savory Fido, ed. *Out of the Kumbla: Caribbean Women and Literature.* Trenton: Africa World Press, 1990.

Edgell, Zee. *In Times Like These.* London: Heinemann, 1991.

Fanon, Frantz. *Black Skins, White Masks.* Translated by Charles Lam Markmann. New York: Grove, 1967.

Gikandi, Simon. "Modernism and the Masks of History: The Novels of Paule Marshall." In *Writing in Limbo: Modernism and Caribean Literuture*, by Gikandi Simon, 168-196. New York: Cornell University Press, 1992.

Glissant, Edouard. *Caribbean Discourse: Selected Essays.* Charlottesville: University Press of Virginia, 1999.

Hume, Kathryn. *Fantasy and Mimesis: Responses to Reality in Western Literature.* New York: Methuen, 1984.

James, Cynthia. "Gender and Hemispheric Shifts in the Caribbean Narrative in English at the Close of the 20th Century: A Study of Paule Marshall's Daughters and Erna Brodber's Louisiana." *Jouvert 5.3.* http://152.1.96.5/jouvert/cyja.htm (accessed April 28 , 2002).

Jansen, Odile. "Women as Storekeepers of Memory: Christa Wolf's Cassandra Project." In *Gendered Memories. Vol. 4 of the Proceedings of the XVth Congress of the International Comparative Literature Association "Literature as Cultural Memory" Leiden 16-22 August 1997*, edited by John Neubauer and Helga Geyer-Ryan, 35-43. Amsterdam: Rodopi, 2000.

Marshall, Paule. *Brown Girl Brownstones.* New York: the Feminist, 1981.

—. *Daughters.* New York: Plume, 1992.

Nunez-Harrel. *When Rocks Dance.* New York: Ballantine, 1996.

O'Callaghan, Evelyn. *Woman Version: Theoretical Approaches to West Indian Fiction By Women.* New York: St. Martin's, 1993.

Patteson, Richard F. "Zee Edgell: The Belize Chronicles." In *Caribbean Passages: A Critical Perspective on New Fiction from the West Indies*, 51-81. Boulder: Lynne Rienner, 1998.

Prasad, Madhave. "On the Question of a Theory of (Third World) Literature." *Social Text*, Fall 2000: 57-83.

Rahming, Melvin B. "Theorizing spirit: The Critical Challenge of Elizabeth Nunez's When Rocks Dance and Beyond the Limbo Silence." *Questia Media America, Inc.* Studies in the Literary Imagination. 37.2 (2004): 1+ Gale Group. (2005). http://www.questia.com (accessed September 21, 2005).

Raiskin, Judith L. "With the Logic of a Creole Michelle Cliff." In *Snow on the Cane Fields: Women's Writing and Creole Subjectivity*. Minnesota: Minnesota University Press, 1996.

Savory, Elaine. "Ex/Isle: Separation, Memory, and Desire in Caribbean Women's Writing." In *Winds of Change: The Transforming Voices of*

Caribbean Women Writers and Scholars, edited by Adele S. Newson and Linda Strong-Leek, 169-177. New York: Peter Lang, 1998.

Toyosato, Mayumi. "Grounding Self and Action: Land, Community, and Survival in I Rigoberta Menchú, No Telephone to Heaven, and So Far From God." *Hispanic Journal*, no. 19.2 (1998): 295-3.

Notes

[1] The study of Caribbean literary development must consider three salient points: Creole writing, which is a type of standard Caribbean English opposed to Jamaican and other islands' English (J. Edward Chamberlin explains the interaction of language in *Come Back To Me My Language: Poetry and the West Indies*[1993]); writing that works with rather than against the Euro-colonial form, for example, Derek Walcott (St. Lucia) and V. S. Naipaul (Trinidad); and cultural and aesthetic value of Caribbean culture in itself. For that reason, the historical background of exploitation, slavery, and colonialism requires a close examination as relevant components which have shaped the development of Caribbean society and, hence, its literature. Eric Williams' *From Columbus to Castro: The History of the Caribbean 1492-1969* (1968) and Gordon C. Lewis' *Main Currents in Caribbean Thought: the Historical Evolution of Caribbean Society in its Ideological Aspects, 1492-1900* (1983) summarize the origins and development of Caribbean society while outlining the main events relevant to the development of Caribbean ideology, which has emerged from the admixture of peoples and beliefs. That background of colonialism and combination of population has produced the multi-cultural, multi-ethnic, and multi-racial influences which Caribbean writers depict in their literary productions. Therefore, the encounter of Amerindian, African, Indian, Chinese, European, and people from the Middle East has produced the themes and ideas essential for the creation of Caribbean narratives as well as poems. George Campbell's poem, "Holy," (*The Penguin Book of Caribbean Verse in English*, Paula Burnett, ed. 1986) illustrates the concurrence of the various cultures and ethnicities as the speaker says, "Holy be the white head of a Negro . . . Heads of Chinese hair . . . Heads of Indians" (178).

Added to the ethnic component, the landscape and the geographical location of the islands have induced writing and a collection of theories, which try to explain Caribbean psychology, colonial dependency, and the geographical feature of smallness and isolation. For instance, Antonio Benitez-Rojo's *The Repeating Island: the Caribbean and the Postmodern Perspective* (1995) yields an analysis of the dynamics that constitute the "Caribbean basin." Through the concept of chaos as that which congregates in the known "(dis)order of Nature" (2), he analyzes the "processes, dynamics, and rhythms" that repeat themselves and which could be found in "the marginal, the regional, the incoherent, the heterogeneous" (3). Caribbean discourse, for him, carries a myth or desire for social, cultural, and psychic integration to compensate for the fragmentation, while Caribbean literature differentiates itself from the European by creating "an ethnologically promiscuous text" which allows a reading of the "polyphony of Caribbean society's characteristic codes" (189). Meanwhile, Edouard Glissant, like Benitez Rojo, examines the Caribbean and the New World as a varied, impressively boundless text. His *Caribbean Discourse: Selected Essays* (1999) deals with the historical ambiguities, multiplicity, and fractures that remain characteristic of the Caribbean *"to pull together all levels of experience"* (4). For him, history is beneath the surface and "landscape is its own monument" (11). His review of history advances from slavery to the present, and includes a revision of the ideas linked to Creole language, colonization, and creativity. He focuses his approach to the role of landscape, community, and the collective unconscious, "tracking down every manifestation of the multiple processes, the confusion of indicators that have ultimately woven for a people" (1-2). In *Poetics of Relation* (1997), he expands the ideas presented in *Caribbean Discourse* (1999) using the concept of "relation" and "the rhizome." As he says, "Rhizomatic thought is the principle behind what I call the Poetics of Relation, in which each and every identity is extended through a relationship with the Other" (11). Based on "the rhizome," he concentrates in concepts such as errantry, nomadism, poetics, and "métissage." Through the collection of essays, prose poems, and commentary, Glissant examines the culturally complex Caribbean society and discourse within the boundless (without center) outlook.

Roberto Fernández Retamar, too, reviews colonialism, capitalism, language, and literature through the vantage point of the Cuban Revolution and the metaphor of "Caliban" within the realm of William Shakespeare's *The Tempest* (1955), but excluding Miranda. His notions about literature and literary criticism deal with imperialism, social class, the "mestizo" and the nation, the European "classics," the nature of the "literary," and influences and similarities between minor literatures. Retamar's ideas gyrate around the question, "Does a Latin American culture Exist?" (3) while he explains cultural trends, Latin America and the concept of "utopia," and "Ariel" as the image of the intellectual. Wilson Harris is another Caribbean writer who has theorized and written about the Caribbean. Harris' *The Womb of Space: The Cross-Cultural Imagination* (1983), as well the collection *Selected Essays of Wilson Harris: the Unfinished Genesis of the Imagination* (1999) theorize about the landscape, time, and history while in *The Palace of the Peacock* (1960). T*he Eye of the Scarecrow* (1965), and *The Secret Ladder* (1963) Harris combines words and concepts in an unpredicted manner to show the undercurrents which impede the occurrences of binary oppositions as he illustrates human psychology and the historical legacies as a spiral development. He also writes critical works such as *Tradition and the West Indian Novel* (New York: St. Martins, 1978) visualizing "a *fulfilment* [sic] of carácter . . . rather than *consolidation*" (28). He sees the West Indian as a "series of subtle and nebulous links" (28). Edgar Mittelholzer's *A Morning at the Office* (1979) is another demonstration of a small Caribbean world as he depicts a time span of five hours of the routine of Caribbean office workers. Mittelholzer develops a catalog of people that resemble Trinidadian society and synthesizes the attitudes of a social world in relation to class, race and its economic circumstances. Mittelholzer captures essential characteristics linked to the components that have shaped the Caribbean and its psychology.

In addition to the geography/landscape/psychology aspects, the study of Caribbean literature requires a review of emigration, immigration, diaspora, and exile. Migrancy and diaspora refers back to the Middle Passage, which started the African Diaspora or the dispersion of a people from their original homeland, for example, when the white-European colonizer forced Black Africans to come to the new world to work in the white-European colonizer's plantations during the period of Euro/Caribbean colonization. As a result, the people underwent a process of displacement and enslavement, a process which has induced themes of uprootedness and dispossession. Kamau Brathwaite's *The Arrivants: A New World Trilogy* (1973) explores the dilemma of the New World through a poetical account and manipulating the language, creates jazz/folk rhythms that recall historical facts through flashbacks, digressions to Europe, New York, Africa, and the fusion of Caribbean present and past, all of which evokes the Middle Passage and its aftermath. Indian and Chinese indenture service, another type of migration, took place when the colonizers brought people to the Caribbean under an employment or service contract. Once in the New World, the people established communities, which Caribbean writers such as V. S. Naipaul portray in their works. In Naipaul's *A House for Mr. Biswas* (1969), the Tulsis represent an East Indian family evocative of Trinidadian society. The narrative, told in retrospect, portrays an Indian descendant who tries hard to have his own house. Through the portrayal of Mr. Biswas' life, Naipaul represents the colonial situation and its effects on society. The novel, in addition, expounds the theme of education and publishing. The colonial model of education was based on the British culture and their literature, full of metaphors (daffodils) not relevant to the islands and reinforcing a sense of "othering" (Austin Clarke's *Growing up Stupid under the Union Jack* (1980), George Lamming's *In the Castle of My Skin* (1953), and Merle Hodge's *Crick Crack Monkey* [1970]).

Publications were limited in the Caribbean and, because of the separation and difficult communication among the islands, many publications remained local. Surmounting difficulties, many magazines, journals, and clubs emerged; for example, Tom Redcam's *The All Jamaica Library* (1904 to 1909), which published a few volumes. During the 1920s-1940s, appeared *Trinidad* and *Beacon* (Alfred Mendes, Albert Gomes, C.L.R. James), *Picong, Progress, Callaloo,* and *Forum*. In the 1940s, appeared *Bim* (Frank Collymore, editor), *Kyk-over-al* (A. J. Seymour), and *Focus* (Norman Manley). *Savacou,* CAM (Caribbean Artists Movement), *Casa Las Americas, Bongo Man, Abeng* (Jamaica), *Moho, Tapia, Manjak,* and *Ratoon* appeared in the 1960s and 1980s. BBC Caribbean Voices indicates the scope of publishing opportunities as well as the migrant/exile tendencies of the times. Naipaul, whose novel was published in 1961, incorporates the inappropriate educational process and publishing limitation in his version of Biswas and his buffoonery. The novel, too, evokes the difficulties in achieving a publication, for Biswas represents an unsuccessful journalist who goes to the

"Ideal School of Journalism," (342) trying to improve his skills. Naipaul's exposition, in a way, highlights the difficulties that a journalist faces, even though his depiction forms part of the tragic/buffoonery of Biswas. Another event, the construction of the Panama Canal, induced Caribbeans to migrate looking for jobs and economic opportunities. Eric Waldron (*Tropic Death* 1926) was one of those West Indians who migrated to Panama. Olive Senior in "Windows," from the collection *Discerners of Hearts and Other Stories* (1995), bases the story on a returnee who had gone to work in the construction of the Panama Canal. As early as the 1920s and 30s, an exodus to London and the United States developed. Claude McKay (deeply linked to the Harlem Renaissance, wrote *Home to Harlem* (1928), *Banana Bottom* (1933), and *Banjo* [1920]) exemplifies the movement to London and the United States. In his novel *Banana Bottom* ([1961] regarded as the first classic of West Indian prose and the first to portray West Indian heroine), he embodies in Bita Plant the transformation resultant from a British education and a migrant experience. Bita, a Jamaican girl given in adoption to Reverend Craig and his wife, represents a "transplanted African peasant girl" (11) educated in England and brought back to her country where she feels attached to her natural roots. Just like McKay, Una Marson (1905-65), who was writing at the same time as Phyllis Shand Allfrey (1908-86), belongs to that migrant category. She became involved in cultural and political activity in England, and during the Second World War, Marson participated in support groups (Salvation Army and YMCA) to West Indians and in feminist organizations in Britain. One of her poems, "Nostalgia" in her collection *The Moth and the Star* (1937), affirms the tendencies of emigration and exile, "Living in sunless reaches under rain/how do exiles from enchanted isles/tend and sustain their rich nostalgic blaze?" (24). In addition to Marson, George Lamming, Sam Selvon, V. S. Naipaul, Andrew Salkey, somehow linked to BBC Caribbean Voices, established themselves in London while other writers, such as Derek Walcott, A. J. Saymour, and Martin Carter stayed in the Caribbean. Austin Clarke (*The Meeting Point* (1967), *Storm of Fortune* (1973) and *The Bigger Light* (1975), migrated to Canada.

Overall, leaving the family and community parallels the experiences of migration and exile in the novels (the Caribbean Bildungsroman) about the child growing up under the influence of the British models of education. Migration from the rural to the urban, and from the Caribbean to the metropolitan centers find expression in Naipaul's *A House for Mrs. Biswas* (1969) and *Miguel Street* (1959); Lamming's *In the Castle of My Skin* (1953); Michael Anthony's *The Year in San Fernando* (1965); Clarke's *Among Thistles and Thorns* (1965) and *Growing Up Stupid Under the Union Jack* (1980); Geoffrey Drayton's *Christopher* (1959); Ian McDonald's *The Hummingbird* (1969); Zee Edgell's *Beka Lamb* (1982); Merle Hodge's *Crick-Crack Monkey* (1970) and *For the Life of Laetitia* (1993); Jamaica Kincaid's *Annie John* (1985), *Lucy* (1990), and *My Brother* (1998); and Marlene Nourbese Philip's *Harriet's Daughter* (1988). Besides the migrant aspect, the aboriginal element originating from the inhabitants of the Caribbean (Arawak, Carib,Taino, Siboney) produces narratives such as H. G. de Lisser's *The Arawak*

Girl (1958); Edgar Mittelholzer's *Children of Kaywana* (1952); and Wilson Harris's *Palace of the Peacock* (1960) and *Heartland* (1964).

The folklore and oral tradition represent a significant element in the study of Caribbean literature. Tales, stories, legends (Anancy), jokes, narratives, folk speech, sermons, beliefs (Obeah), religious instruction, customs, funeral rites, cookery, crafts, arts, customs, and medicine were passed from generation to generation, and later on integrated to Caribbean texts. C.L.R. James' *Minty Alley* (1936), Ismith Khan's *The Obeah Man* (1964), Roger Mais' *Brother Man* (1954) and *The Hills Were Joyful Together* (1953), Sam Selvon's *The Lonely Londoners* (1956), and Claude McKay's *Banana Bottom* (1933) incorporate folkloric elements in their texts. Further on, writers began experimenting with dialect or some type of linguistic-English continuum, Creole, or "Nation language," as Brathwaite calls it in his essay, *History of the Voice: The Development of Nation Language in Anglophone Caribbean Poetry* (1984). In *Caribbean Verse: an Anthology* (1967), O. R. Dathorne sustains that even today West Indian poets remain linked to the folk traditions. Dathorne asserts that McKay and Louise Bennett's dialect verse could not exist without the folk tradition. V. S. Reid's *A New Day* (1949) and Sam Selvon's works (1950s-1980s) exemplify the incorporation of some type of folk expression. Patricia Powell in *The Pagoda* (1998) incorporates a Jamaican dialect or continuum through the world of a Chinese immigrant. Besides the folkloric/dialectical element, the representation of the white West Indian creole has induced the depiction of situations and feelings of characters as cast out by the ones who were below them in the social hierarchy. Some works represent black people calling white creoles "white cockroaches" and "white niggers." Lady Nugent's *Journal* (1839), Phyllis Shand Allfrey's *The Orchid House* (1953), J. B. Emitage's *Brown Sugar* (1966), Geoffrey Drayton's *Christopher* (1959), and Jean Rhys' *Wide Sargasso Sea* (1966) include white creoles in their works.

Furthermore, within the study of Caribbean literature, the African theme demands a close examination. The sources for a vast number of literary works come from African languages, concepts, and dialects. African cultures and traditions, (ideas, religion, foods, ethos/pathos), patterns of social structure and organization (family structure, woman as a chief role in family, matrilinearity, matrifocality), questions of race and color, and the Black emigrant/immigrant, the concept of "African diaspora," and Anancy as African folk-character permeate Caribbean literature. In sum, to study Caribbean literature means to review the literature keeping in mind the intersection of the various trends encountered in the Caribbean and how authors represent them in their writings. The information was compiled from Louis James' *Caribbean Literature in English* (1999), Richard F. Patteson's *Caribbean Passages: A Critical Perspective on New Fiction from the West Indies* (1998), Kenneth Ramchand's *The West Indian Novel and its Background* (1970), and *Frank Birbalsign's Frontiers of Caribbean Literature in English* (1996), among others.

[2] Nowadays, Caribbean literature transmits historical information derived from the events stemming from colonialism. After Christopher Columbus encountered the Caribbean, countries such as England, France, and Spain invaded and took control

of the islands promoting the movement of individuals to the recently found land and enforcing a policy of colonization. Once the islands obtained their independence, the countries influences (traces of trade, education, products, qualities, and characteristics) remained developing into a neocolonial effect. Colonialism has passed, but neocolonialism still affects the islands and their inhabitants.

[3] Other authors such as Erna Brodber, Olive Senior, Patricia Powell, Maryse Condé, Jean Rhys use memory and dreams in their narratives and poems.

[4] A paper, "In Search of the Self: Paule Marshall's Daughters and Zee Edgell's In Times Like These" by Aida Luz Rodríguez was published in The Atlantic Literary Review Quarterly. 4.4, 2003.

[5] Sigmund Freud in his psychoanalytic theory of personality explains that the personality has three components within the sub/conscious: the Id is the organic part and functions in the subconscious, the superego is the ethical and moral part, in essence is the conscience, and the ego is the psychological part, which controls, selects and decides. (Allport, G. A. et. al. *Teorías de la personalidad*. Argentina: Editorial Universitaria de Buenos Aires, 1971).

[6] Whenever we talk about Caribbean identity, we have to keep in mind that Europeans traveled to the Caribbean as colonizers and that Africans were forced to come as slaves. At that time, the African Diaspora began. That's why most of the inhabitants of the Caribbean islands were migrant people who, living under deprivation, emigrated, mostly, to the metropolis.

[7] In *The Location of Culture* (London: Routledge, 1994). Homi K. Bhabha says, "Three conditions underlie an understanding of the *process of identification*. First: to exist is to be called into being in relation to an otherness. . . . It is a demand that reaches outward to an external object. . . . Second: the very place of identification, caught in the tension of demand and desire, is a space of splitting. . . . Finally, the question of identification is never the affirmation of a pre-given identity" (44-45).

[8] Frantz Fanon in *The Wretched of the Earth* (New York: Grove, 1963) talks about the gaze of the colonized: "The look that the native turns on the settler's town is a look of lust, a look of envy; it expresses his dreams of possession—all manner of possession: to sit at the settler's table to sleep in the settler's bed, with his wife if possible. The colonized man is an envious man. And this the settler knows very well; when their glances meet he ascertains bitterly, always on the defensive, 'They want to take our place.' It is true, for there is no native who does not dream at least once a day of setting himself up in the settler's place" (39).

[9] In "The Other Question . . . Homi K Bhabha reconsiders the Stereotype and Colonial discourse," Bhabha identifies the stereotype "as the Lacanian schema of the Imaginary . . . The imaginary . . . is the transformation that takes place in the subject at the formative mirror phase" (29). For Bhabha, this is "*problematic,* for the subject finds or recognizes itself through an image [,] which is simultaneously alienating and hence potentially confrontational" (20).

[10] Robert Young, in *Colonial Desire Hybridity in Theory, Culture and Race* (London: Routledge, 1995), explains hybridity in relation to culture and race. He discusses theories about racial difference, culture, and civilization. Derek Walcott,

in "What the Twilight Says: An Overture," in *Dream on Monkey Mountain and Other Plays* (New York: The Noonday, Farrar, Straus and Giroux, 1970) acknowledges himself as "this hybrid, this West Indian" (10). Also, Fanon in *The Wretched of the Earth* (1963) talks about the "nationalist militant who had fled from the town in disgust at the demagogic and reformist maneuvers of the leaders" (147).

[11] In *Representation: Cultural Representations and Signifying Practices*, Stuart Hall (London: Sage, 1997) discusses "systems of representation" and how "Because we interpret the world in roughly similar ways, we are able to build up a shared culture of meanings and thus construct a social worldThat is. . . . why 'culture' is sometimes defined in terms of 'shared meanings or shared conceptual maps'" (18).

[12] In "Migrant Character in Michelle Cliff' *No Telephone to Heaven*" (*Global Diasporistic & the United States: Exile, Migration, Race, Ethnicity: Selected Papers*. Ed. Anthony Julian Tamburri. Florida: Center for Interdisciplinary Studies, 2005) Aida Luz Rodríguez outlines the migrant experiences of Clare's parents Kitty and Boy Savage.

[13] In "Caliban," (*Caliban and Other Essays*. Minnesota: UP, 1989) Roberto Fernández Retamar distinguishes between "exotic Creole" and the "authentic mestizo." He refers to José Martí and his term "'our mestizo America" (4). Meanwhile, Jean Bernabé, Patrick Chamoiseau, and Raphaël Confiant in "In Praise of Creoleness," (*Callaloo* 13 (1990) 886-909) explain "la créolité" as an inclusive term referring to aspects of race, language, history, and culture. The term alludes to a consciousness rooted in colonial history but linked to migration, "Creoleness is the *interactional or transactional aggregate* of Caribbean, European, African, Asian, and Levantine cultural elements, united on the same soil by the yoke of history" (891). As well, in "With Logic of a Creole," (*Snow on the Cane Fields: Women's Writing and Creole Subjectivity*. Minnesota: UP, 1996) Judith L Raiskin sums up, "Creoleness, then is a mixed culture connecting all Caribbeans with each other and with the multiple countries of their ancestral origins" (182).

[14] In "If I Could Write This in Fire, I Would Write This in Fire," the narrator establishes the relationship to the land, location, and race, "There was land. My grandparents' farm. And there was color" (65). The narrative voice speaks in the first person switching between present and past tenses, "We were standing . . . I visit her . . . Her husband beats her . . . " (63-69). At the same time, the narrator recalls from memory her life story as if they were dreams, reflections, stories, anecdotes, including colonizing details and historical fact, using the Jamaican native language as well as traditional English. Based on that, then, the narrative could parallel the speaker's quest as she reaches self-awareness, "I and Jamaica is who I am. No matter how far I travel" (81). Definitely, the narrative develops a consciousness and illustrates the feelings of a creole who comes to terms with her heritage and her identity.

[15] In "Nobel Lecture" (1992, Reprint in "The 1992 Noble Prize in Literature: Derek Walcott," by Edward Halsey Foster. *Dictionary of Literary Biography Yearbook: 1992*. Ed. James W. Hipp. Detroit" Gale, 1993. 5-19), Derek Walcott points out

how the Antillean geography conveys history in its vegetation. He mentions the sea, the cane, the Middle Passage, and the erasure of African memory.

[16] In the essay "Narration at the Postcolonial Moment: History and Representation in Abeng," Simon Gikandi says that Michelle Cliff "Instead of seeking to establish a unique Caribbean narrative of history . . . [she]seeks to write what amounts to a schizophrenic text" (235). Referring to Abeng (1984), he adds, "the meaning of Caribbean history arises from the tense conjunction between manifest and celebrated Eurocentric meaning and a repressed Afro-Caribbean hermeneutics" (242). Incidentally, Gikandi's comments on Abeng (1984), in a way, hold true for the text of her work, Free Enterprise (1993), which seems to be a record of historical knowledge interpolated within the representation of life and struggle among slaves, blacks, Creoles, and whites. Thus, the "Caribbean narrative of history" becomes chaos as Cliff develops a representation influenced by the interaction of the Euro/American-African/Caribbean tensions.

A close examination of the text shows Cliff's manipulation of the phrases within the historical exposition. First, Cliff uses the word, the cities, and the states mentioned in the text, to place the action within an American context. Immediately, right from the title, Cliff evokes the country of the free enterprise, The United States. Moreover, the vocabulary she employs such as "investment (9) . . . Industry (28) . . . common goods (45) . . . company (69) . . . profiting off the trade" (78) refers to the *Free Enterprise* (1993). The fact that Cliff intermingles the expressions mentioned, scattered throughout the text, adds to the chaotic sensation because within the exposition of the characters, appears an evocation of the American theme, "'[b]ecause in this world, Captain, property, ownership equals power'" (144). Therefore, her book becomes an enterprise that allows her to combine history narrative with poetic techniques.

The section "U.S. Public Health Service Station #66," illustrates Cliff's manipulation of narrative to mix the historical events with Annie Christmas story: After the nuns died off, or were sent on, the place was taken over by the United States government, whose Public Health Service runs it today.

At Carville, Annie Christmas entered the grounds through a tear in the wire fence, through which two lepers had once run off to get married (39).

This way, a disruption in the narrative, changes the tone, the place, and the situation to create a schizophrenic sensation and developing chaos on the narrative. The insertion of dialogue, letters, and poems interrupts the narrative flow, too. Further, the change of point of view and narrators or speakers increases the feeling of disorder. The narrative, then, becomes emblematic of the chaotic and fragmented Caribbean. It is Annie who confirms the notion of historical chaos, "'that the history of my people, the history of my part of the world, is of the one-step-forward, two-step-back variety" (52). To add to the schizophrenic feeling, Cliff intermingled the languages, "Let us bless the Highest/For bread . . . Dios bendiga . . . " (184-185). But, besides the chaos, there is lyricism, "Standing one afternoon under several of the flags which had claimed the colony, before the British prevailed once and for all, efficiency conquering all, on the very same verandah in Runaway Bay, Annie's mother made a speech to her" (9). She inserts poems, too, "Ye gods./Talk about disgrace./It saved her life. That blackened skin" (9).

In synthesis, *Free Enterprise* (1993) records historical knowledge inserted within the character's life stories and struggles among slaves, blacks, Creoles, and whites. Hence, Caribbean history, as it is narrated, becomes a representation of chaos influenced by the interaction of the Euro/African/Caribbean tensions, especially British/American.

[17] In "Imagined Communities in the Novels of Michelle Cliff," (*Homemaking Women Writers and the Politics and Poetic of Home*. Ed. Catherine Wiley and Fiona R. Barnes. New York: Garland, 1996) Meryl Schwartz argues that the human subjects begin politically with needs and desires. She says, "this dimension is the question of what *general* conditions would be necessary for our particular needs and desires to be fulfilled" (23).

[18] Bob Corbett in "Selected Voodoo terms," defines Voodoo as "the dominant religion and cultural reality of Haiti. The Voodoo religion is native to Haiti, having been fused from an uneasy union of African and Roman Catholic elements." (http://www.webster.edu/~corbetre/haiti/voodoo/terms.ht m. 23 September 2005).

[19] The affinity with the landscape evokes Wilson Harris *The Palace of the Peacock*. (London: Faber and Faber, 1960).

[20] Thelma B. Thompson-Deloatch discusses romantic love in "Fire and Ice: The Socioeconomics of Romantic Love in *When Rocks Dance* by Elizabeth Nunez-Harrell," *(Arms Akimbo: Africana Women in Contemporary Literature*. Ed. Janice Lee Liddell and Yakini Belinda Kemp. Gainesville: UP of Florida, 1999.) She refers to "The Love Axe/l: (Developing a Caribbean Aesthetic 1962 — 1974)," in which Edward Kamau Brathwaite talks about the doubleness of love. She also mentions that to explain a Caribbean aesthetic he coined the term "love Axe/l." She says that love acts like an axe and that Nunez-Harrell's representations of love, substantiates Brathwaite's reflections. All the characters in the novel are linked through love, (an axel).

FEODOR DOSTOYEVSKY AND CLAUDE MCKAY: CROSS-CULTURAL DIALOGUE WITH THE DOMINANT WESTERN ETHNOCENTRISM

TATIANA TAGIROVA

Russian literature of the nineteenth century plays an important role in McKay's formulation of a solution to his dilemma of a dual cultural identity and in his development as a writer. It is not a coincidence that Ray, the Haitian narrator of *Home to Harlem*, reads Dostoyevsky's *Crime and Punishment* and considers him to be a creator of genuine art. His engagement with Dostoyevsky in *Home to Harlem* and his subsequent internal dialogue with Tolstoy in *Banjo* reveal the influence of these writers on McKay's artistic development. Parallel to Dostoyevsky who contests the positive effects of Western rationalism and individualism and affirms his Russian culture, McKay creates a distinct difference between Caribbean and Western modes of thinking.

The alienation of the educated from the uneducated, the connection of "real art" with "contemporary reality"[1] and the seminal role of the writer in the development of the nation are some of the Russian themes that influenced McKay's formation. Instead of imitating Western standards of his time, he turns to the indigenous Caribbean and African American culture and its people as the main source of his literary inspiration. Along with *Crime and Punishment*, *Home to Harlem* and *Banjo* illuminate an understanding of "a native culture that had been hidden from view and held in bondage to narrow Western standards of civility and literacy."[2] A return to the "native soil" and an affirmation of his own people and their culture are some of the ultimate values that McKay shares with his Russian predecessor.

The search for black identity and the influence of the dominant European ethnocentrism are some of McKay's most characteristic tensions. In *The Souls of Black Folk*, W.E.B. Du Bois points to the African American man as someone who is born with a veil and "a sense of always looking at one's self through the eyes of others." (38) When McKay read this book as a student at Kansas State, it shook him "like an earthquake."[3] Du Bois's statements about the lack of true self-consciousness among North American blacks who could see themselves only "through the revelation of the other world" encouraged him to confront "his own deepest ambivalence as a black colonial reared in both the folk and the British imperial traditions."[4] As a poet and an individual who had the previous experience of living between two worlds, the world of the Jamaican black peasants and the world of the British literary and cultural traditions, he understood African Americans who always felt their "two-ness—an American, a Negro; two souls, two thoughts, two unreconciled stirrings."[5] In his best-selling novel celebrating Harlem's black masses, he gives importance to the notion of double consciousness and applies it to his West Indian background.

The two different identities within one to which Du Bois refers is not just an African American or Caribbean phenomenon. Due to profoundly parallel socio-historical conditions, Russian writers, like their Caribbean and African American counterparts, acknowledged the notion of double-consciousness resulting from Peter the Great's westernization of Russia. The czar's transformation of the Russian gentry into military and civil services as well as his recruitment of masses of armed workers from the peasantry created major problems for these two groups of people. The service caste that Peter formed from the Russian nobility was to benefit the state that was attempting to become westernized and the heavy taxes that the peasants had to pay deprived them of any financial independence.[6] These reforms further separated the Russian masses from the gentry. In *The Notebooks for The Possessed*, Dostoyevsky describes this process in the following way:

> The people were not considered essential at the time, but were looked upon as raw material, and as payers of the poll tax. Sure, they were closely guarded, but as to internal, proper life, it was left to them in its entirety; and though the people had to suffer a lot, they finally ended up by loving their own suffering. (146)

While the majority of the Russian population was left with its own traditions intact, the Russian nobility became westernized. As Dostoyevsky acidly states, "the entire upper class of Russia ended up being transformed into Germans, and, uprooted, got to love everything German and to hate and despise everything of their own." (146) Catherine the Great, Peter's most faithful follower, continued this process and instructed Russians to turn to the West as a source of intellectual knowledge. Influenced by the European Enlightenment, she considered

France to be "the supreme model of civilization."[7] The Russian nobility that aspired to become European then desired above all to become Frenchmen. This adoration of French civilization continued in the nineteenth century "undiminished even by the war with Napoleon."[8] While France became the most important source of Russia's enlightenment, Germany, Britain and Italy also contributed to the development of the emerging Russian intelligentsia of that time.[9]

Feodor Dostoyevsky, a founding "native soil" member, was among the first ones to reject foreign impositions and to show the duality of the Russian identity created by means of this influence. Mikhail Bakhtin describes the innovative, non-European type of writing that Dostoyevsky created:

> Thus, all the elements of novelistic structure in Dostoevsky are profoundly original; all are determined by that new artistic task that only he could pose and solve with the requisite scope and depth: the task of constructing a polyphonic world and destroying the established forms of the fundamentally *monologic* (homophonic) European novel. (8)

Discussing the pluralism within Dostoyevsky's writings, Bakhtin continues,

> Here in Russia the contradictory nature of evolving social life, not fitting within the framework of a confident and calmly meditative monologic consciousness, was bound to appear particularly abrupt, and at the same time the individuality of those worlds, worlds thrown off their ideological balance and colliding with one another, was bound to be particularly full and vivid. In this way the objective preconditions were created for the multi-leveledness and multi-voicedness of the polyphonic novel. (20)

The absence of the monologic consciousness and a polyphonic type of thinking to which Bakhtin refers are also characteristic of McKay's Ray, who searches for his own voice among the "multi-leveledness" of other voices presented in *Home to Harlem* and struggles to reconcile his African identity with Western influence. Commenting on his belonging to a black race, he states,

> These men claimed kinship with him. They were black like him. Man and nature had put them in the same race. He ought to love them and feel them (if they felt anything). He ought to if he had a shred of social morality in him. They were all chain-ganged together and he was counted as one link. Yet he loathed every soul in that great barrack room, except Jake. Race. Why should he have and love a race?[10]

Even though Ray understands that white civilization and Western education have negative effects on black people, he cannot fully reject them. Despite his intellectual knowledge of African history and culture, he demonstrates an ambivalent attitude toward blackness by his desire to belong to a white nation:

> Great races and big nations! There must be something mighty inspiring in being the citizen of a great strong nation. To be the white citizen of a nation that can say bold, challenging things like a strong man. Something very different from the keen ecstatic joy the man feels in the romance of being black. Something the black man could never feel nor quite understand.[11]

He is alienated from the black masses of Harlem due to the cultural and intellectual background that makes him feel superior. The European voice is one of the prominent ones among which he has to discover his own.

In *Home to Harlem* and *Banjo*, Russian writers of the nineteenth century are central influences on Ray's inner drama. Similar to those different individuals who enter Raskolnikov's inner speech as "a symbol of a certain orientation to life and an ideological position, the symbol of a specific real-life solution to those same ideological questions that torment him"[12] they exemplify a type of art that Ray would like to create in *Home to Harlem*. As he thinks of achieving an original form in his writings, he engages in an internal dialogue with them:

> Dreams of making something with words. What could he make . . . and fashion? Could he ever create Art? Art, around which vague, incomprehensible words and phrases stormed? What was art, anyway? Was it more than a clear-cut presentation of a vivid impression of life? Only the Russians of the later era seemed to stand up like giants in the new. Gogol, Dostoievski, Tolstoy, Chekhov, Turgeniev. When he read them now he thought: Here were elements that the grand carnage swept over and touched not. The soil of life saved their roots from the fire. They were so saturated, so deep-down rooted in it.[13]

Parallel to Dostoyevsky's characters, whose main tasks in the novels are to "find one's own voice and to orient it among other voices, to combine it with some and to oppose it to others, to separate one's voice from another voice with which it has inseparably merged,"[14] Ray realizes his allegiance to both European and African cultures and influences and understands the difference between himself and the uneducated masses of Harlem. McKay's fascination with the nineteenth-century Russian writers indicates that they offer him "a compelling counterpart to the European example."[15] They are the voices that play an important role in Ray's formation. Like the influence of new points of view in the writings of Dostoyevsky that present a resolution to the questions of "Who am I?" and "With whom am I?,"[16] they help Ray to find answers to some of his questions.

The alienation of the educated from the uneducated is one of Dostoyevsky's most vital concerns. According to Leonid Grossman, in prison he became aware for the first time that "the cosmopolitan, socialist dreams of his youth were remote from and even contrary to the nationality newly revealed to him through his contacts with the oppressed Russian people."[17] During that time he started to think about a specific problem of the Russians—the alienation of the educated and uneducated, of the upper and lower classes. Later on, he incarnates this alienation in Raskolnikov, the main character of *Crime and Punishment* who is attracted to Sonia, a representative of national culture rooted in the Russian Orthodox Church. Unlike her, he is an embodiment of "two opposing characters that he describes in his article on crime" whose very name suggests that he is "split in two."[18]

Raskolnikov's divided personality that is the result of foreign influence is revealed from the opening pages of the novel. He is a simultaneous representative of "ordinary" and "extraordinary" people that he describes in his article on crime published in the *Periodical Review*.[19] He thinks that ordinary men must live in submission and have no right to disobey the law.[20] On the other hand, extraordinary ones may "transgress the law" as they seek "the destruction of the present for the sake of the better."[21] He believes that the first category "preserve the world," while the second "move the world and lead it to its goal."[22] According to Richard Peace, Raskolnikov's theory has merely externalized his internal conflict:

> Thus from the very first the reader is made aware of the disharmony in Raskolnikov between a ruthless side and a meek side. This dichotomy is present in scene after scene throughout the novel. The behavior of Raskolnikov is now self-assertive, now self-effacing; now rational, now irrational; now "bad," now "good," and his own ambivalence is both reflected and heightened through the characters and situations he encounters. (35)

When he is drawn to Napoleon, he acts with coldness and rationality. Other times, he demonstrates kindness and compassion. In his actions, he is simultaneously "the man of the present" and "the man of the future" that he describes in his article.[23] Both superiority and inferiority complexes are Raskolnikov's inherent characteristics:

> Symbols of aggression evoke in Raskolnikov feelings of submission; symbols of submission bring out his aggressiveness. The coin of Raskolnikov's inner realm, bearing on one side the head of Napoleon, on the other side, the effigy of a louse, spins in a constant game of "heads and tails" with his surroundings.[24]

Contrary to Raskolnikov, Sonia does not believe in the theory of extraordinary men. In her opinion, there can be no rationalization of murder because no human being has the right to kill another. She completely rejects his theory and demands that he interpret his act as a crime that he needs to confess. His rationality and individualism are juxtaposed to Sonia's morality and inner understanding of right and wrong that comes from her faith in God. While he is alienated from the common people, Sonia is embedded in Russian culture and religion. Through her Dostoyevsky presents a challenge to Raskolnikov, a representative of the Russian intelligentsia who has drifted away from his national morals. The novel asserts that Sonia's example of unconditional love and submission to God is much more valuable than that of Napoleon. Dostoyevsky's condemnation of Raskolnikov's rationality, cruelty and individualism and his praise of Sonia's faith in God, sacrifice and morality are clearly seen. Even though Sonia is a prostitute who can only fit the "louse" description in Raskolnikov's theory, her inner goodness and integrity are superior to his values. She is the one who finally helps him to find a solution to his agonizing problem.

While adherence to Napoleon creates adversity in Raskolnikov's life, Sonia's spirituality, rooted in the Russian Orthodox Church, brings about a change in his life. Through these two characters, Dostoyevsky presents his criticism of blind fascination with the West. As Ellen Chances states in "The Superfluous Man in Russian Literature," the westernized heroes of Dostoyevsky's fiction must take "a journey through doubt and rational thought in order to come to an acceptance of Russian spiritual values." (33) Like Alyosha and Ivan, two protagonists of *The Brothers Karamazov*, Sonia and Raskolnikov represent two different value systems to which the Russian intellectuals of the nineteenth century were exposed. One is that of sacrifice, consideration for others and submission to God and the Russian Orthodox church. The other is that of Western rationality, egotism and isolation. Like Ivan Karamazov, a character uprooted from the Russian soil who questions the very existence of God, Raskolnikov believes that "all is in a man's hands."[25] In his opinion, it is justifiable to kill a human being in order to make the world a better place. On the other hand, Sonia and Alyosha Karamazov share a deep and sincere faith in God and believe that happiness can never be built on the unhappiness and tears of other human beings.

Even though at the beginning of the novel Raskolnikov is a proud, Western-oriented rationalist who imagines himself to be independent of Russian spirituality, his ideas change towards the end. At first he decides to follow the path of Napoleon, but later on he returns to the second path. The epilogue replaces his rationality and egotism with the religion and love of Sonia, who accompanies him into exile. His decision to follow her example shows his final rejection of the Napoleonic theory:

> Raskolnikov's controversial conversion in Siberia to Sonya's ethic of submissive and limitless love for mankind, although it strains credibility to the limit, is meant to conclude his journey from evil to good, from a rebellious individualism in which "all is permitted" to a pious acquiescence in the way things are, however painful and unjust.[26]

The novel's structure and development admit the possibility of Raskolnikov's ultimate conversion. Through Sonia and her faith in God, Dostoyevsky demolishes "successful layers of rationalization" and shows that the Napoleonic type of thinking is "evil and insane."[27] Even though Raskolnikov separates himself from "love, from God, from Russia, and from mankind" when he decides to act upon his theory,[28] he is not a completely cold, selfish, and rational egotist devoid of any inner morality:

> Although the epilogue has struck many excellent critics as contrived and extraneous, it emerges from a thorough examination as an essential component of *Crime and Punishment*. Raskolnikov is psychologically capable of the metamorphosis he is destined to undergo. He is impelled by a preternatural force to conceive, commit, and confess the crime. Furthermore, the numerical motifs, the Lazarus theme, and the nature imagery of the novel all prepare the reader for the concluding scene. The epilogue is the inevitable result of all that precedes it and is, in Robert Louis Jackson's felicitous phrase, the "transformation of ends into beginnings."[29]

The positive side of his inner nature creates the possibility of his salvation. Like Sonia, he chooses morality and God through his final acknowledgment of the negative effects of the calculating type of thinking.

Dostoyevsky's return to the common people and his realistic portrayal of their everyday reality are some of his most important contributions to the development of Russian literature. He not only theorized about art, but also actively strove to bring art and reality together. The secret of his popularity lies in "that truthfulness (*pravda*) which looks at us from every page of his books and gives them such irresistible force."[30] A return to the "soil," to the common Russian folk, to their culture and strength is his "constant theme."[31] In an 1861 issue of *Vremya* (*Time*) Dostoyevsky writes,

> We have come to realize the necessity of our joining with our native soil and with the people, . . . because without them we cannot exist. We feel that we have wasted all our forces in a life led separately from the people.[32]

He realizes the importance of his connection with the Russian masses and their spirit and urges other writers to turn to the common people and the culture that they represent. In the February 1861 issue of *Vremya*, he insists of a realistic portrayal of their lives:

> The important thing is that art is always faithful to reality to the highest degree, its deviations are fleeting and temporary; art is not only faithful to reality but cannot be anything else but true to contemporary reality. Otherwise it would not be real art. The mark of real art is that it is always contemporary, urgent and useful . . . Art which is not contemporary and doesn't answer contemporary needs cannot exist. If it does exist, it is not art, it becomes shallow, degenerates, loses its power and all artistic value.[33]

The alienation of the educated from the uneducated is one of the main areas of McKay's affinity with Dostoyevsky. He expresses his own ambivalence and tensions through the protagonist who reads *Crime and Punishment* in *Home to Harlem*. While Ray's friend Jake has a free and unregulated approach to life, Ray displays the dilemma of a "civilized" West Indian intellectual. By juxtaposing Raskolnikov with Sonia and Ray with Jake, both Dostoyevsky and McKay question the positive effects of Western influences on their national identities. Even though Sonia's irrationality is rooted in the Russian Orthodox Church and Jake's is found in his closer ties to Africa, both writers convey their preferences for their national sentiments. Parallel to Dostoyevsky's *Notes from the House of the Dead* and Du Bois's *The Souls of Black Folk* that share a "deep affinity" and bring to light "the previously devalued and veiled expressive culture of an ethnic majority still in bondage to the sovereign contempt of modern Western civilization,"[34] *Crime and Punishment* and *Home to Harlem* reestablish the importance of Russian and Afro-Caribbean cultural values.

Similar to his Russian predecessor who pointed to the importance of common folks as the true keepers of Russian culture, McKay searched for a positive identification of black life among the masses of the African diaspora, whom he considered to be preservers of African roots. He not only wanted to contest the constraints on the previous black writers, but also "hoped to define the black experience in the West in terms of the Negro's African roots."[35] McKay encouraged African Americans to follow cultural values and traditions that their ancestors brought from Africa for he believed they could help his characters to cope with their "torturous lives in the West."[36]

McKay turns to the folk culture and expresses his sympathy with oppressed Jamaicans and African Americans in his poetry and prose. Even though Ray feels alienated from the black masses of Harlem, in no way does he laugh at his race or caricature it. Like the policeman-narrator of McKay's poem, "The Heart of a Constab," who wants to return to his "people, my people, me owna black skin" and vows to never part from "de country, de love o' me soul,"[37] he desires to come closer to Jake, an Afro-American keeper of Negro roots. The narrator of "The Heart of a Constab" and Ray find beauty in their African heritage and common people. Besides McKay's celebration of "the freedom, spontaneity, and sensuality of the black lower classes,"[38] his peasants and workers deserve respect and admiration for their hard labor, integrity, sincerity, and perseverance.

His commitment to common folks, initiated in *Home to Harlem*, continues in *Banjo*, his second novel. In the Vieux Port or "the Ditch" of Marseilles, Ray meets the black Diaspora from the United States, the West Indies and Africa. The French port becomes the international setting for McKay's search for a "revitalised diasporic black culture" that can challenge postwar colonialism and imperialism.[39] Situated between Africa and the rest of Europe, it brings together "two kinds of transatlantic passages in the postwar world: international commerce and itinerant blacks, both transported by ships."[40] In Marseilles, they represent a "new post-Emancipation, postwar phenomenon: the diasporic exile community of blacks" that offers an alternative to modern civilization.[41] *Banjo* exposes "the problems of blacks in general in a world dominated by hostile, insensitive and profligate whites"[42] and contrasts "the free life of common Negroes with the frustration of those caught in the more sophisticated web of modern civilization."[43] Once again, as in *Home to Harlem*, the writer's sympathy is with the lower-class blacks.

Ray perceives France as a part of Western civilization that dehumanizes black people and makes them "labor under its law," yet lacks "the spirit to tolerate them within its walls."[44] Unlike Goosey, who feels protected from racism in France, he understands the effects of the "world-wide domination of occidental civilization."[45] The French consider themselves to be "the most civilized nation in the world" that treats black people much better than the Anglo-Saxon nations, yet Ray deems the French police to be "the rottenest of the whole world."[46] In his opinion, there is "no such animal as a civilized nation."[47] In France, as in Anglo-Saxon nations, he finds discrimination against his people:

> Ray looked deeper than the noise for the truth, and what he really found was a fundamental contempt for black people quite as pronounced as in Anglo-Saxon lands. The common idea of the Negro did not differ from that of the civilized world in general. There was, if anything, an unveiled condescension in it that was gall to a Negro who wanted to live his life free of the demoralizing effect of being pitied and patronized.[48]

In *Banjo*, McKay further develops his indictment of white "civilization." He praises the lifestyle of his black characters and questions a stereotypical approach to race:

> Ray refused to accept the idea of the Negro simply as a "problem." All of life was a problem. White people, like red and brown people, had their problems. And of the highest importance was the problem of the individual, from which some people thought they could escape by joining movements.[49]

In Ray's opinion, the Negro presents a challenge to Western civilization. In his race, he finds a sincerity and openness that he admires:

> From his experience, it was white people who were the great wearers of veils, shadowing their lives and the lives of other peoples by them. Negroes were too fond of the sunny open ways of living, to hide behind any kind of veil. If the Negro had to be defined, there was every reason to define him as a challenge rather than a "problem" to Western civilization.[50]

Through Ray, McKay contests Du Bois's definition of ordinary African Americans as wearers of veils. While, according to McKay, a civilized white person or an educated African American or Caribbean intellectual that strives to be white may have to see himself through the eyes of the others, the Caribbean and African American masses are free from that restraint. Contrary to Du Bois's opinion of the "history of the American Negro" as the struggle to "attain self-conscious manhood, to merge his double self into a better and truer self," (17) McKay's characters are worthy of respect, dignity and admiration just the way they are. Unlike those influenced by Western education and culture, they don't feel a need to lose their identity in order to escape white society's stereotypes.

In *Banjo*, McKay continues the realistic portrayal of the Negro masses first started in *Home to Harlem*. Again his voice is heard through his main character, Ray. In response to Goosey's advice to write about "race men and women" who make a good living in Paris, he states that he is not a reporter for the Negro press and cannot keep up with black "society folk" of Paris who might prefer to have Monsieur Paul Morand, "a society writer," describe them.[51] He does not think that upper- or middle-class black folks are good examples of his race:

> I can't see that. They say you find the best Negro society in Washington. When I was there the government clerks and school-teachers and the wives of the few professional men formed a group and called themselves the "upper classes." They were nearly all between your complexion and near-white. The women wore rich clothes and I don't know whether it was that or their complexions or their teaching or clerking ability that put them in the "upper class." In my home we had an upper class of Negroes, but it had big money and property and power. It wasn't just a moving-picture imitation. School-teachers and clerks didn't make any ridiculous pretenses of belonging to it. . . . I could write about the society of Negroes you mean if I wrote a farce.[52]

Ray finds the imitation of the upper class by the middle-class North American Negroes amusing. He attacks their hypocrisy and snobbery:

> Gee! I remember when I was in college in America how those Negroes getting an education could make me tired talking class and class all the time. It was funny and it was sad. There was hardly one of them with the upper-class bug on the brain who didn't have a near relative—a brother or sister who was an ignorant chauffeur, butler, or maid, or a mother paying their way through college with her washtub. If you think it's fine for the society Negroes to fool themselves on the cheapest of imitations, I don't. I am fed up with class.[53]

This comical imitation irritates Ray. He prefers the truth rather than lies, pretensions and hypocrisy. Therefore, he turns to the masses that he finds to be much more honest and real.

Ray believes that until black intellectuals acknowledge their racial heritage, they will never produce a real renaissance:

> And I wonder how we're going to get it. On one side we're up against the world's arrogance—a mighty cold hard white stone thing. On the other the great sweating army—our race. It's the common people, you know, who furnish the bone and sinew and salt of any race or nation. In the modern race of life we're merely beginners. If this renaissance we're talking about

is going to be more than a sporadic and scabby thing, we'll have to get down to our racial roots to create it.[54]

In Ray's opinion, building up from one's own people is "not savagery. It is culture."[55]

Through his narrator, McKay criticizes privileged Negroes' acquisition of a white man's education that has taught them to despise their own people:

> Then when you come to maturity you realize with a shock that you don't and can't belong to the white race. All your education and achievements cannot put you in the intimate circles of the whites and give you a white man's full opportunity. However advanced, clever, and cultivated you are, you will have the distinguished adjective of "colored" before your name. And instead of accepting it proudly and manfully, most of you are soured and bitter about it—especially you mixed-bloods.[56]

Ray suggests turning for example to "whites of a different type" and recommends that they turn their backs on "all these tiresome clever European novels" and study the Irish cultural and social movement, the struggle of the Russian peasants, the great Russian novelists up to the time of the Russian Revolution, the story of Gandhi and his contribution to the masses of India and "the simple beauty" of the African dialects.[57]

His challenge to take pride in Negro roots also extends to the West Indian elite. In chapter XVI of *Banjo*, "The 'Blue Cinema,'" McKay shows that "the coloniser's myth of cultural superiority" has been used to divide West Indians from Africans.[58] At the beginning of the chapter, Ray meets a student from Martinique who is proud of the fact that Empress Josephine was born in his island. He thinks that most people from there are Creole rather than Negro, and "the best people" of Martinique speak a "pure French."[59] When Ray asks the Martinican to meet an African from the Ivory Coast, he refuses to go with him to the African bar, saying that the white French changed their attitude toward black people because of the Senegalese who came to France.[60] Ray challenges his superior attitude:

> You must judge civilization by its general attitude toward primitive peoples, and not by the exceptional cases. You can't get away from the Senegalese and other black Africans any more than you can from the fact that our forefathers were slaves.[61]

He goes on to tell the Martinican student that his white education is the source of his blindness:

"You are like many Negro intellectuals who are belly-aching about race," said Ray. "What is wrong with you-all is your education. You get a white man's education and learn to despise your own people. You read biased history of the whites conquering the colored and primitive peoples, and it thrills you just as it does a white boy belonging to a great white nation."[62]

Yet Ray feels that he is caught in between two worlds, that of his African heritage and that of Western civilization. That is why he thinks that it is easier for Banjo, someone who "in all matters acted instinctively," to be himself in the white world.[63] It is much more difficult for him, a black intellectual, to act "with an intellect standing watch over his native instincts to take his own way in this white man's civilization."[64] In spite of this, however, he doesn't want his intellect to take control over his soul:

> But of one thing he was resolved: civilization would not take the love of color, joy, beauty, vitality, and nobility out of his life and make him like one of the poor mass of its pale creatures. Before he was aware of what was the big drift of this Occidental life he had fought against it instinctively, and now that he had grown and broadened and knew it better, he could bring intellect to the aid of instinct.[65]

In conclusion, similar to Dostoyevsky who strove to portray the Russian people of the nineteenth century truthfully, McKay worked towards a unique and distinctive depiction of the Caribbean and African American masses of the twentieth century. A return to the "native soil" and respect for his own people and culture are some of the tendencies that he shares with his Russian predecessor. The "penitent nobleman" desires to come close to the masses and becomes "creatively active" in the Russian literature of the nineteenth century.[66] McKay's Ray also gains strength through contact with the cultural treasure of Africa and with ordinary black folk.

However, unlike Dostoyevsky's Raskolnikov, who finally rejects the Napoleonic type of thinking and returns to his national sentiments embedded in Russian Orthodoxy, Ray cannot fully reject Western education in defining his Afro-Caribbean identity. He is an alienated West Indian intellectual who desires to come closer to the masses, but though fascinated with Tolstoy, who "had turned his back on the intellect as guide to find himself in *Ivan Durak*,"[67] he is not able to fully assimilate his example. He understands the contradictions between intellect and instinct, but doesn't want to forsake either one of them. While his contact with the black community of *Banjo* brings him closer to his African-based roots, he is unable to undergo a complete change.

Bibliography

Bakhtin, Mikhail. *Problems of Dostoevsky's Poetics.* Minneapolis: University of Minnesota Press, 1984.

Baldwin, Kate. *Beyond the Color Line and the Iron Curtain: Reading Encounters Between Black and Red, 1922-1963.* Durham and London: Duke University Press, 2002.

Chances, Ellen. "The Superfluous Man in Russian Literature." In *Reference Guide to Russian Literature*, ed. Neil Cornwell and N. Christian, 29-35. London: Fitzroy Dearborn, 1998.

Cooper, Wayne. *Claude McKay: Rebel Sojourner in the Harlem Renaissance.* Baton Rouge: Louisiana State University Press, 1987.

Du Bois, W.E.B. *The Souls of Black Folk: Essays and Sketches.* Greenwich: Fawcett, 1961.

Dostoyevsky, Feodor. *Crime and Punishment.* New York: Amsco, 1970.

—. *The Notebooks for The Possessed.* Ed. Edward Wasiolek. Chicago and London: University of Chicago Press, 1968.

Dowler, Wayne. *Dostoevsky, Grigor'ev, and Native Soil Conservatism.* Toronto: University of Toronto Press, 1982.

Fabre, Michel. *From Harlem to Paris: Black American Writers in France 1840-1980.* University of Illinois Press 1991.

Frank, Joseph. *Dostoevsky: The Mantle of the Prophet 1871-1881.* Princeton and Oxford: Princeton University Press, 2002.

Jones, Bridget. "With 'Banjo' by My Bed: Black French Writers Reading Claude McKay." *Caribbean Quarterly* 38:1 (1992): 32-39.

Mathewson, Rufus. *The Positive Hero in Russian Literature.* Stanford, California: Stanford University Press, 1975.

Matual, David. "In Defense of the Epilogue of *Crime and Punishment*." *Studies in the Novel* 24.1 (Spring 92): 26-34.

McKay, Claude. *Banjo.* New York: Harcourt, 1970.

—. *The Dialect Poetry of Claude McKay.* Plainview, New York: Books for Libraries, 1972.

—. *Home to Harlem.* London: Black Classics, 2000.

Peace, Richard. *Dostoyevsky: An Examination of the Major Novels* Cambridge: Cambridge UP, 1971.

Pedersen, Carl. "Olaudah Equiano, Claude McKay, Caryl Phillips and the Extended Caribbean." In *Prospero's Isles: The Presence of the Caribbean in the American Imaginary,* ed. Diane Accaria-Zavala and Rodolfo Popelnik. Oxford: Macmillan, 2004.

Peterson, Dale. *Up from Bondage: The Literatures of Russian and African American Soul.* Durham: Duke UP, 2000.

Singh, Amritjit. *The Novels of the Harlem Renaissance: Twelve Black Writers, 1923-1933*. University Park and London: The Pennsylvania State University Press, 1976.

Smith, Robert. "Rereading *Banjo*: Claude McKay and the French Connection." *College Language Association Journal* 30.1 (Sept.1986): 46-58.

Ward, Bruce K. *Dostoyevsky's Critique of the West: The Quest for the Earthly Paradise*. Waterloo: Wilfrid Laurier University Press, 1986.

Zenkovskii, V.V. *Russian Thinkers and Europe*. Trans. Galia S. Bodde. Paris: Young Men's Christian Association, 1926.

Notes

[1] Dostoyevsky as quoted by Wayne Dowler, *Grigor'ev, and Native Soil Conservatism*, 117.

[2] Dale Peterson, *Up from Bondage: The Literatures of Russian and African American Soul*, 6.

[3] Claude McKay, *A Long Way from Home*, 110.

[4] Wayne Cooper, *Claude McKay: Rebel Sojourner in the Harlem Renaissance*, 68-69.

[5] Du Bois as quoted by Copper, *Claude McKay: Rebel Sojourner in the Harlem Renaissance*, 69.

[6] Bruce K. Ward, *Dostoyevsky's Critique of the West: The Quest for the Earthly Paradise*, 11.

[7] Bruce K. Ward, *Dostoyevsky's Critique of the West: The Quest for the Earthly Paradise*, 67.

[8] Ibid.

[9] Ibid., 13.

[10] Claude McKay, *Home to Harlem,* 106; hereafter cited parenthetically as *HH*.

[11] Ibid., 106.

[12] Mikhail Bakhtin, *Problems of Dostoevsky's Poetics*, 238.

[13] Mc Kay, *HH,* 158-159.

[14] Mikhail Bakhtin, *Problems of Dostoevsky's Poetics*, 239.

[15] Kate Baldwin, *Beyond the Color Line and the Iron Curtain: Reading Encounters Between Black and Red, 1922-1963,* 26.

[16] Mikhail Bakhtin, *Problems of Dostoevsky's Poetics*, 239.

[17] Leonid Grosman as quoted by Wayne Dowler, *Grigor'ev, and Native Soil Conservatism*, 66. In 1849 the secret police of Nicolas I arrested Dostoyevsky and other members of the Petrashevsky circle for their adherence to the European revolutions of 1848 and their criticism of the Russian social order. Following the arrest, Dostoyevsky was sent to Siberia, where he lived in prison camp for the next four years (Frank 7-8).

[18] Peace, *Dostoyevsky: An Examination of the Major Novels*, 34.

[19] Feodor Dostoyevsky, *Crime and Punishment*, 201.
[20] Ibid., 203.
[21] Ibid.
[22] Ibid.
[23] Feodor Dostoyevsky, *Crime and Punishment*, 203.
[24] Peace, *Dostoyevsky: An Examination of the Major Novels*, 36.
[25] Feodor Dostoyevsky, *Crime and Punishment*, 1.
[26] Mathewson, *The Positive Hero in Russian Literature*, 20.
[27] Ibid.
[28] Ibid., 102.
[29] Matual, "In Defense of the Epilogue of *Crime and Punishment*," 33.
[30] Zenkovskii, *Russian Thinkers and Europe*, 155.
[31] Ibid., 158.
[32] Ibid.
[33] Dostoyevsky as quoted by Dowler, *Dostoevsky, Grigor'ev, and Native Soil Conservatism*, 117.
[34] Peterson, *Up from Bondage: The Literatures of Russian and African American Soul*, 80.
[35] Singh, *The Novels of the Harlem Renaissance: Twelve Black Writers, 1923-1933*, 42.
[36] Ibid., 43.
[37] Mc Kay, *The Dialect Poetry of Claude McKay*, 63.
[38] Wintz, 198.
[39] Pedersen, "Olaudah Equiano, Claude McKay, Caryl Phillips and the Extended Caribbean," 144.
[40] Ibid.
[41] Ibid., 145.
[42] Smith, "Rereading *Banjo*: Claude McKay and the French Connection," 48.
[43] Cooper, *Claude McKay: Rebel Sojourner in the Harlem Renaissance*, 305.
[44] Claude McKay, *Banjo*, 314; hereafter cited parenthetically as *B*.
[45] McKay quoted by Fabre, *From Harlem to Paris: Black American Writers in France 1840-1980*, 109.
[46] McKay. *Banjo*, 274.
[47] Ibid.
[48] Ibid., 275.
[49] Ibid., 272.
[50] Ibid., 272-273.
[51] McKay. *Banjo*, 116.
[52] Ibid.
[53] Ibid., 116-117.
[54] Ibid., 200.
[55] Ibid.
[56] Ibid., 201.
[57] Ibid.

[58] Jones, "With 'Banjo' by My Bed: Black French Writers Reading Claude McKay," 34.
[59] McKay, *Banjo*, 199.
[60] Ibid., 200.
[61] Ibid.
[62] Ibid., 200-201.
[63] Ibid., 164.
[64] Ibid.
[65] Ibid.
[66] Zenkovskii, V.V. *Russian Thinkers and Europe*, 115.
[67] Mc Kay, *Banjo*, 322. The Russian word *durak* that McKay uses in *Banjo* is translated as "the fool" in English. Ivan *Durak* or Ivan the Fool is a Russian folkloric character that often outwits those who consider him a fool.

THE IMAGINED NATION IN CRISTINA GARCÍA'S *MONKEY HUNTING*

RAQUEL PUIG

Benedict Anderson, in his seminal book *Imagined Communities*, describes nation as an imagined community where people who never have met or will never meet are brought to think of each other as belonging to the same family.[1] That concept of nation as construed or "imagined" is pivotal in a story dealing with a Chinese indentured servant, Chen Pan, who arrives in Cuba during the middle of the nineteenth century, manages to escape the plantation where he is no more than a slave, and becomes a respected and wealthy merchant in Havana's *Barrio Chino*. Cristina García's *Monkey Hunting* poses the problem of "nation" through the character of Chen Pan and his more than forty years in his adopted country, Cuba. Chen Pan's life in Cuba comprises a span in that country's history that is definite for its construction as a nation. Emancipation and independence from Spain are some of the historical moments Chen Pan witnesses, and sometimes actively supports. Gordon K. Lewis expresses the importance of the construction of national ideology in Cuba thus:

> Put together in the period between Céspedes declaration of gradual slavery abolition of 1868 and the Ley Monet of 1882, it [national ideology] lays down the leading imperative of all Cuban nationalist thought ever since, reinforced by the official line of fidelista revolution a century later: that Cuba is to be seen, not as a pluralist society in which different ethnic groups venture their own separate cultural sovereignties, but as a unitary society with all owing fealty the national mainstream culture. Ethnic identity gives way to national patriotism. The group gives way to the nation. (291-292)

Considering that Chen Pan's life in Cuba runs parallel to the construction of this country's nationhood, it is pertinent to examine Chen Pan's trajectory and how this positions him in the nascent homogenizing concept of the Cuban nation.

The story of Chen Pan is the story of countless Chinese who were lured, kidnapped, tricked with worthless contracts, and loaded onto

Chinese indentured laborers' ships modeled on African slave ships, where they suffered the same middle passage. After the abolition of the African slave trade in the British Empire, there was a shortage of labor in the New World and South China became the West's destination to find replacement for the African slaves. In 1847, the first significant trafficking of Chinese indentured labor reaches Cuba (ten years previous to the arrival of Chen Pan) in the Spanish ship Oquendo that brought 212 Chinese men to Havana. This cargo was brokered by British traffickers and Spanish Cuban buyers. The network of Chinese indentured labor brokers, shippers, buyers, and investors crossed lines of colonial empires, including monied interests of the British, Americans, Portuguese, French as well as the Spanish Cubans. To launch the indentured trade in Cuba, planters used a company called the Real Junta de Fomento y Colonización. The Real Junta then contracted Julieta y Cia. of London. The two main labor agents in Asia were Fernando Aguirre based in Manila and Mr. Tait in Amoy/Xiamen. After 1855, Aguirre and Mr. Tait were replaced by the Cubans with their own offices in Havana, London, Macao, and Amoy /Xiamen. In 1859, the Cuban finance and insurance firm La Alianza entered Chinese indentured trade and provided much of the financing for Chinese importation. In the 1870s, Julieta y Cia. re-emerged as contractors of the Real Junta. It is estimated that from 1847 to 1873 some 124,873 to 150,000 Chinese indentured labor arrived in Havana on 342 ships. Most of them ended concentrated in the sugar plantations of Matanzas, the central province of Cuba.[2]

Some of the methods utilized for procuring Chinese labor involved kidnapping or decoying peasant men, and luring laborers and ex-prisoners to gambling houses. Gullible young men went to "recruitment agents" and afterwards discovered that they were not employed as laborers but were to be sold as slaves. Often, fellow countrymen were employed by colonial traffickers to trick Chinese men into signing deceiving contracts. Once onboard, it became clear that the "recruited" had signed his life to a contract that under the guise of indentureship was no more than an enslavement sentence. The conditions on board were so detrimental and the treatment was so demeaning that the mortality rates were higher than the rates for African slaves: from twelve to thirty percent, sometimes reaching as high as fifty percent. The main cause of death was violence: rebellions, crew assassinations, suicides, thirst, suffocation, and sickness were the main reasons for the decimation of the human cargo. The Chinese called the ships the "devil ships" because as Alexander Laing, a writer who wrote about the ship Sea Witch aptly stated: "[it] was a Dantean dream; it had become the lid of Hades, and the damned were below."[3] Of more than 140,000 Chinese that sailed for Cuba, more than 16,000 died during the journey. A testimony in the China-Cuban Commission Report[4] describes the treatment the Chinese received thus:

> al salir de Macao, fuimos confinados en la bodega: algunos fueron incluso encerrados en jaulas de bambú, o encadenados a postes de hierro, y unos pocos fueron seleccionados indiscriminadamente y azotados hasta la saciedad como medio de intimidación para los otros . . . el tratamiento a bordo era malo y el agua apestaba . . . [5]

> [Upon leaving Macao, we were confined to the bilge: some were even held in bamboo cages, or chained to iron posts, and a few were selected indiscriminately and whipped extensively as a means of intimidating the others . . . Treatment on board was bad and the water stank.] (My translation)

Once on land, in Havana, conditions were no better. They were mistreated and sold as slaves:

> al desembarcar, cuatro o cinco extranjeros a caballo, armados con látigos, nos condujeron como a una manada de ganado al barracón para ser vendidos . . . cuando nos pusieron en venta en el mercado de hombres, fuimos divididos en tres clases . . . y obligados a desnudarnos para que nuestras personas pudieran ser examinadas y pudiera fijarse precio. Esto nos cubrió de vergüenza. [6]

> [Upon disembarking, four or five foreigners on horseback, armed with whips, led us like a herd of cattle to the barracks to be put on sale. . . . When we were put on sale on the men's market, we were divided into three classes. . . . And forced to strip naked so that our persons could be examined and the price determined. This covered us with shame.](My translation)

The working conditions on the plantations attest to the miserable condition that will plague them beyond the eight years that the indenture contract decrees.[7] Another testimony in the Commission Report describes the working conditions for the Chinese indentured laborer "We labor 21 hours out of 24 and are beaten . . . On occasion I received 200 blows, and though my body was amass of wounds I was still forced to continue labor . . . A single day becomes a year . . . And our families know not whether we are alive or not.[8]

One of the consequences of such horrendous treatment to Chinese indentured laborers was the high incidence of suicides. Due to the quantity of Chinese suicides, Cuba exhibited the highest rate of suicides worldwide, one for each 4,000 inhabitants. From 1850 to 1860 for each one million inhabitants in Cuba, the proportion was of 57 suicides among the white population, 350 among the African population, and 5,000 among the Chinese population.[9] Apart from suicide, other methods of rebellion were used by defiant Chinese. There were plantation rebellions, cane field burnings, assassination of overseers and escape. Maroonage in Cuba's Chinese population began as soon as the first Chinese arrived to the island. It is estimated that the proportion was five to seven times higher than in the African population. Apparently, they had help from the Spanish authorities who for a few *pesos* would provide false documents that enabled the Chinese indentured laborer to choose a new employer or join a free working crew.[10]

Cristina García in *Monkey Hunting* inserts Chen Pan in the history of the indentured Chinese in Cuba. From Amoy, China, his birthplace, he travels on a slave ship to Cuba and undergoes the hardships of the plantation. But, what is Chen's story? Does it fit the official history? To answer these questions it is pertinent to examine how Chen Pan's history is written in *Monkey Hunting*. Is Cristina García providing her main character, Chen Pan, with a reconstruction of history that includes filling the gaps that linear history so succinctly avoids? García follows closely the official history of the Chinese in Cuba which, fortunately for Cuba's history, can draw from the personal testimonies of Chinese indentured laborers in the Chinese-Cuban Commission Report. To a certain extent, this Report captures the oral histories of countless voices that would have remained silent otherwise. A further examination of Chen Pan's narration will determine aspects not revealed officially, and how Chen Pan's conception of his history places him in the Cuban nation that is developing astride his own evolution as a wealthy merchant in Havana's *Barrio Chino*.

Chen Pan begins his story in Amoy in 1857 where he is invited for tea by "a slope shouldered man with drooping whiskers"[11] who serves a tea that was hot and "heavily sugared."[12] Early on in the story there is a reference to the sugar that was provided to the English through a system of slavery that Chen, unwittingly, would soon join by signing a contract he believed would procure for him the money to return to Amoy "a wealthy man, perhaps a stronger man if the story about the drinking water wasn't a lie."[13]

Like so many before and after him, Chen suffers and witnesses mistreatment and atrocities during his voyage. Chen Pan's experience aboard ship is a recapitulation of the testimonies of Chinese indentured laborers to the Cuban-Commission Report. The same violence and conditions are present: mutinies, suicides, lack of food and bad water. But, it is not until he reaches Cuba that his dream starts to fade with the realization that he was brought there to cut sugarcane and that, previously a free man, now he was owned by a Spanish landowner. Brought to a plantation on Central Cuba, probably Matanzas where most of the indentured labored, and suffering the unfortunate destiny of his African counterparts in the plantation of La Amada, he kills the overseer with a stone the same way he had killed an "enormous macaque monkey"[14] in China. After a sojourn in the plantation which must have lasted around two years, Chen Pan "slipped away from the other slaves during a march to weed a distant field,"[15] and simply walked away. So begins his history as a maroon, spending nine months in the forest battling the spirit of his mother that haunted him in the form of an owl. Chen Pan thought that his mother was distraught because he had left China without leaving her money or producing a grandson.[16] When the owl finally leaves he makes the decision to stay in Cuba based on a mental game with himself: "If he succeeded in killing it [the jutía], Chen Pan decided, he would remain in Cuba."[17]

From 1860 to 1867, Chen's trajectory is a mystery that García chooses not to historicize. How Chen becomes a wealthy merchant in Chinatown is a puzzle that has to be reconstructed in *Monkey Hunting*. The scant information offered by García regarding this mysterious time frame of seven years that spanned between Chen's stay in the forest and his arrival to the *Barrio Chino* reads thus: he spent one year in the forest and "It had taken him four months more to work his way to the capital-hauling scrap metal, grooming gamecocks, and furiously gambling."[18] García also adds that Chen Pan, who, basically, was an ambulatory merchant who "dragged his refurbished wares from door to door in his dilapidated cart,"[19] saved Count de Santovenia from an assault and in return the count offered him protection for life. Chen obtained a Letter of Domicile that guaranteed his freedom, and with the count's support and with money gained gambling opened his shop, the Lucky Find. So, it took him less than seven years to become a wealthy man in the *Barrio Chino*. Chen Pan arrives in Havana in 1860, the epoch that coincides with the beginnings of what later would be called *Barrio Chino*.

It was in 1858 when the first Chinese merchants established themselves in Calle Zanja. A Chinese *fonda* is the first establishment in conjunction with a fruit stand owned by Lan Si Ye. During the 1860s, Chinese from California, with a strong commercial culture and economic resources, immigrated to Cuba and established themselves on Zanja Street.[20] The combination of the Cuban-Chinese merchants and the California merchants provided the basis for the *Barrio Chino*. Chen is thus part of this development, and prospers by it. He has found a place where he feels he belongs. For him "the sight of Havana with its seductive curve of coast, stirred in him [the feeling] that it was where he belonged."[21] This is the first time in *Monkey Hunting* that Chen Pan feels a sense of belonging. Havana changes his perspective, and the question asked ten years before, when he was stripped in the market and examined for strength: "Here he could no longer rely on the known ways. Who was he now without his country?,"[22] gives way to a feeling of freedom: "Chen Pan, however, wasn't the least bit nostalgic. He was most grateful to Cuba for this: to be freed, at last, from the cycles of the land. He'd carried both books and a hoe in his youth. He preferred books."[23] It is interesting that Chen feels liberated when, at the same time, he is well aware that he does not partake of the hegemonic Cuban society:

> Chen Pan knew that the Cubans would have preferred that he still worked for them in the fields, or sold garlic at their kitchen doors. The manner in which they spoke to him-and expected to be spoken to in return- infuriated him. But he had learned to control his temper. A gracious tip of the hat was more unsettling to the enemy than a stream of curses, and impossible to retaliate against.[24]

Society constitutes itself as an entity by excluding the multitude. According to Michael Hardt and Antonio Negri "the multitude is an inconclusive constituent relation, the people is a constituted synthesis that is prepared for sovereignty. The people provide a single will and action that is independent of and often in conflict with the various wills and actions of the multitude. Every nation must make the multitude into a people."[25] Ever since his arrival in Cuba, Chen has belonged to the excluded multitude, which according to Hardt and Negri does not belong to the center (the people) where sovereignty takes place. His condition as a slave/ indentured servant presupposes his exclusion from that center, and as a free man, his condition as a Chinese positions him in the peripheral multitude. The fight for Cuban independence from Spain is fought with the aid of the multitude conformed by African slaves and indentured servants that are granted their liberty in exchange for their patriotism, and active involvement in the uprisings that are known as the Ten Years War. Chen Pan joins by buying fifty machetes and heading "east, toward the war, to deliver the machetes to Commander Sian."[26] During the War for Independence, thirty years later, Chen Pan again wants to join the fight against the Spaniards, but is convinced by Lucrecia, his wife, to stay home. Instead, he sends the rebels all the money he had acquired through business with the Spaniards. Once the Cuban flag is raised and the nation is formed, Chen Pan experiences the black uprising of 1912 where the rumor is that "*los negros* were rising up, arming themselves with muskets and machetes, readying to launch a bloody race war that would leave the criollo dead."[27] Chen Pan's reaction to these rumors is telling of his awareness of belonging to that periphery that helped the formation of the sovereign nation and then was excluded: "Chen Pan didn't believe this [the rumor] was true. But what did his opinion matter? He saw how the *chinos* were treated, even the respected ones like Lorenzo. When the criollos needed medical attention, they were very solicitous of his expertise- it was Doctor Chen this and Doctor Chen that . . . When the times grew difficult or the jobs scarce, he knew well enough that they were just *chinos de porquería* [filthy Chinese]."[28] The Afro-Cuban fight for the right to form a political party produces deep emotions in Chen, who acquiesces that "What choice did they have. Men grew tired of tolerating misery, of waiting for better days."[29] Chen knows that he has a bond with the black population, and this bond is the same bond that existed when he was working and suffering side by side with them in La Amada. Fifty-five years have elapsed since his arrival in Cuba and his engagement as a slave, but the feeling of exclusion is strong in him. He realizes that it would only be a matter of time before the Chinese "no longer would be welcomed in Cuba. In times of economic necessity, they were usually the first scapegoats. This infuriated Chen Pan because thousands of *chinos* had fought hard for the country's independence."[30] That independence and the resulting sovereignty escapes people like Chen who will never truly belong.

The "imaginary plane" of the nation, which eliminates differences, corresponds according to Hardt and Negri "on the practical plane to racial subordination and social purification."[31] This "imagined community"[32] that is formed by the hegemonic nucleus, or the people, exists because it creates 'otherness.' This 'otherness' is based on differences that the nucleus is not willing to include. The "unitary experience of a nation-subject"[33] needs to exclude the oppositional differences. Its survival rests in the exclusion and oppression of the multiplicity. The story of Chen Pan is thus a story of exclusion that begins with his arrival in Cuba. First as an indentured laborer, he is ostracized and exploited. He is conveniently used to fill the gaps that British prohibition of the African slave trade left in a society that desperately needed sugar workers in order to survive. His situation after his release from indentured slavery and his commitment to the libertarian cause confirm Hardt and Negri's affirmation that "The flip side of the structure that resists foreign powers is itself a dominating power that exerts an equal and opposite internal oppression repressing internal difference and opposition in the name of national identity, unity, and security."[34] Chen, almost at the end of his life, suffers from an ambivalent sense of nationalism. He does not belong in China, neither does he fully belong in Cuban society. The unified "imaginary community" may have built a monument to the *chinos mambises* (Chinese freedom fighters) who bravely fought in the insurrection against Spain, but once sovereignty and nation are achieved, they become the instruments of exclusion. And, Chen Pan, as countless others are left in the periphery of that excluded multitude.

Bibliography

Anthrobase. "Benedict Anderson." *Dictionary of Anthropology*. www.anthrobase.com/Dic/eng/pers/anderson_benedict.htm

García, Cristina. *Monkey Hunting*. New York: Alfred A. Knopf, 2003.

Alonso Gallo, Laura and Fabio Murrieta, eds. *Guayaba Sweet*. Cádiz: Editorial Aduana Vieja, 2003.

Hardt, Michael and Antonio Negri. "Sovereignty of the Nation-State." *Empire*. Cambridge: Harvard University Press, 2001.

Helly, Denise. "EL Reporte de la Comisión de Cuba." *La Habana Elegante, Segunda Época*. http://www.habanaelegante.com/spring2004/PanópticoDos.html

Lewis, Gordon K. *Main Currents in Caribbean Thought*. Baltimore: The Johns Hopkins University Press, 1983.

Pastrana, Juan Jiménez. *Los Chinos en las Luchas por la Liberación Cubana 1847-1930*. La Habana: Instituto de Historia, 1963.

PBS. "Ancestors in the Americas." <http://www.pbs.org/ancestors in the americas/program1_2.html>

Pérez de la Riva, J. *El Barracón y Otros Ensayos*. La Habana: Editorial de Ciencias Sociales, 1975.

Yun, Lisa and Ricardo Rene Laremont. "Chinese Indentured Laborers and African Slaves in Cuba." *Journal of Asian American Studies* 4:2 (2001): 99-122.

Notes

[1] Anthrobase.
[2] Lisa Yun and Ricardo Rene Laremont, "Chinese indentured laborers and African Slaves in Cuba," 99-122.
[3] Ibid., 112.

[4] The exploitation of the Chinese indentured laborers became so alarming that the Chinese government sent representatives to question the laborers directly. The result was an 1874 report that documented the kidnapping or deceiving of Chinese and their subsequent inhumane treatment in Cuba. The Chinese government, upon receiving the Report, became indignant and tried to curtail further Chinese indentured traffic.
[5] Denise Helly, "El reporte de la Comisión de Cuba," 3.
[6] Ibid., 3.
[7] Indenture contracts, which were supposed to last for only eight years, were routinely ignored and unenforced in Cuba. The 1854 regulations permitted the Chinese indentured to purchase the remainder of their contract at any time, but only after they had compensated the master for the purchase price, the value added since the time of the purchase, any clothing, loss of labor due to sickness, and the inconvenience for finding a replacement for the Chinese laborer. Chinese indentured laborers were paid four pesos monthly and, from that sum the cost of travel from China was deducted, and the provision of clothing and food. Thus, by the time the Chinese indentured laborers's eight year-term expired, he owed his employer. Then, the master could invoke a clause in the contract to renew the contract, thus keeping the Chinese indentured laborers unfree until his death. (Yun 115)
[8] PBS, "Ancestors in the Americas," 1.
[9] J. Pérez de la Riva, *El barracón y otros ensayos*, 481.
[10] Ibid., 491.
[11] Cristina García, *Monkey Hunting*, 4.
[12] Ibid.
[13] Ibid., 5.
[14] Ibid., 33.
[15] Ibid., 38.
[16] Ibid., 39.
[17] Ibid., 42.
[18] Ibid., 62.
[19] Ibid.
[20] Juan Jiménez Pastrana, *Los chinos en las luchas por la liberación cubana 1847-1930*, 46.
[21] Cristina García, *Monkey Hunting*, 62.
[22] Ibid., 21.
[23] Ibid., 81.
[24] Ibid., 81
[25] Michael Hardt and Antonio Negri. "Sovereignty of the Nation-State," *Empire*, 103.
[26] Cristina García, *Monkey Hunting*, 87.
[27] Ibid., 184.
[28] Ibid.
[29] Ibid., 194.
[30] Ibid., 246.

[31] Michael Hardt and Antonio Negri, "Sovereignty of the Nation-State," *Empire*, 103.
[32] Ibid., 105.
[33] Ibid.
[34] Ibid., 106.